FEARLESS

Psychic Self-Defense

Transcend the Fear of Spiritual Warfare

JAI

FEARLESS

Psychic Self-Defense

Transcend the Fear of Spiritual Warfare

FEARLESS: PSYCHIC SELF-DEFENSE
Transcend the Fear of Spiritual Warfare
by JAI

Copyright © 1990-2018 by JAI (Dream Universal Media)

ISBN-13: 978-1-7324068-3-4

Edited by: Timothy Rodd
            D. Christopher Rodd
            Devahni Lopez

Disclaimer:

The materials contained in this text, and related recordings, are provided for general information purposes only and do not constitute medical or psychological professional advice. The author nor the publisher accepts responsibility for any loss which may arise from inappropriate reliance on information contained in this text.

The contents of this book and the recordings of the meditations herein are protected by copyright under international conventions, and the reproduction or retransmission of the contents of this text and/or related recordings and/or artwork is prohibited without the prior written consent of the author.

The content of this text and related recordings, including all music, all text, all downloads, all music samples, and all other material are owned or controlled by *dreamuniversalmedia* and their content and technology providers. ALL RIGHTS RESERVED. Unauthorized duplication or distribution of this content is strictly prohibited.

A Note of Caution:

If you are experiencing thoughts of harming yourself or others, or seized by overwhelming emotions, attempting Mystical Meditation that involves Self-Inquiry, or the witnessing of the mental process through meditation and contemplation, is NOT advised as it may cause these feelings to intensify. You are encouraged to seek the immediate help of a licensed therapist or healthcare practitioner.

The information in this text is for informational purposes only and not intended to diagnose, treat, cure, or prevent any disease or disorder. If you are experiencing symptoms of depression or physical problems, it is advised that you see medical and psychological professionals for evaluation.

Consecration

May the words of my mouth and the meditations of my heart be acceptable to The Most High, Creator of all the worlds. I pray that my will and Thy Will become as One. I write from that Oneness.

I offer this book in the Name of the One Holy True and Eternal God, Lord of all the worlds and Timeless realms, in all of their physical and nonphysical appearances. We seek to know the Oneness of The Divine and not be distracted by the divisive labels that seek to define what cannot be defined. I bear witness to the truth of Timeless Wisdom delivered by the prophets, apostles, messengers, saints, angels, and servants of The Divine Light.

My soul is grateful for The Protection, Love, and Guidance of The Comforter, The Holy Spirit. I accept that The Faces that have been shown us as Manifestations of The Creator, known and unknown, seen and unseen, were, and are, among us … never departed, yet is returned, as we prepare ourselves for our rightful place among the worthy.

I offer this journal from no position of authority. I am but a traveler, a student, a seeker, lifting my pen and voice to express praise and thanks to The Almighty, The Most High, for the blessing of this opportunity to share this journey with you.

I have learned
so much from God
that I can no longer
call myself
a Christian, a Hindu, a Muslim,
a Buddhist, a Jew.
The truth has shared so much of itself
with me
that I can no longer call myself
a man, a woman, an angel,
or even a pure Soul.
Love has
befriended Hafiz so completely,
it has turned to ash
and freed me
of every concept and image
my mind has ever known.

~ Hafiz ~

The message of FEARLESS: PSYCHIC SELF-DEFENSE, Transcend the Fear of Spiritual Warfare, has been revealing itself with inspired structure and intention over the course of many years. Much like my book THE TIMELESS NOW, it wrote itself line for line, experience for experience, true stories woven together by the fragile threads of awakening. It is a sharing. It is a pointing. It is an invitation, an offering to you, as it was to me. I did not sign up for this. Very few do. The mystical world is not separate or set apart, in any way, from the one we think we know. It is the animating breath that sustains all we know and that which we do not. To navigate our journey through the many realms of it, all we need do is breathe. Sooner or later, as I did, you will need this book. Read it *before* you need it.

Acknowledgments

I thank The Most High for that first trip to the other side for evidence that there is no "veil" between worlds. You showed me that the realm of Maya was just the tip of the iceberg. You smiled Transcendence upon me from one dimension into the next. Thank you for opening the portal to the Mystic and showing me that this is not all there is. You showed me that death is only a figment of the collective imagination. You taught me that people really can change. You've shown me a Higher Love.

My mother, Dorothy Louise Warren (Raushanah Hassain) was one of the most powerful mystics I have ever known. I thank her for teaching me that there is no such thing as death, as her life still breathes through me, along with all of the lives she so lovingly touched. I am so grateful for all of the love she brought to my life. She was my biggest fan and I was her's. She was a warrior … a peacemaker … a counselor … a healer … a real, live angel. I thank The God every day for ever having known her.

Many thanks to Timothy Rodd for opening your Third Eye wide enough to see a finish line I almost lost sight of, and for tirelessly helping me cross it. Thank you for sharing your energy and refusing to stop just short of the journey's victory. Thank you for the graphic design, cover art, and all of your editing work.

Christopher … Thank you for your help with some of the most brutal bouts with research and editing ever. Thank you for helping with the conquering of the "devil in the details";

Jamil … Thank you for your intuitive guidance in marketing and distribution. Because of the wisdom you shared, many people who might not otherwise have been able to access this offering will be given a chance to embrace a healing, spiritual perspective;

Nicholas … Thank you for lending your beautiful voice to the I Die to My Ego Self Meditation. The vibration of your voice brought a powerful healing spirit to the meditation. Thank you for believing in me and pushing me to reach higher;

Rahmon … Thank you for your help with sound engineering, your invaluable research, and thank you for your prayers. The Light you each have brought into my life will always illuminate my path and give me a sense of purpose.

Thank you, Richard Allen, for pulling me out of the perfect storm. I give thanks for the braided twists and turns of fate and circumstance the Universe delivered to my doorstep that caused our paths to cross. Your spiritual strength and guidance helped me to bear the unbearable. The Natural Mystic is alive and well in your heart of hearts.

Thank you, Joe Stecher, for your introduction to the concept and practice of the I AM Meditation in the tradition of Gurdjieff. It was deep, insightful, and contributed greatly to directing my path toward the perspectives of Advaita consciousness, out of which much of the Light of this book emanated.

Daniel Hernandez, my teacher … my friend. Thank you for all you shared with me and taught me. I will never stop reeling from the shock of your passing. Now you live in every star I see in the sky. I miss you.

Arthur Hakalani Pacheco … Mahalo! I miss you! Thank you for teaching me more about death than I ever wanted to know. I will always remember your radiant smile, your melodic laughter, and looking forward to current stories of your dramatic interdimensional journeying, each with a new metaphysical twist. Thank you for sharing your ethereal world until we could see that we can see it too. You made such a graceful dance of living in the Light and singing the blues at the same time. You poured out more Light and Love than anyone could contain all at once.

Akihiro (Calvin) Moriwaki … I scanned the final edit of this book and felt your spirit alive on every page. There is no way to measure how much of your wisdom and magick you shared with me. I was truly blessed to have even known you, not to mention to have had you as one of my 'awakening' teachers. You are appreciated, loved, and missed. I thank you for helping drag me kicking and screaming into the Timeless understanding of what is beyond the veils between the limitless dimensions of consciousness. Goodbye feels like just another ash rising from the fires of impermanence. I know you are still here.

Reverend Harley Robert 'Hal' Beagle of Religious Science/Science of Mind Church, Honolulu, Dr. William Hornaday of Science of Mind Church, Los Angeles … Thank you for making me understand that a rapport with the spirit world is a practical and very normal part of the physical world.

Matthias Swaby – I thank you for your prayers. Your life is a testament to the power of The God over life and death. I thank The God for you and for the spiritual intervention that performed a profound healing in my life. I can never repay you for your bravery, persistence, and courage, fearlessly confronting demons with the touch of an angel of The God. Your humble manner and your chosen surrendered life are a soul's inspiration. I am blessed to have been welcomed into your spiritual family.

Night Shift Editing Team – Thank you all for your energy, time, and diligence. The devil is in the details. Thank you for following it through to the last breath of exorcising that beast.

I give thanks to my ancestors, who remembered me before I was the thought that is me, who delivered me to my understanding, who speak from their watery and earthly graves from the realm of the Timeless to remind me there is no such thing as death. You are the vibration of an ancient drum beating itself into Ultimate relevance, telling true stories time wrote in the Ether of their erasure. The Spirit of cultures of origin occupied, set aside, and buried under the earth from which a new world rises, snatching Light back from thieves and raiders, grave robbers, and soul traders. Scientists, still unsure of what the magic means, can only wonder as it surfaces in dreams of clandestine things that rise like the phoenix to be known again. This magic cannot be burned down with a library. It will not be mocked. It breathes a sacred breath that cannot be choked out or gunned down with silver bullets. It is airborne and cannot be buried, disguised, or replaced with lies. It flows through the bloodline of the body of consciousness that is waking up from this dream. The mouthless whispers emerge from a mosaic of inspired visions of prophetic graffiti, inscribed upon the walls of what will not be forgotten. Voices ride the whirlwinds of the unborn realm into the eye of the cyclone, that place of stillness and silence and Light. Thank you for your voices. Thank you for your sacrifices.

The Light Meditation

Written by JAI
Tim Rodd: Narration, Copy Editing, Post Production, Cover Design
Rahmon Muhammad: Sound Engineer
Sebastian Robertson: Sound Engineer
Levi Chen: Chinese Harp or Zither

I Die to My Ego Self Meditation

Written by JAI
Narration: Nicholas Rodd, JAI
Tim Rodd: Copy Editing, Post Production, Cover Design
Rahmon Muhammad: Sound Engineer
Sebastian Robertson: Sound Engineer
Levi Chen: Chinese Harp or Zither

Many thanks to prolific composer, producer, visionary musician, and performing artist … the heart and soul of Yin Yang Records and Liquid Gardens, Levi Chen. Dream Universal extends immense appreciation, love, and light for your participation in our healing Mystical Meditation journeys. The East meets West meets the Cosmos, ethereal soundscapes of Meditation of my Soul, featuring the interplay of ambient electric guitar textures and the traditional Gu Zheng, Chinese harp, formed a sound that perfectly complements our catalog of healing meditations.

FEARLESS: PSYCHIC SELF-DEFENSE
Transcend the Fear of Spiritual Warfare

TABLE OF CONTENTS

Protect and Heal the Light Body

Featured Meditation: THE LIGHT MEDITATION

In this text, an initial uppercase "L" for the word Light is distinguished from an initial lower case "l" as a reference to or an association with the realm of Divinity.

The upper case "M" in Mirror is distinguished from the lower case "m" of the mirror of mundane reality. Mirror herein refers to the Mirror of the Higher Self that has no physical image to reflect, reflecting only our Divinity. The mirrors of the perishable realm can only reflect the vanity of our ego self.

An upper case "S" refers to the Self that is connected to and alike in Essence to the Most High, Creator God, by the Breath of Spirit and Light that we are at the core of our being. It refers to the Higher Self that has reached the highest potential and subtlest, stateless existence, actively cooperating with the fulfillment of God's Will and purpose for our being. A lower case "s" refers to self-serving, shallow values accompanied by a preoccupation with physical plane, so-called reality. It is a perspective that tends to trap us in a state of distraction by the mundane. This distraction robs us of the depth and meaning of the life we are capable of manifesting. There is a pettiness about the "self," the thought of I, me, my, and mine. There is a lack of discipline and accountability, often leading to the desecration of the Temple of Self. The lack of control over the animalistic nature of the physical self can eclipse the Light of the vessel on the path of eventual becoming.

On some paths of Western mysticism, some change the spelling of the word magic to magick to distinguish magical tricks from mystical practice. There is a thin line between the mystical and the magickal.

All gender references to The God in this text reflect terminology that is not necessarily intended to be gender-specific. I accept that the Holy Names of The God and the Holy Attributes of The God, both known and unknown, know nothing of contradiction in opposites of polarities … only the Union of Spirit. Both the Yin and the Yang energies must exist to be our Cause and continuation. The masculine and feminine energies are compelled to engage in this grand mystical dance of existence equally respected and acknowledged as being mutually responsible for the emanation of all creation in its myriad glorious forms. The God is called by many names from many traditions. My focus remains on The One … That Which defies our marginalized, limited comprehension, that which cannot be named, known, or defined.

WHAT IS
PSYCHIC SELF-DEFENSE?

What is Psychic Self-Defense?

As the golden dawn of a new age teases the horizon of modern civilizations in decline, we are being required to seek answers to the questions of our souls more independently than ever before. We are witnessing a Time of stark transformation of consciousness, unprecedented evolution and regression spinning in the same Time and Space. It has become our spiritual and moral responsibility to energetically assist in issuing in this new, yet ancient age, declaring that the hereafter is here now. We are here at this crossroad and turning point in history to participate in the healing of the spiritual despair that is overspreading the entire planet. It seeks to diminish the high vibration of our essential Selves and to extinguish the Light that we are.

Regardless of how we choose to package or label it, it is a societal and spiritual imperative that ancient wisdom is resurrected and examined for its relevance to our survival. The unsustainable pseudo-reality we have created for ourselves threatens to culturally reduce our humanity to levels lower than the animal kingdom. We have allowed the lowest planes of our consciousness (our animalistic nature or lower self), to define us and confine us to a cage of our own construction. We have forgotten who we are and embraced illusory identities, false labeling, and branding, causing us to lose sight of the fact that we are all connected. We are all the same essentially formless, nameless, genderless, Eternal Beings, energetically connected to all there is, without any defining narrative. The "I" of the true Self is the I AM within the "I" that we perceive ourselves to be. Who we really are is that conscious awareness that witnesses our carnal "self." We are the birthless, deathless, conscious awareness, behind that mask of flesh. We are Truth expressing itself as us. To perceive ourselves differently creates the worst form of existential suffering.

We cannot always rely on finding every answer and solution in traditional places of worship or schools of thought. They as entities are seeking the same answers and solutions that we are. We must seek to become the answer rather than just another question waiting to be asked, the sought after more than the seeker, the charitable more than the needy. We must trust the Third Eye (Psychic Eye) vision of our higher Selves and allow its secrets to weave the fabric of this mystical journey. We will open our hearts, souls, and minds to be the reflectors, the workers of Light. It reduces our phenomenal potential to settle for being just another shadow cast upon the temporal world of transient silhouettes that come and go, without a trace, without a footprint, without a face, without the realization of that sacred place within.

Psychic Self-Defense is the study and practice of enabling a powerful defense system that protects against energetic, spiritual, and psychic attack. Issues around the theme of Psychic Self-Defense surface when outer or inner forces wage an attack against that sacred place within. Many dramatic phenomena are associated with this type of predatory energy, even spilling over into the experiences and circumstances of our practical, everyday lives. It is wise to embrace the study of the subtleties and dynamic charm of this sacred dance of Light, shadows, and the thought-forms that cast them. Here we will examine the realm of the formless for its relevance to our lives on both the physical and nonphysical plane. We will learn techniques that raise our vibrational frequency, making us unavailable for such sophomoric games as psychic target practice.

Our scope will extend from the foul glint of an "evil eye" from the cashier at the supermarket, to the attack waged from the elaborate altar of a practicing occultist with a grudge. The source of relentless assaults against our psyche can be very diverse. They can sprout from the depths of our own subconscious mind and that of others or extend to the subliminal thought-forms peppering the messages and influences of predatory media. We will establish here that an ounce of prevention is worth a pound of cure, sharing modern and ancient methods of managing the energies that affect our lives. These energies can express themselves in mind-boggling extremes. It is hard to know if we are being too paranoid or not being paranoid enough. Our goal is to survive with our minds, bodies, and souls intact. Our goal is to realize who we are and never forget. Our own Self-Realization is our ultimate defense and will free us from the bondage of justifiable fear. We will pursue the knowledge of our true Self, that Eternal, indestructible, formless field of conscious awareness that we are, and ask ourselves, "Who are we protecting in our practice of Psychic Self-Defense? Are we seeking to defend the physical manifestation of our self, or do we actually believe we need to defend the True Self that we really are? Does the Realized Self need to be defended by anybody?"

On the threshold of spiritual self-sufficiency, our confessions are to the Mirror. We, each in our own way, seek and find a Temple of refuge in the heart of our higher Selves. Every face will turn to the rising Sun, and every knee will touch the Earth. Every tongue will confess the meditations of our hearts and bear witness to the Soul and Origin of all Creation, affirming that, in essence, we are One with the Most High. Ours is the Temple within. We turn within, knowing that we are not alone. By the Will of the Most High, our angels, guides, and ancestors are all around us. They are assisting, guiding, and protecting us, whether we are consciously aware of them or not. They are certainly aware of us.

The changeless nature of our Higher Self will always be a mighty warrior standing tall in our defense. That same perspective of our present being is an individuated field of conscious energy, just as much as those on the other side of the veil between worlds. We stay in a positive relationship with it as we exercise the muscle of remembering who we are through spiritual practice and the meditative exercise of Self-Inquiry. It is our nature to be distracted by the rise of physical manifestations and the enchantment of phenomena. There is so much freedom in embracing the subtle shift of identification as the I AM ... the True Self. Our challenge is to remain there. From that formless, nameless, stateless perspective, we are free. We are safe. We are pure.

The clock of a Timeless dimension is ticking faster than ever before. Its hands are spinning faster and faster, bringing humanity nearer to the end of one cycle, and the glorious dawn of another. Violence, hatred, crime, and poverty, on this plane of existence have reached Biblical proportions. The individual and group Karma of the people and nations of the world race toward completion in this accelerated Time warp of dramatic transition, revelation, and transformation.

Much of humanity has succumbed to a skillfully programmed, electronic, digital, automated, and computerized state of unconsciousness that has locked us into a high-tech prison of our own design. The chilling cultural climate is such that it has become difficult to even communicate with one another as human beings. We compete and gloat over how many things we can do, all at the same time, under the label of "multi-tasking." Humans have begun to function like robots. We are becoming more and more unfocused, unhappy, lonely, isolated, and empty, stuck on remote control, and auto-pilot. In the face of our high-definition Wi-Fi culture, we have become the androids we covet. We are rapidly losing definition as human beings.

We are inundated with, and hypnotized by every manner of social media and sophisticated technology that has left us more out of touch with one another than ever before. We have internet surfed our way into a virtual reality mindset, devoid of human contact and connection. Before this book reaches you, there will probably be obsolete technology dumping sites full of the same devices I am using right now, after we have been seduced into believing we cannot live without any of them. We are losing our social skills, our manners, families, friends and our sense of Self. We are increasingly unable to calendar appointments into our skin-tight schedules just to spend time with our families and friends. As the years pass, the epidemic level of loneliness is deadening our humanity, and robbing us of what matters the most in life ... ourselves and one another.

This is not rocket science. Studies have already shown that the brain requires downtime and that there is a price to pay for not conducting our lives accordingly. There are disturbing similarities between the symptoms and behaviors associated with addiction to drugs and the compulsive use of common technological, social networking tools. World culture is becoming increasingly reliant upon this fast-lane cyber mentality. Perhaps it would be better that we returned to carrier pigeons, considering the human price we are paying.

This is not a judgment. I am as guilty as the next person. As I write this, I sit before six active computer monitors, engulfed in blue light. I have been fortunate enough to have missed many years of the onslaught of this technological revolution. I lived outside of so-called first world culture for nearly fifteen years, often in areas where hot water, electricity, and a phone signal were not to be taken for granted. I eventually returned to my city "home," where a breath of fresh air and a quiet moment is a luxury. The communications of people had begun to sound like computer-generated, electronic, digital static. Distracted, blunt, abrupt, monotone, monosyllabic, bottom-line style tweet language offered no patience for a relaxed conversation or meaningful dialogue. We hardly make eye contact anymore. Our minds have become so fragmented that we cannot sustain the strength of our energy fields sufficient to protect ourselves from the energetic assaults of others. We have even forgotten how to breathe. There is no Space or Time to seek the refuge of a quiet meditation discipline.

When I returned to fast lane, big city life, after years of rural island life, I was completely overwhelmed by the technological and cultural changes. I fell deep into culture shock to the point I could hardly function, and there I remain as a voyeur peeking from under the bleachers of this game of life, rather than being a player on the field. The radiated conversations of computer-generated voices settle like dust on these virtual lifestyles, while our energy fields are polluted, damaged, and wide-open, defenseless against attack.

Our lifestyles have become so brutally inhumane that one flaw in an overcrowded calendar could have the power to topple lives like dominoes falling. Even our food has to be so fast that the value of good health takes no precedence over speed. The stress is deadly. There is no importance placed on the ability to focus and concentrate on anyone or anything singularly. If we do not schedule appointments and reminders for the balance and freedom of a quiet meditation, we will break. We will rupture those connecting threads between the shell, the spirit, and the soul of our being. We will effectively burn the bridge between dreams. We will sacrifice our humanity, Orwellian style, scramble our frequencies, and damage our electromagnetic field, a precursor to disease on all levels of our being.

An undistracted counter-culture is forming, focused on the spiritual healing of the physical, mental, and emotional self. People are suffering and have begun to seek to transcend the noise of this chaos, moving into the stillness, the silence of the inward journey toward Self-Realization.

With the realization of Self comes an inherent commitment to the responsibility for protecting every aspect of this Self. At some point in our lives, we have all heard references to matters of psychic attack and self-defense. Psychic Self-Defense is not limited to those who chose to study or practice magickal, mystical, or spiritual paths. We can all improve the quality of our everyday lives by forming habits based on an understanding of sound spiritual protocol. A student of mysticism engaging in as basic a practice as meditation, or a yoga class, must consider the study of Psychic Self-Defense a mandate.

How can we responsibly protect ourselves if we do not know who we are? An awakening or Self-Realization can take place in the blink of an eye. One of the most powerful instant meditations I can think of is to breathe deeply and relax into a gentle shift of perspective. Release all superficial identification. Go beyond the mind of the lower-self perspective into the perspective of the Eternal I AM, the indestructible I AM, the Higher Self. Begin the Self-Inquiry with the question,

"Who am I, really?" Witness the lower self, the physical self, and its ongoing list of desires. Just like a graveyard, there's always room for one more. Don't judge. Don't correct. Observe, witness objectively, without trying to change anything. Identify life's changeful things. Release any attachment to controlling the changefulness of changeful things. Identify what is unchanging. Stand in that formless, Timeless, spaciousness. Witness every detail of our senseless struggle in an attempt to fulfill our list of demands. Feel that freedom. Then ask, "What witnesses the witness that I am? What sees the seer?" That is the beginning of the most sacred of journeys, the journey to the Higher Self.

It is comforting to affirm that we are of the same Essence as That Which Created us, and we are powerful enough, wise enough, to lovingly protect this beautiful being that we are. Whatever our motivation, this study will lead to a stronger sense of security as we navigate the obstacle course our lives have become. We fearlessly lift the thin veil between worlds to the realization that we are That. We are the Seer and the seen. We have nothing to fear in the embrace of the Ultimate I AM.

The Meaning of the I AM

The I AM defies definition. We are dreams born of the sacred realm of the I AM delicately clothed in matter. Only the blind spots of our own vision would make us believe otherwise. There are many common names for the energy of this subtle and powerful field of conscious energy. There are many manifestations of the I AM. It is the object of our Self-Inquiry, that conversation between the ego self and the Higher Self. The energy of the formless, eternal, transcendent being of pure consciousness is the Higher Self that we are. The I AM has deep significance in many mystical traditions and goes back into antiquity thousands of years, representing a pure, Timeless, formless Self that witnesses the physical expression of Itself as us. We manifest in form as the clay creatures we are, driven by That Sacred Breath, powered by That Light of Origin, sustained by the same. The heart must embrace this perspective to be released from the bondage of self-identification with transient forms covered with labels and become a truly Self-Realized being. This is not an event. It is a path through the mystical gates of Self-awareness, into the eternal domain of the I AM that we are.

The I AM seems to represent something different to everyone. Historically, the I AM has no definition since its presence precedes those who might seek to define it. It has come to represent a cry for home, for freedom from captivity and slavery, a cry for The God. As a key element of regular spiritual practice, many metaphorically burn or "chant down" all of the false identities assumed in our efforts to assimilate into this theatre of shadows. The simple act of ignoring false precepts and concepts of Self facilitates the burning away of counterfeit inner and outer realities that lead us to our spiritual corruption and destruction.

The vibration associated with the I AM can be maintained through disciplined spiritual practice, faith, and reliance on the seen and unseen for guidance. It, in this text as a dimension of consciousness accessible to all of us, for we are the temple that houses the energies of the Eternal I AM, the Creator of all we are, and all we know. It is only a matter of exercising and flexing the muscle of remaining in the I AM, pulling ourselves back from every cage of bogus definition we assign to our true Self. Even though notions of Eternal existence are commonly associated with a past life, a future life, or an afterlife, it can be entered without experiencing what we call death. To view existence as the I AM or to remain within the myopic vision of a one-dimensional self-concept is a choice. When we have suffered sufficiently from this limiting and terrifying perspective, we expand our focus to explore the nature of who we really are.

Who we really are is not limited to that reflection we see in the mirror. Even the mirror has enough sense to know that our reflection is not who we are, so it does not cling to anything we show it. It accepts and releases. It does not look for yesterday or tomorrow. It does not record or identify with that image. It is our own minds that tend to do that. But we are not the mind. We are not the body. We are That … That which preceded the mirror and all false concepts of the "I." The real "I" is that Formless, Timeless, Storyless being expressing itself as the form it witnesses in the mirror. "That" is the I AM. From that perspective, we ask, "Who am I?" From this perspective, we affirm that there is no death, no time, no story, no form. Then, after the rush of freedom we feel from that realization, we must ask, "Can the seer be seen? Can the witness be witnessed? What witnesses the witness?"

At this point, Self-Inquiry begins. The fire is kindled, and the process of awakening to freedom has begun. Time is escaped. The bullying of the flesh is checked and put in its place as a cooperative subordinate to the Higher Self and the Most High. From a state of consciousness mimicking a coma, we awaken to the dawn of every new day, rejoicing that we are blessed with the opportunity to renew our commitment to the purification of our hearts. We commit ourselves to cleanse the controlling, manipulative energies of desire, attachment, and aversion. There are many roads to the spiritual mindset of the I AM. There are many names ascribed to the Ultimate Witness. Opinions, cultural conditioning, and choices only

10

add to the diversity of the colorful mosaic of our collective journey. The fact that someone else is traveling a different path than our own does not mean that they are lost. There should be no unfavorable comparisons, nor should these paths and respective deities be set up in competition with one another for rightness. If we have images, qualities, or even the intonation of a name, that reference is still not of the Ultimate I AM, the Unknowable, and most subtle in density.

In the Baha'i temple in Wilmette, Illinois, one of the most beautiful I have ever seen, there are nine doors, each representing a different faith. Each of the doors represents a path to the experience of what is characterized in this text as the realm of the I AM, the realm of the Sacred. There is nothing that must be done to earn one's place as the I AM, only to strive to gracefully master the balance of unconditional acceptance of the perfect balance inherent in creation. Everything has a balance that must be kept to progress from negative into positive existence. There is no such thing as all good or all bad. That type of duality is subjective, relative, and can turn on a dime.

The Yin Yang is a sacred symbol that represents all of life as a circle, rather than seeing it as linear. A horizontal timeline suggests that there is a distinct beginning and at some point, an ending. A vertical timeline may suggest the same. But there is no end within the circle, especially this circle. It is divided into two parts, not in a straight line, but an "S" shape. One side is black illustrating the Void from which the Light emerged. The white side illustrates the Light. The two small circles of opposite polarity on each side mean that nothing is just one way. Duality is our nature and the nature of creation. It requires us to be more merciful and compassionate in our judgments of everything including ourselves. Everything and everyone is a composite of two sides, each necessary to the other.

Whatever name you want to call it, and there are many, our souls are well familiar with the energies of I AM, naturally seeking its serenity for survival. The longing is the connection. If prayer were a government, its name would be, I AM.

Its flag and national anthem would be "The Eternal OM." Its race of people is the *human race*. The President's name could only be expressed by silence. The I AM is our safe refuge from the evil influences and attacks of mischievous creation. The streets on this sacred journey are littered with broken hearts and vanity-based dreams. That Which Created us is sufficient to guide us through the challenging experience of material form and will be there waiting to welcome our grateful spirits home. Unconditional Love is the Soul of the I AM.

Yin Yang

The outer circle represents the circle of life in perpetual motion

The two dots indicate there is no absolute yin or yang. Each contains the essence of the other

The Wu Ji is the point of stillness. The calm in the eye of the storm

Qualities of Yin

night
dark
cold
negative
passive
female

Qualities of Yang

day
light
warm
positive
active
male

13

Protect the I AM

The Light essence of the I AM is sustained more easily when the body Temple has been cleansed of the toxic, negative energies that collect in the normal course of our daily lives. The nature of the I AM is a request for the respect and purification of our physical bodies, as a vehicle of transportation assigned to our immortal soul by The Creator for this temporal experience. The essence of our immortal soul is one with That of The Creator I AM, the One that is the Witness of the seer of the experience of our form. Our physical form or container represents the temple of The Creator. Our indifference to the desecration of the temple of The God will cost us in all ways because we are not our own. In some ways, we take ourselves too seriously. In other ways, we do not take our real Self seriously enough. We are unique and peculiar in creation, and respect should be born of healthy spiritual self-esteem.

In the process of the cleansing of our temple, physical, mental, and emotional balance can be maintained by surrounding ourselves with the supportive energy of like-minded people. There is no need to become anti-social in relationship to people we determine to be unlike ourselves. Some fulfill this basic need in the environment of a church or spiritual organization of people. Others are fortunate enough to find it within their families and circle of interpersonal relationships. The Internet can even provide a safe and effective way of communicating with like-minded people. It is most important to know that the temple of our soul is within. Yet, a social journey can provide powerful revelations of The God and The God within ourselves and others, holding that delicate balance between Heaven and Earth, clay and Ether. Even though the strongest spiritual connection is kept through focused prayer and meditation, the nature of the I AM can occur harmoniously as a chord, rather than exclusively as one single note. Those who have chosen to submit to the Divine Will of The God can be a choir in celebration rather than a form of sacrificial, solitary confinement.

The body is as much affected by loneliness, grief, fear, anxiety, and stress as it is by toxins and chemicals that we ingest and are exposed to every day of our lives. Regular physical activity and a daily practice of some form of transcendental physical disciplines such as Yoga, Martial Arts, Chi Gong, or Tai Chi as a form of meditation, is highly recommended. This discipline will assist in the maintenance of a fit and worthy vessel to host the energy flow of the I AM. These activities can be done in a group to keep the spirit stimulated by new input and new acquaintances.

The path of the Natural Mystic on the road to the realization of the Self can lead us to peace with no borders. It can also lead us to bouts of loneliness and the isolation of spiritual solitude. A social circle that is either too small or too large is not healthy if it becomes a form of bondage. A well-chosen social environment, which respects the integrity of our immortal soul, is a taste of the "rapture" on this physical plane of existence. The journey takes on a synergy that multiplies and intensifies our individual energies by our association with the energy of an entire group with the same focus and tuned in on the same frequency. However, I quote a well-known Spanish saying, "Mejor solita que mal acompañada" … "Better alone than in bad company." Group Karma can be experienced because of the company we keep or groups we energetically align ourselves with.

The I AM can be associated with many of our considerations of heaven and the afterlife. Heaven, like hell, can exist as a dimension or frequency. As with the abyss, once we have gazed into the realm of the I AM, it has also gazed into us. We have to keep reminding ourselves that as the forces of good are realized in the I AM, so are the forces of evil well anchored in their I AM. Both frequencies can be tapped into at will or may choose to tap into us if we are open and available. For that reason, becoming well-versed in Psychic Self-Defense is very important, as we pray for the virtue of spiritual discernment to continually grace our lives. There is no reason to live life fearfully. Fear is nourishment for negative energies and entities. They feed on it. That Which Created us is sufficient to protect us from

15

anything outside of Divine Will. Nothing outside of Divine Will exists.
Consequently, protection is a lifestyle, not an occasional ritual. Anchored in the
energy of our Higher Self, nothing can do us harm. The I AM is pure awareness
and cannot be harmed.

The 'self' that needs protection is not real.

~ A Course in Miracles ~

I AM Consciousness Rising

The human condition requires that we observe the first law of nature, Self-preservation. Survival of the fittest has always extended beyond physical boundaries into the invisible realms. Knowledge is power. The belief that what you don't know can't hurt you can invite disaster as you've never imagined. You do not need to be involved in any type of mystical studies or practices to require the knowledge of Psychic Self-Defense. We are energy, and there are energies all around us all of the time that can, and will, affect our lives on many levels. These energies rise from many physical and nonphysical sources. They can rise to personally target us, or it can be a matter of being in the wrong place at the wrong time. We will examine many forms of attack that I am familiar with. They are not necessarily from a physical source. Many are smokeless fire elementals from the jinn kingdom, angels, discarnate beings, and their countless manifestations.

In this text, we approach the subject of spiritual warfare from apparently physical sources, asking, "Who is being attacked?" The answer is … A person who is presumed to lack the knowledge of who they are. Who defends? A person who does not know who they are. Who is the attacker? A person who does not know who they are. All of those questions and answers lead to the revelation that we have nothing to fear. If we know who we really are, and the power associated with living as our Higher Self, then we know we have nothing to fear. From that perspective, we accept that we are made of the same Eternal Essence of That Which created us. We are That. What should we fear? "Nothing!" … answers the I AM Consciousness Rising. It does not matter how many candles you have to light. It does not matter how many mantras you know to chant. It does not matter how much sage you burn. Nothing will save you more than knowing who you really are.

In psychic development classes I have taught, I spend a lot of time and energy dispelling the fears associated with mystical studies. Knowledge is the best cure for fear. This particular type of fear can be the result of negative programming and cultural propaganda. One factor in the propagation of such fear is the judgment and oppression imposed upon seekers, by some who claim to represent the "Truth" of "God." Some organized religions and spiritual paths tend to regard certain types of spiritual independence as threatening, dangerous, and even evil.

I could drop a defensive posture on the issue and say, not all warnings about the dangers of certain prepackaged mystical practices are completely unfounded. I could take the offensive and condemn them according to their own Law, which leaves all Judgment to God, not to someone who decides to play God. However, I now see both sides. I know that there are undeniable dangers, particularly to impressionable, gullible, naïve, or spiritually compromised people. I now know there are undeniable dangers to spiritually sound, strong, and stable people as well.

Certain mystical paths and studies can cause us to become magnets for phenomena that can be disturbing, at least. The more common victims of potentially dangerous spirituality tend to be those who profile themselves as outcasts … vulnerable loners estranged from family, friends, and social contacts that could provide balanced feedback. These people are often drawn to philosophies offering the well-baited hook of "home" and "family." A diverse support system can provide a caring voice of reason that serves as a reality check from many perspectives.

Many of us have found out the hard way, through tragedy or trauma, that there are things in this life beyond our control or explanation. Feelings of helplessness can fully engage a desperate pursuit for the power to survive it. It can then take on the spirit of a power monger attracted to radical mystical paths to manipulate the events and circumstances of life. Some just want attention and embrace controversy as a means to achieve that end. Whatever it takes to drive us to these studies, know that approaching it with an ego-based agenda will not yield good results.

A major event may prompt a quest to control the things we can, no matter how inconsequential, often manifesting as OCD (Obsessive Compulsive Disorder) behaviors. Others just want what appears to be "something for nothing" or a quick fix instead of putting in the spiritual work required for healing. Real change requires adopting a sustainable, holistic lifestyle that supports a more evolved consciousness. This is not for cursory study or entertainment. I can relate to many of these psychological and character profiles and confess that control issues made me embrace and travel spiritual paths of study and practice that could have been dangerous to me. By Divine Grace, my soul's path ultimately led me full circle, back to my mother's favorite prayer as a child, the 23rd Psalms from The Bible (KJV), representing a cornerstone of faith and spiritual practice.

Yea, though I walk through the valley
of the shadow of death,
I will fear no evil, for thou art with me

It is no wonder that the study of the mysteries has come under intense scrutiny and criticism by spiritual conservatives. But we are the honest ones. We are the sovereign ones. Many practices may be "judged" by some to be unacceptable, yet they are powerful and spiritually correct. With *all* paths, there are positives and negatives, and even that determination is a judgment to some degree. On this sacred journey, the path is the destination. Most important in essence is that the path is focused on the pursuit of a beautiful, loving relationship with Universal Law and That Which Created all. Any path can lead to detours and confusing crossroads. I don't believe that in all cases throwing the "baby out with the bathwater" is required. They all may have their merits. To choose to travel NO path defies the Laws of a Universe that is in perpetual motion, evolving, expressing, unfolding in its revelation of who we essentially are.

Whether we are studying mysticism or just trying to carve out some sacred space in a whirlwind life, it is important to know how to protect ourselves, not so much in a defensive way, but more so, in a preventative way. One of the most important recommendations is to exercise sound discretion and critical judgment in our choices of associates and friends. Friends are like clothes; they say a lot about us. Everyone has heard the horror stories of cultish organizations and irresponsible rogue spiritual groups. We must make sure we know, as best we can, the spiritual orientation of those from whom we seek spiritual classes, friendships, or advice.

Imagine what life could be like vibrating at a frequency where there was no way to hide wickedness behind cloaks of good intention, where all is seen, all is known, and all is Divine Love. Imagine a world with no ambition to strive every day to subject beings to needless suffering.

We are people of many dimensions. On one side our imagination, on the other its visible manifestation. We are free. We walk our path in knowledge, not fear, of ourselves or anyone else. We walk the path of the Natural Mystic with those who have traveled before us. We merge as energies with those receiving guidance through the relationship we maintain with The Creator. In every dimension of our Ultimate Reality, we are loved and protected by The Most High. Our greatest danger is our own ignorance.

Many of the mystical experiences people report make the concept of Spiritual Self-Defense as important as breath. Most of us have, at some point in our lives, had a spiritual experience; some good, some ecstatic, some scary, some threatening, some even dangerous. After such experiences, one cannot expect to ever be the same again. It can represent the first stirrings of the evolution of spirit, a quickening, a confirmation of our connection to the world of nonphysical existence.

There are safety issues on this unpredictable spiritual path when mingling with energies, entities, and unseen forces. We address these issues as they arise with the wisdom of the ancients as our problems represent a modern spin on old themes. There is nothing new under the Sun. Understanding this works to our advantage in matters of Psychic Self-Defense. It allows us to access the wisdom of the ages and appropriately apply this knowledge and improve the quality of our lives.

The first step to spiritual protection is our wise and discerning choices regarding the company we keep and what we choose to share with other people. Being friendly with a person does not necessarily mean they are our friend. Uncensored disclosure of personal mystical experiences can open the doors to ridicule or judgment and expose us to danger. That is why it is so important to pay attention to the company we are in before beginning a spiritual or any other type of self-expose. I believe these things to be private and have no place in common, casual conversation. It is unwise to feel too free to engage in random small talk about our spiritual experiences, among people who have no foundation for understanding such issues. We must first look at the spiritual and cultural mindset of the people around us and ask ourselves if these are people we really want to disrobe our soul in the presence of. If not, we should respect boundaries regarding the depth and extent of our disclosures, depending on who we are talking to.

We must accept the fact that it is "normal" to have what some see as paranormal experiences. It is far more common than we may think. Some try to explain away mystical phenomena as evil or crazy. It is to our advantage to pursue and embrace an understanding of the spirit realm and its relationship to the rich world of mystical practices and study. It will make our lives make more sense as we expand our understanding of the many dimensions of our temporal life. We are complex mystical beings, challenged to discover that within the context of physical experience.

Life is a gift to be examined, cultivated, and preserved. The spirit of ourselves is who we really are, apart from our clever packaging. Many of us get emotionally attached to the packaging. Many never rise above a dirt level consciousness that anchors our spirit to the perishable, then breaks our spirit because it cannot conform to the concrete boundaries we set in place. We cannot endure our physical reality if we refuse to broaden our vision of Self to include the imperishable, immortal duality of our nature.

The Mystical Path to Self-Realization

It is possible, and common, to be physically alive and spiritually dead at the same time. It is not difficult to distinguish the living from those who are dead to the consciousness of Self. Many of us are walking dead, worshipping the dead, trapped in the revolving door styled graveyard of the material world, feeding upon any sign of life, like vampires. It is also possible, and common, to be physically dead and spiritually alive and well, shining a Light that cannot be diminished, by the grace of That Which Created It. There is a thin line that divides one side from the other. It is sad to drift toward the expiration date of our perishable form without embracing the knowledge that there are two sides of our existence. They can overlap, allowing us to be able to blink from one to the other, often without realizing that it happened. A death-like state of consciousness is the cruelest death. It does not offer the finality and closure associated with physical death. It is a form of purgatory. There is comfort in knowing that resurrection can occur in the length of time it takes to choose it.

We cannot awaken a person who is pretending to be asleep. The awakening and realization of Self will occur whether we like and want it or not. In that inevitable moment between closing our eyes in one world and opening them to another, we will know then. The gift is to know now. No one wants to hear the eleventh-hour battle cries of the rudely awakened. There is a price to pay for hitting that snooze button over and over again, with no sense of personal responsibility for the storm of consequences that follows. Those who sought to stir our awakening process may want to know; Where were you when I needed a friend, someone to talk to and share my journey with, through the many levels of consciousness I traveled, often feeling alone, ridiculed, called crazy, teased, disregarded, avoided? Where were you then? Where were you when worldly vanity was stripped away to raw bone to leave me exposed, afraid, and vulnerable, with nothing left of who I thought was me, with nothing but the knowledge that I had not lost myself. I had found myself!

The profoundly sacred existential loneliness of the seeker on the path to enlightenment is the archetype of the Hermit. The Hermit progressively sheds the need to be validated by mischievous, opinionated clay vessels passing in the night of our corporal journey. The Hermit has not withdrawn from the world as much as he or she has embraced the True Self, The Ultimate Light of Ultimate Healing, The "I," the connection between humanity and Divinity. I share with you, The Hermit, an excerpt from my book on Mystical Meditation and Archetypal Healing for contemporary relationships. From FACELESS: THE SACRED RELATIONSHIP, the Hermit seeks to be understood.

Nine
IX
The Hermit

The darkness is my solitary playground. Isolation is my shelter from the raging storms of the outer worlds. My heart seeks in silence the secrets of the void from the lowest realms of the abyss, to the most exalted realms of Light Consciousness, searching within the deepest and highest aspect of myself for that which I could not find in others. I face the East and travel the path of the Mystics, the ancient ones. I navigate my journey in between worlds, exploring the mysteries of creation and Creator.

I turn within dissolving into translucent shadows of my most private Self. I am the Hermit. I am moving into profound seclusion, beyond the mist that drifts into time and twilight. What some call a cold and lonely cavern in the most desolate hours of the soul, I call my sanctuary of inner peace and Temple of quiet refuge for the healing of my fractured spirit and the illumination of my soul. Obscured from sight, I retreat into the cocoon of the Hermit.

From behind my cloak of concealment, I beg for your patience and understanding. I turn away. I need some transpersonal space. Please let me go, that I may hibernate, evolve, and heal. Let the Greater Silence enfold me. I will emerge transformed, out of a Light shower of epiphanies, Love, and songs of redemption.

Profile of The Hermit Archetype

The Hermit awaits the glorious first light of an inner awareness that crouches, dormant, and half-asleep in a locked closet of consciousness. His is the somber ecstasy of the stillness of inner space. Upon the threshold of enlightenment, his weary spirit stands, finally.

Wrapped securely in the cloak of solitude, the Hermit finds the courage to face his own nakedness, no longer suffocating in the polluted atmosphere of mindless diversion, and empty noise of the crowd. He turns his back on the chaos and hollow chatter of a world in stark denial of its own madness. In search of The Ultimate, seeking only The Unattainable ... he would rather be alone. He meditates;

*When the last grains of sand in my hourglass
sift through the short narrow time tunnel of my life
to whom shall I beckon with outstretched hand and say,
"Come with me?"*

*Who, then, would say,
"I will?"
Herein lies my final truth
I am born into this life as spirit alone
As spirit alone, I shall leave it*

25

Being alone
and being lonely
is not the same reality
There is no lonely soul
that is One with The God
My soul, alone, in the shimmering triple darkness of its solitude
is only closer to the beginning, closer to the end, and thus,
much closer to The God

The Hermit recoils, retreats into the womb of the Universe, into the school of its most sacred wisdom. The innermost essence of the being of the Hermit archetype seeks shelter, nourishment, and protection, in the same manner as the fetus during its period of gestation in the development of the human form. The Hermit learns to accept, embrace, and love the many aspects of his higher and lower consciousness on his voyage to the center of his being, through meditation, contemplation, committed study, and introspection. His withdrawal from the materialistic, carnal-minded world may extend beyond healthy limits. If this "retreat" spirals into indifference, morbid isolation, depression, and fearfulness of life, the Hermit should seek the counsel of the Hierophant or be swallowed into the Abyss and become lost in purgatory without windows or doors, ceilings or floors.

As the archetype of the Hermit, we must have wisdom enough to identify those times in our lives when we must withdraw from the external theater of a world that seeks turmoil and suffering, cleverly masqueraded as entertainment, rather than peace. It is being channeled into our world through every conceivable medium. If we were to judge based on the "programming" that we subject ourselves to on a daily basis, we would believe that there is no hope for this world. It extends from the individual to the family unit, within our communities, between our countries, even into the elemental and spiritual realm. The panic resulting from this negative meditation is enough to force our withdrawal and shift from one perspective or frequency into another. To step outside of the matrix of programming is to step into the world of the Hermit.

The Hermit may suggest that we retreat into internal illumination for as long as it takes to heal from the damage caused by the negative, destructive energy of the systems and mindset of outer and inner confusion. There is nothing abnormal about these feelings, as despondent as they may make us. It is only our soul's yearning for the Sacred, for connection or union with The Creator. Though there may be feelings of urgency associated with this longing for connection, there is solace in knowing that *the longing is the connection. The longing IS the connection.*

The Hermit archetype has strong associations with both esoteric and mundane forms of fertility, gestation, and healing. It is symbolic of the alchemy of mysticism's inner journey. As sacred as the descent of Spirit into matter, equally sacred is the ascension of Spirit from the prison of matter to higher realms. Sacred is the magick created through connecting once again with its Eternal Source and manifesting Divine Will on this plane, as we were created to do.

The Hermit can represent the fertilization of our mind, spirit, and body, nurturing to maturity the positive seeds we plant. This may indicate entry, reentry, or initiation into an institution of higher learning, for mental, physical, or spiritual growth and development. It may represent the healthy retreat of the over-stimulated mind into an environment where thoughts are gathered, reorganized, and our unique beauty is rediscovered. The Hermit *always* represents a withdrawal of some sort, motivated by passage through the inner planes on the subtle frequency of a Vision Quest, destined for higher ground.

The individual who is transitioning to the level of The Hermit toward spiritual maturity either chooses to evolve, or is pushed to a brighter Light than that which guided him to that point. He then becomes a beacon of Light from the Source of creation as he generously shares it with others. To evolve The Hermit

27

mystically reinters the symbolic womb of the Eternal to reexperience gestation and rebirth.

The Hermit's archetypal energy is that of a sacred, solitary withdrawal into the silence that precedes illumination. The soul is Timeless. It is Unknowable. Seeking to understand the nature of it is essential to our physical existence. We are required to examine it and contemplate its relevance to the experience of our daily lives. What is this mysterious presence, and how is it on an adventure within us? Is it our True Self, from our True Origin? Is it indeed an adventure or are we in exile? Ask the Hermit, and then ask the I AM, the Higher Self, to remember the Light that we are, and the Creator of that Light.

We have the responsibility of developing and nourishing our own spirits toward the goal of sharing our Light. It is a blessing to be able to help others learn to slip in and out of the windows and doors of the perishable world. We get to enjoy this spiritual adventure. Our meditation and prayer discipline give us strength and protection in the face of predictable phenomena that will naturally accompany breakthroughs in awareness on our Vision Quest. We all have the potential to grasp glimpses of Ultimate Reality, fearlessly, for the depth of our knowledge robs it of its shock value and serves to open our Third Eye vision.

Do understand that we do not have to be on any "path" as a "seeker" to be drawn into a world of experience that is completely beyond our comprehension or perceived control. We are all only one small incident away from opening a Pandora's Box that we cannot close. On the path of spiritual studies, even something as apparently innocent as Mystical Meditation is not for the cowardly, or those who are satisfied with a mere cursory knowledge of basic Psychic Self-Defense. We don't have the luxury of entertaining a single thought of existential randomness, coincidence, or fear in our perceived reality. Some experiences may occur that could frighten us and lure us back into the world of the spiritually unconscious, searching for a false sense of security and the bliss of ignorance. That kind of fear can lead to a crisis of faith if we are forgetful of who we really are and our relationship with That which created us. The point where the two meet and find out that they are One, and that there never was two … that is the emergence of freedom from illusion. This book presents an overview of experience and instruction from many cultures and schools of thought. A basic understanding of mystical phenomena that one should reasonably expect to occur prepares us for a resurrection of consciousness.

Though it can be very disturbing, science fiction drama from the spirit world is not our greatest threat. The greatest problem I have encountered on my mystical life journey is with the *spiritually* dead or 'undead' people. They believe they are real, based only on their physical presence. They snipe from a cowardly distance, regularly firing bullets of malignant energy into the heart of our awakening. They seek to turn spiritual growth into a spiritually incorrect joke, in league with classism, sexism, racism, religionism, and all of the "ism's" that seek to divide and conquer. Our goal is to transcend energies and judgments that keep us from seeing one another as the same.

Thoughts are things. Words are weapons. It is important to identify disruptive behavior threatening our peace of mind in our circle of friends, family, and associates. We may have to choose to keep our circle small. We may lose friends. We may make friends. The Hermit has released all attachment to seeking the approval of others, the opinions of others, or compromising a spiritual standard to bargain for the friendship of others. He or she resists being influenced, in any way, to become popular and accepted by others. This introverted archetype does not opt for a "sheep" mentality in a world full of wolves. The Universe will conspire to restore and renew the life of the Hermit based on Destiny, and according to Divine Will. After the intended lessons are learned, confidence will return, strong enough to become Self-defined, and Self-affirming. The Hermit ends up being far better off since we have become cooperative and proactive in the process of our own spiritual rebirth and development.

29

The first sign of Self-Realization is the *awakening*. There are many signs of an awakening or 'quickening' of spirit. Our spirit and soul will stir when it is shown true purpose and destiny manifesting in our lives. There is always a purpose and reason for everything. It is up to us to find out what it is and do what we came here to do. The next level is the *recognition* of the changes in our own energy. Based upon that recognition, we will seek our own energetic levels in our associations and friendships, holding to exacting standards. That initiates the *gathering*. When it happens, it is a gift of the Divine, and we will know. It is undeniable, unmistakable energy and we will recognize it on contact. It then becomes our responsibility to acknowledge this gift and never take it for granted. Our quickened vibration causes our rise into the realm of higher frequencies of thought and action. We will find positive connections with like-minded people who will become bringers of Light for ourselves and others, increasing the numbers of our circle.

It is not wise to develop co-dependent relationships or fall into emotional bondage with "shadows" because we must never forget that our most powerful resource is our independent connection with That Which Created us. We do not need to form a cult or join one to maintain our circle of spiritual comfort. Nothing we allow to stand between The God and us is worth the consequences. There are times we will find ourselves on our own, with no support group around us of people on our same wavelength. It tends to be a rite of passage. Often, we are placed in a position of aloneness so that we can witness the extent to which *we are not alone*. We will grow in strength and contribute to the strength of others as we become well prepared to defend ourselves and submit our ego selves to the voice of silence. We will prevail, and still be more than just conquerors. We must strive to cultivate and maintain our healing abilities, even when challenged by discordant energy.

Signs of Natural Psychic Abilities

Some people are more psychically sensitive than others. These people are sometimes forced into the study of Psychic Self-Defense just to manage energies that are a normal part of their lives. They are not strangers to sometimes disturbing mystical and paranormal experiences. They are magnets for it. This is not an exposé about horror stories of rampant wickedness and how to fear it. It is a holistic collection of suggestions from many paths, beliefs, and experiences. Only what resonates with the energy of your Higher Self should be considered. On any path of mystical study, many have experiences that are difficult to explain. These experiences are a natural part of our multidimensional existence, both perishable and imperishable, as they demonstrate our dual and transcendent nature.

Some unsettling experiences may include, but are not limited to:

- The sensation of being pulled out of body by an unseen force, feeling paralyzed and unable to "get back into" the physical body. This may occur just before falling asleep or being lulled into deep sleep. It can begin as a lucid dream, nightmare, or Sleep Paralysis;

- Dreamlike visions or apparitions;

- Dreams that come true, either literally or symbolically;

- Dreaming in color and experiencing Lucid Dreams with an unusual, surreal feeling;

- Strong feelings toward certain people, either positive or negative that turn out to be a sign or warning;

- Having thoughts about someone and they call or visit soon after;

- Having seen an illumination of varied colors or aura surrounding the body of a person;

- Having mysterious knowledge of unknown events with no apparent reasonable explanation;

- Recognizing and having knowledge or memories of places never visited before;

- Having the feeling of recognizing a person unknown on a conscious level;

- Dreaming about someone unknown and later meeting them and recognizing them from the dream;

- Having recurrent dreams or visions of another time period wherein there was a feeling of having been present;

- Sensing an unseen presence;

- Having heard a voice that had no possible physical source;

- Having seen someone, or something, a light or shadow, in the peripheral vision, then turning to look and finding nothing;

- Identifying a scent with no possible physical source;

- Having canceled or altered plans for trips or appointments without having a conscious reason, only to discover later that something happened that you would have chosen to avoid;

- Having had memories of life before the age of three;

- Having known what other people were going to say before they say it;

- Having felt the sensation of freezing cold pass through the entire body, with no apparent physical cause or source;

- Having become extremely angry with someone and they have experienced an unfortunate and unusual turn of luck soon afterward;

- Having dreamed certain details of another part of the world and subsequently traveled to that place and recognized those details to be accurate;

- Having seen things move with there being no physical cause;

- Having traveled to places without physically being there (astral travel);

- Having experienced physical death and being revived, mental faculties intact, with the experience of having traveled to the "other side";

- Having had the experience of being transported to another place, either in or out of body, and communing with what appeared to be aliens, spirit beings or deities;

- Having felt that prayers or touch was a factor in the healing of someone suffering from an illness;

- Being born with a "veil" (a sheath of skin) over the face;

- Having had premonitions of events to come and they actually occurred;

- Having dreamed or had visions of information that have caused a win in a game of chance;

- Being regularly singled out of a crowd and asked for advice;

- Having had dreams of flying and experiencing a shocking feeling of falling when awakened;

- Having experienced intuitive feelings knowing that it is logical to override worldly explanation;

- Having had physical symptoms (headaches, nausea, itching, burning, panic attacks, shortness of breath, dizziness, diarrhea, unusual bleeding, insomnia, choking, or heavy pressure on the chest) seeming to correspond with some unexpected event;

- Having some unusual identifying mark on the physical body, believed to be spiritually significant;

- Having had many compliments on beautiful or unusual eyes;

- Having had an emotional reaction to being in a certain place, around a certain person or coming in contact with certain objects (uncontrollable crying, fear, laughing, panic, sadness, grief, loneliness, peace, comfort, or relief);

- Having looked in the mirror and seeing images of people or places on the other side of the mirror;

- Having looked into a glass or body of water and seen images of people or places in the water;

- Having written unfamiliar things and not having any conscious recollection or control of the writing;

- Having always been curious and attracted to the mystical;

- Having a strong belief of having lived before;

- Having felt that energy directed by mind or emotion has affected the operation of electronic or mechanical equipment (blowing out light bulbs, stopping clocks and wristwatches, draining batteries, altering the functions of televisions, radios, cars, etc.);

- Having appeared to cause animals to behave strangely;

- Having moved objects with the mind;

- Having seen or had communication with an apparition of someone known to be dead;

- Having had a spiritual or religious experience and given a communication directly from The God or angels;

- **Having been instructed by voices with no physical source, to do something that was completely against moral belief, and following, or not following their instruction. This is particularly true of messages suggesting self-harm or harming others.**

- **Having experienced the sensation of an energy, entity, or spirit entering and controlling the physical body with or without consent.**

You would be surprised to know how common all of these experiences are. It's not something that people are anxious to communicate to one another for fear of being called insane. It would be most unusual if we did *not* experience these types of phenomena. The more of them we have experienced, the easier and more rewarding the study of Psychic Self-Defense will be. It offers spiritual independence and freedom from our fears.

Some of these experiences may be quite frightening or even devastating. However, I believe that by the time you have finished reading this book, you will at least have a better understanding and frame of reference. Acceptance of the diverse manifestations of nonphysical reality is much easier if there is a sound knowledge of just how common it is. It is fascinating to study how to control it, banish it, or even embrace it.

There are two exceptions about embracing it. If you have experienced any of the **bolded** phenomena from the basic checklist above:

- **Having been instructed by voices with no physical source, to do something that was completely against moral belief, and following, or not following their instruction. This is particularly true of messages suggesting self-harm or harming others.**

- **Having experienced the sensation of an energy, entity, or spirit entering and controlling the physical body with or without consent.**

Please know that if the experiences listed in **bold** letters should occur, it is cause for great concern. You must consult physical, mental, and spiritual professionals for help. **Consider any variation of these particular experiences an issue of great urgency and seek help immediately.** It would *not* be a good idea to engage or continue any type of mystical study without consulting physical, mental and spiritual professionals to determine the cause of and remedy for this type of Spiritual Emergency. Your highest priority should be the study of how to get your life and your soul back

If you have experienced any of those above, consider yourself among those for whom the veil between the worlds of spirit and matter is very thin. You are not necessarily crazy. You are not necessarily evil. You are not necessarily weird. These abilities, however, can be very disruptive and counterproductive to leading a "normal" life. Choose to see these experiences as a gift and a blessing even during times it may feel like a curse. Embrace these Timeless, priceless adventures and use them to benefit the highest good for yourself as well as others. Wisdom would warn us to be cautious about oversharing our experiences, and with whom we chose to do so. There are some who are not spiritually open-minded enough to accept or even discuss unfamiliar spiritual reality without judgment and fear.

Spiritual gifts are not to be abused. There is a thin line between "use" and "abuse" and a very large, tedious, gray area in the interpretation of "use." One rule of thumb is to determine whether or not you are using your gift to harm, take advantage of, or manipulate anyone against his or her Free Will. If you feel you have done or intended to do this, approach the issue in prayer and ask for guidance and forgiveness. It is not worth the consequences of crossing the line.

Don't risk turning a gift into a curse. Many do not understand the serious consequences of choosing to be a negative energy that causes others to require Psychic Self-Defense to protect themselves from being attacked. Energy is neither good nor evil. It just is. It is the intention and the outcome that makes the difference. Any energy directed into the lives of others to cause harm will effectively turn into a boomerang that returns to the sender. The only one we curse in the end is ourselves.

Any energy that seeks to force issues and manipulate Divine destiny will be fruitless. There is nothing that we should desire outside of Divine Will. However, the reality of creation is, there is nothing we *can* do other than what is permitted by Divine Will. None of our mystical practices can transcend or change the Permission of That Which Created all. The result of the *desire* to impose our vain personal will upon ourselves or others will return three times into our lives. If the intention is to consciously cause harm to, or manipulate the Free Will of another, the Karmic Cause and Effect consequences will return it to us three times three. It is not worth anything we could think to gain, knowing that we are bargaining and playing dangerous games with all we truly are … Our souls and our connection to The Source. Imagine a world full of gifted people who choose to direct their powerful spiritual energies to bring love, healing, and peace to creation. Imagine a world full of gifted people who choose to act just out of love for and connection with The Creator, The Source of all gifts. Imagine!!

Spiritual Warfare

We are energy. Our electromagnetic energy field can be affected by other energies. Many mystical practices cause energetic shifts that affect us on every level of our being. Energy is neutral. It is neither positive or negative, good nor evil. What differentiates positive mysticism from negative mysticism is *intention* and *outcome.* Some call it black magic and white magic. On some paths of Western mysticism, some change the spelling of the word magic to magick to distinguish magical tricks from mystical practice. There is a thin line between the mystical and the magickal, but drawing that line is not the purpose of this text. I choose to call it either positive or negative mysticism. Any thought or act intentionally committed to creating a negative outcome is referenced here as "negative mysticism." Any thought or act intentionally committed to creating a positive outcome will be referred to as "positive mysticism." If the *intention* is negative, regardless of the outcome, it is considered negative mysticism. At the same time, if the outcome is negative, regardless of positive intention, it is still negative mysticism.

A judgmental, jealous, envious, or hateful thought about another can be a projection of negative energy associated with the practice of negative mysticism. This projection of condensed negative energy can take on a life of its own as a 'thought-form.' It can be used as a weapon as damaging as a bullet fired from a gun. It feeds upon the energy resources of its target. Thought-forms can, and do, create havoc, discord, and illness. They can even present life-threatening issues by way of subtle frequencies and powerful energy currents influencing the electromagnetic energy field of the intended victim. Some know this as a psychic attack. It qualifies as the practice of negative mysticism because a projected intention has caused harm to someone. Some of us even psychically attack ourselves by entertaining our own negative thoughts!

Some of the most flagrant practitioners of negative mysticism are many of the very same people who are its most judgmental critics. Even the most sacred of practices, such as prayer, chanting, and meditation can be used in such a way as to cause harm. That is why having only a cursory interest and knowledge of certain spiritual paths can be dangerous.

The irresponsible throwing around of projected energy can corrupt any spiritual practice, *including* meditation and prayer, which both *seem* to be absolutely benign. Meditation and prayer hold the potential power required to make any magick work. We are the magick that we seek, but we must be careful. Many of the rules of Western magick trace their roots to ancient mysticism and can operate within the same framework, except that with mysticism there is no frame. Our positive intention, cooperative with Divine Intention, will manifest the experience in life that we seek.

We determine what type of mysticism we are practicing. Any time the mind becomes focused upon anything or anyone, the object of that attention has somehow been affected or changed. If it is anger, hatred, envy, or jealousy that is focused or meditated upon, then projected at the object of this negative emotion, it is as evil as a wicked magical spell. These attacks can occur subconsciously if the practitioner is in a state of denial. The subconscious attack can be more dangerous than the deliberate attack. What is not consciously known cannot be easily controlled. It must first be identified to exercise power to control it. If the same projection of energy is positive, sending loving, healing, protective energy, it would be one of the strongest forms of prayer.

Many of us frequently practice positive mysticism without realizing it and may call it by a different name. The most powerful form of positive mysticism is prayer. It has been said that Jesus was known as one of the most brilliant positive mystics that ever lived. It is said that he performed healings. He had the gift of prophecy. He walked on water. He communicated with the spirit world. He resurrected the dead. He even rose from the dead. Certainly, these phenomenal feats qualify as positive mysticism, at the very least. Jesus taught that we, too, could perform such feats and miracles with sufficient faith and trust in The Divine One ... faith the size of a mustard seed ... faith like that of a child. The prophets and messengers from most spiritual paths have been ascribed to have possessed mystical powers.

We must keep in mind that The One God protects us all and is everywhere present in our lives as we consider the dangers of spiritual practices as innocent as meditation. Prayer is essential to our protection from the unpleasantness of the spirit world and the physical world. Every one of us has had unpleasant encounters with the phenomena associated with negative mysticism, whether we know it or not, even if we have never practiced mysticism of any kind. The veil between the worlds is quite thin. I do not intend to evoke fear, only to inspire awareness and commitment to study. We will discover that in the process of our spiritual evolution, we will become increasingly sensitive to the subtlest of energies, their patterns, and their many manifestations. The energies that we are uncomfortable with can be avoided and banished. There are spiritual cleansing practices that are recommended in most traditions. Hopefully, this text will cover many that will keep this spiritual journey of ours cleansed of both Astral and Earth Plane garbage. Refer to the section on "Prayer" for a mosaic of protection prayers from many traditions. The Light Meditation audio recording is provided with this text to perform before daily prayer and meditation rituals.

Signs of Positive Mysticism

Positive mysticism, in any of its many forms, either intentional or unintentional, can emerge from the following common human tendencies:

1) There is an overwhelming desire to connect with The God and submit to Divine Will and the Divine Plan for our lives. This is not about religion. It is about a glorious sense of confidence in the connection between the I AM that we are, and that which created us, of Its Own Essence;

2) The commitment to improve the quality of life of self and others is a resounding sign of positive mysticism;

3) There is a desire to be a conduit of healing and an instrument for transmissions of sacred wisdom. The expression of this longing manifests in many creative forms;

4) There is a commitment to the study and research of our connection with the Earth and nature.

5) There is an evolved understanding of the forces of nature we are at the effect of;

6) There is a desire to commit random acts of kindness and compassion;

7) There is a desire to be a part of solutions rather than the voice of problems;

8) There is a desire to be co-creator of miracles;

9) There is a desire to create peace in the face of discord;

10) There is an innate consciousness of the Natural Mystic that dwells within;

11) There is a belief in The Creator and rejection of all that is not That;

41

12) The commitment to improve the quality of life of self and others is a resounding sign of positive mysticism;

13) There is a desire to be a conduit of healing and an instrument for transmissions of sacred wisdom. The expression of this longing manifests in many creative forms;

14) There is a strong interest in the study of the ancient mysteries;

15) There is an evolved understanding of the forces of nature we are at the effect of;

16) There is an empathic connection with the energies of others. There is an innate desire to alleviate needless suffering and extend kindness and compassion;

17) There is a desire to be a part of solutions rather than the voice of problems;

18) There is a desire to create peace in the face of discord;

19) There is an innate consciousness of the Natural Mystic that dwells within;

20) There is a belief in The Creator and rejection of all that is not That;

21) A strong sense of Kismet, Synchronicity, Serendipity, Fortune, Fate, and Inner Guidance;

22) There are excursions in consciousness that become commonplace;

23) Visitations of angels, ancestors, loved ones on the 'other side,' and prophetic revelations are common in Lucid Dream events;

24) The practice of Reiki and forms of Energetic and Remote Healing;

25) Mystical Meditation (Meditations that inspire mystical phenomena).

Signs of Negative Mysticism

Negative mysticism, in any of its many forms, either intentional or unintentional, can be the result of the following common human tendencies:

1) There is a tendency to shoot a fly with an elephant gun, and swat elephants with fly swatters, based on transient erratic emotional states. Such compulsions can be an indicator of a conscious or subconscious psychic attacker. We must have a committed prayer and meditation practice in place to give us strength in these days of unprecedented spiritual warfare. We must approach petitions for protection as basic as a prayer with impeccable discernment to avoid creating an unpredictable outcome or an attack against innocent people. One must have 20/20 Third Eye vision, seeing all perspectives and choose to act with sound judgment, which, by definition, means someone can get it twisted and try to play god. The Karmic debt incurred is not worth the fleeting satisfaction of revenge. Vengeful, unforgiving, grudge-holding people must elevate their frequency through prayer and meditation to avoid attracting negative energy and providing a place for it to land. Allowing unresolved conflict to cause psychic energy to spin out of control, harms both the sender and the target. A wise mystic controls their energy and avoids either over or under-reacting to the challenges of life. Seek fair and equitable conflict resolution in a timely manner. Practice forgiveness;

2) There is a tendency to seek to avoid destiny by attempting to alter it, whether it be at their altar or in the spinning thought-forms of their obsessions. We can manipulate fate, but it is an exercise in futility to attempt to manipulate destiny. To fulfill our destiny, whatever it may be, is among the most profound of human goals and achievements. Nothing but Divine Grace can alter destiny. Nothing good can come from efforts to stand our personal willfulness up in opposition to destiny. It is a waste of energy. At the same

time, know that you need to keep an open mind with regards to determining what your true destiny is. The process of awakening is a natural one and cannot be conformed to the rules we often play by;

3) There is a desire to manipulate or control the fate and will of others, regardless of how noble we perceive our intentions to be;

4) There is a tendency to suppress or deny deep subconscious feelings, to the extent that when we approach our mystical practice for intervention, we may meditate on a wave and create a tsunami of pent up emotions;

5) There is a tendency to avoid responsibility. If a failure is experienced, there is an inclination to blame external forces, blame the process, but never blame ourselves for having created the cause. Journaling is a very important tool to help us review our documentation objectively, connect the dots, and understand the circular nature of time and the relationship between events. Journaling makes it easier to observe the Law of Cause and Effect at work. If we feel our spiritual practice is not as effective as we would like it to be, it is because we were a cause, or at least an influential contributing factor, that resulted in the compromised outcome. If a lamp is plugged into a fully functioning power source and it doesn't work, we check the lamp for the defect because we are sure that the source works. If we ask for something in prayer and don't get it, don't assume the prayer was not heard. All prayers are heard. Perhaps the answer is simply "NO." The Source is all-powerful and knows all things, including how and when to say no. Let your journaling be the cause of new good habits forming, after observing consistent Karmic patterns;

6) There is a tendency to want to be a "member of the club" without paying dues. Spiritual endeavors require a tremendous commitment and investment of energy, study, and practical experience. Shortcuts and quick fixes disrespect the process and can ultimately lead to disaster;

44

7) There is a tendency to deny the Natural Mystic of the "I in I," the unfathomable power of the Higher Self. If we do not see ourselves as *being* the magick, we seek to create in our mystical practice, our most energetic efforts are futile, and will render negative results. When we cannot see the spark of the flame of The God … the "I in I" that we are … we are limited in our efforts to love ourselves unconditionally. To love the Self can be complicated if we insist on seeing ourselves as the "s"elf, in its changeful revolving door of identities we find in the mirrors of our minds. The knowledge of Self gives us the unlimited ability to emit a higher frequency of love for all beings and becomes an example of what beautifully mystical beings we all are;

8) There is a strong tendency to see Universal Order as a phenomenon that occurs outside of the self. There is a Self-observing-self perspective that would better serve us. We are the keepers of the Universal Order that we are. Our choices dictate our relationship with Universal Order. Choose for the Eternal being that we are, not the perishable form that rises like a wave on an infinite sea. We *are* a phenomenon, seen and unseen. When the manifestations we seek to create are aligned with our destiny, the Universe will align itself behind the strength of our commitment to fulfilling that destiny;

9) There is a tendency to give permanent reality to temporary conditions and situations. Toward an effort of avoiding personal responsibility for our lives, we can trivialize the major issues we need to address while maximizing the importance of trivia. The mystical process of prayer and meditation ritual is sacred and should not be treated profanely with spiritually empty, vanity based transient pursuits. We approach all ritual as the I AM with love for all beings, affirming that the Self cannot be harmed. Like all beings, we would prefer an attack free life, yet attack cannot become our central point of focus. These situations come and go. They may spark annoying and even disturbing

events, but the worst thing we can do is give too much attention to the phenomena. We must maintain focus like a laser beam on how to detect and dismiss negative energies. Our center of attention must be focused on being that field of energy that is our Higher Self. We are learning here how to defend ourselves above the storm and under the radar against any form of attack;

10) There is a tendency to deify physical manifestations and give too much energy and significance to them to the point of distraction. The ultimate of all manifestations is the knowledge and understanding of the multi-dimensional, phenomenal beings that we are. We don't have to chase phenomenal experiences to convince ourselves or anyone else of anything. If we can embrace our real Self, the I AM, as the observer of the self of our conditioned perception, our energy field is fortified against attackers. Extend to observing "What" observes the observer and the real inquiry has begun. What can attack consciousness engaged in that elegant dance and win? The battleground and the common ground of our lives begin in the formless realm. It is amazing how some create a beautiful altar and then begin to worship the forms and objects they place upon it. It is like worshiping a telephone as a friend, rather than seeing it as an instrument that facilitates communication between friends;

11) There is a tendency to conform the accounts of rare occurrences to substantiate our beliefs rather than proceeding on the strength of faith and trust in Divine Providence. These events are to be expected. The application of *any* given force affects the object at which it is directed. It is up to us to determine the nature of the force that would best suit our intention. We then place our trust in the fact that the application of it will create change by the Will of The Most High. The Universe has nothing to prove to us. If we paid as much attention to what we can contribute to the Universe as what we demand of it, our names might outlive our self-imposed boundaries. There is

46

no spiritual integrity in practicing Psychic Self-Defense only when there is fear of attack. One's lifestyle must reflect respect for the wisdom traditions that teach us how to manage the energies that affect our lives;

12) As an old saying goes, there is a tendency to try to "plant corn and get wheat." We cannot attract anything other than what we are. If we seek to refine what we are, that which we attract to ourselves will be of higher refinement. We are that which we seek. We cannot be a spiritual warmonger and think that we get to live in peace. The most powerful form of Psychic Self-Defense is DO GOOD;

13) There is a tendency to see the nature of a "should be" as being real enough to divert our attention from the truth of what is. Often in the face of what appears to be chaos and suffering, our greatest spiritual growth is underway. We are not to seek to use mystical practice as a "quick fix" to escape from the work involved in facing the challenges of life. Consider that the way it is is the way it is meant to be right now, for a reason. Challenging that can result in transforming mysticism as a positive energy, into a negative force. Be careful what you wish for. Be even more careful of what you demand;

14) There is a tendency to be controlled by anger, jealousy, desire, greed, obsession, fantasy, and illusory romanticism. These are very strong emotions that create strong force fields of hungry, predatory, toxic energy. It is a powerful discipline to master resisting being controlled by our emotions;

15) There is a tendency to have a complete disregard for consequences. There is a wide range of manifestations, from a dysfunctional personality all the way to mental issues that venture into psychosis, sociopathic narcissism or even spiritual possession;

16) There is an instinctive knowledge of magic and mystical sciences often triggered by expressions of negative emotions. The transmission of mystical knowledge can occur in many ways. We may receive messages in dreamtime,

in meditation, from past life, and genetic memories. I don't spend a lot of energy reflecting on past or future lives. I choose to keep my awareness firmly in the now. But it is common that past life memories sometimes bleed through into present life experience. With that can come uncanny mystical knowledge that can't be explained away. That remembered knowledge is accompanied by accountability for our actions, and the causes and effects we create. We are mystical beings. We all have natural mystical powers. We must use them to heal and never to harm. If we are being harmed, we seek refuge in The God, the Protector of the I AM that we are. If we find ourselves tempted in any way to allow our willfulness or anger to energetically harm ourselves and others, we seek refuge in The God from our own transgression;

17) In the practice of "magic" or "magick," as it refers to the mystical sciences, we participate as co-creators in the manifestation of some desire in our hearts. Before you are faced with a pressing matter that inspires you to go beyond common prayerfulness and take a work to task at your altar, ask yourself a few questions. What is the nature of this manifestation? What is the nature of this heart which seeks this manifestation? What is the motivation behind this work? Why is a formal ceremonial approach believed to be required to accomplish it? Against what odds do you strive to manifest this work? Are you sure it is in cooperation with the Divine Plan or is it an attempted manipulation of it? What are the known and unforeseen consequences of this work, as manifested within the timeframe of the worker?

We must be careful when we arbitrarily decide that we know what is best for the highest good of everyone concerned in an attempt to manifest a new reality. If we find ourselves working outside of the framework of Universal and Divine intention, we are treading on dangerous ground. It is not like there is a possibility that our ambition alone would lead us to our imagined success. Nothing can be manifested unless it is permitted by Universal Law and Divine Plan, regardless of the worker's skill or best intentions.

48

When our personal ego willfully flies out of control, and we feel we know beyond the Knowing of the Knower of all things, because of an emotion, an opinion, a judgment, a fleeting desire … It is just not worth the consequences of a momentary rush of a power trip that promises to do a U-turn, derail, crash, and burn.

At the risk of sounding preachy, it is just not worth the dangers involved when the Karmic turnaround presents. The energy will boomerang in mind-boggling ironic ways. If it goes beyond a prayer of surrender, it is a red flag. These subtle energies are sacred. When that sacredness is violated, the entire Universe and the very Essence of The God that created it will rise up against us. Do not *practice* magic. Become it.

Spiritual Emergencies

There are many manifestations of what is classified as a "Spiritual Emergency." I have attempted to cover as wide a range of possibilities and probabilities as my own experience and studies can confirm. What constitutes a Spiritual Emergency is the disturbing occurrence of phenomena that are impossible even to attempt to explain or describe to *anyone* outside of the direct experience of it. It can mean becoming so overwhelmed with such life-altering, crippling fear, and panic, that one may feel cast into some sci-fi realm of the unknown while knowing for a fact that it is all quite real. It more than likely means that you can't confide in family, friends, acquaintances, or colleagues, without the risk of compromising relationships and being called insane. It means that seeking help from the average therapist can get you diagnosed, labeled, and drugged, if not locked up. It can mean that you can't even get help from most sources of spiritual counsel without being victim-blamed and exorcised of some perceived demon that you are judged for having somehow invited in. Sometimes helpful and knowledgeable sources of spiritual support are practitioners of secret arts beyond your comprehension. You may not be ready to step into a shared energetic field with some of them, or the entities and energies they wrestle with constantly, as a part of their own practice.

Spiritual Emergencies Induced by Spiritual Practice

There are precautionary warnings on every spiritual path regarding protocol associated with mystical experiences and practices. I am not demonizing or casting shadows upon the traditional spiritual practices I mention or inferring that they are dangerous. Some are no more triggering of nonphysical phenomena than an afternoon nap. Others require that you become knowledgeable of possible or probable risk factors. Some that come to mind are: Yoga; Meditation; Vision Quests; Soul Retrievals; Ceremonial Sweat Lodge; the use of any consciousness-altering substance in mystical/ceremonial practice; hypnotism; past-life regression;

future-life progression; trance channeling; clairvoyance; clairsentience; clairaudience; psychokinesis; oracle reading; Ouija boards; music with backward masking; visits to certain sacred sites or spiritually charged places with residual haunting energies; profound grief because of a loss of some sort; visitations with energetic or disembodied, nonphysical beings or entities; giving or receiving energetic healings; out of body experiences; lucid dreaming; astral projection and travel; remote viewing; non-observance of basic spiritual and Feng Shui protocol. All of these mystical gifts and practices can trigger what appears to be random phenomenal events in the home or in the person. *Anything* that would cause a trance/altered state of consciousness, whether or not it is substance-induced, intentional, or spontaneous, can serve as a powerful trigger. Being the target of an energetic attack, or even on the receiving end of some random projection or influence, can leave even unintended targets vulnerable to the experience of a Spiritual Emergency.

There are signs to watch for in a necessary practice of Self-witnessing. Many of the red flags and indicators of possible spiritual emergencies are: depression; feeling haunted; feelings or signs of being possessed; changes in eating or sleeping patterns, having visions or hearing voices that make disturbing suggestions and communications; anti-social behavior and feelings of alienation, isolation, shutting out family, friends, and peers; relinquishing personal power to the control of someone or something outside of Self.

Group Karma

Group Karma can be experienced when a mystical interest becomes aligned with groups of others on the path. It is wise to be cautious with regards to mystical groups that are exclusionary, dogmatic, and cult-like, seeking to micromanage the lives of members. Beware when initiatory degrees or rites of passage are introduced which engage in any manner of violent hazing. Overt or covert manipulations and influences are often accomplished using methodical mind-control techniques and reward/punishment scenarios. The lure of fraternity and belonging to a like-minded "family" is attractive to people who feel displaced. Approval and acceptance seeking begins with the destruction of past self-concepts while cultivating and nurturing the evolution of a new self. When social isolation/exclusion, breaking bonds and ties with family, friends, peers, and distancing members from any manner of support group outside of the "family" becomes a factor, it is a cause for concern. It is of particular concern when kept in place with the connective cords of fear, guilt, humiliation, peer pressure, and loss of identity. At the breaking point, letting go of the former "self" may take on the form of confessional self-hatred and self-judgment in exchange for an illusory promise of a "new self" to become. Some of the conforming methods used are sleep deprivation, food deprivation, control of attire, control over sexual expression. Often initiatory rites of passage or rebirth, involving oaths, agreements, and renunciations, serve to commemorate the slaying of the former self.

Doctrines that employ certain elements of brainwashing are used to maintain the state of mind that has been set in place, for example; Memorization, Repetition, Re-languaging (using language only known and understood by the group), Isolation and Resocialization. All social reference points are redefined. Powerful control is taken over even the most strong-minded individuals using threats of shaming, harsh discipline, ostracizing, or excommunicating the victim. These threats are usually made with references of Divine approval. If the victim seeks understanding or guidance with regard to feeling misaligned, often cruel and degrading techniques like "gaslighting" and "stonewalling" are used in a manner that discredits questions and the questioner.

Highly disciplined and restrictive lifestyle choices may well be conduct associated with a Hermetic Order to anchor a cleansing, spiritual practice. A path of renunciation does not necessarily constitute a cult. However, if it is represented as the *only* path to spiritual enlightenment, to the exclusion of all others, or if harm is done to anyone, that is indeed an obvious red flag.

Spontaneous Kundalini Awakening

Kundalini is a Sanskrit term for the primal energy that sleeps, coiled like a snake at the base of the spine, in the area of the Root Chakra. It is the source of latent concentrated power, grounded strength, and profound will. The uncoiling of the Kundalini is the manifestation and realization of optimum potential as a complex being. As this powerful energy rises, it revitalizes and transforms all of the chakras in a manner that can spark a spiritual paradigm shift that reconstructs the experience of everything.

The Root Chakra (the first of the column of seven energy centers of the body) has a shadow side when it is out of balance. Care is to be exercised in meditations that concentrate on the clearing or activation of this area. A spontaneous Kundalini Awakening event is an experience that some have not survived intact. I experienced this phenomenon after a spiritual breakthrough in my studies. I retired from a night of intense study and was awakened by what felt like a bolt of lightning, violently surging up from the base of my spinal column and out through the top of my head. I shook for over twenty minutes as if gripped by a seizure of some sort. After medical professionals failed to explain what had happened to me and ruled out any physical cause, I consulted a trusted spiritual professional and established the connection between that experience and an overwhelming spiritual epiphany that occurred prior to it.

In certain cases, a spontaneous Kundalini Awakening, such as the one I experienced, can be considered a Spiritual Emergency and can have extreme and unpredictable manifestations and consequences. The process of raising the Kundalini force up through the Chakra System should be a gradual one. It can however, be much more complex.

My cursory research using basic classes and internet sources, primarily Wikipedia, yielded so many energetic elements of so many spiritual and traditional paths, that they all began to collide. Each path had different languages, traditions, and cultural twists and turns, but at the bottom line, they are more alike than they are different. Terminology associated with *Yogic and Tantric traditions (Indian)* is becoming more mainstream every day in Western cultures. The *Tan Dien* and the *Dantien* are referring to the same thing (some English spellings are phonetic). *Nadis* and *Channels* are the same thing. These terms were not unfamiliar to me because of years of mixed Martial Arts training growing up. My Martial Arts practice was also my first exposure to mystical healing paths of meditation.

- *Dantien* literally means "elixir field," but a better translation might be "energy center." It is located in the area of the lower abdomen. It is a natural reservoir for storage of the body's vital energy. These are important focal points for meditation, t'ai chi ch'uan, qigong, and other Martial Arts and energy healing techniques in Traditional Chinese Medicine (TCM);

- *The Lower Dantien* is about three finger widths below and two finger widths behind the navel. It is called "the golden stove" where the process of developing the elixir by refining and purifying essence (jing) into vitality (qi, chi) begins;

- *The Middle Dantien* is at the level of the heart, which is called "the crimson palace," associated with storing spirit (shen) and with respiration and health of the internal organs, particularly the thymus gland. This cauldron is where vitality (qi, chi) is refined into shen (spirit);

- *The Upper Dantien* is on the forehead, in the area between the eyebrows, known as the Third Eye. It is associated with the pineal gland. This energy field is where spirit (shen) is refined into Wu Wei (emptiness);

- *The Hara* is in the area of the stomach. In the Japanese medical tradition and in Japanese Martial Arts traditions, the word Hara is used as a technical term for a specific area (physical/anatomical) or energy field (physiological/energetic) of the body. The hara is a core power-source that resides beneath the auric field of the human body. It is housed inside the tan tien, existing on the level of intentionality. The hara is also known as the core star connection;

- *The Nadis/Channels* transport Life Force energies, the cosmic, vital, seminal, mental energies, (collectively described as *prana*). In the physical body, the nadis are channels carrying air, water, nutrients, blood, and other bodily fluids. They are similar to the arteries, veins capillaries, bronchioles, nerves, lymph canals etc.;

54

- *Nadis – Sushumna, Ida, and Pingala*, pull from reservoirs of the latent, potent, energy of animation of the Three Tan Dien, to distribute throughout the body.

  The Sushumna Nadi – connects the *Muladhara* Chakra to the *Sahasrara* Chakra, and is the path for the ascent of *Kundalini* energy up the base of the spine into the Sahasrara. It is considered the central channel for the flow of prana throughout the body and unites all other chakras in the body.

  On either side of the Sushumna Nadi, are two other Nadis that partner together and cross over the spine, meeting in the center of the Sushumna Nadi:

  Ida Nadi – located to the left of the spine and carries feminine lunar energy. Starts in the Muladhara Chakra and ends in the left nostril;

  Pingala Nadi – located to the left of the spine and carries masculine solar energy. Starts in the Muladhara Chakra and ends in the right nostril.

When done in the prescribed manner, as a highly evolved Sadhana (committed spiritual practice), it can be a transformational, healing meditation experience. However, in the case of a sudden involuntary awakening of the Kundalini energy, it can occur as a traumatic event that can feel like an implosion, and look like a seizure. After experiencing such an awakening, I approached the line of study that I believe sparked the event, with more caution. A sound meditation practice begins with studying under a knowledgeable and experienced teacher and guide … someone you feel you can trust.

Use this information more as a glossary than a course of study on this specific subject, because it is cursory and contains just enough information to accomplish nothing at all. This is hardly more than a casual mention, considering the profound depth of all of these sacred, ancient traditions that will never cease to fascinate me. Use these terms for your own research and join me in the effort to be a student for life. An entire book could be written about each topic. Our survival depends on incorporating the transcendent wisdom of these powerful paths into our daily lives.

The Three Major Nadis(Channels)

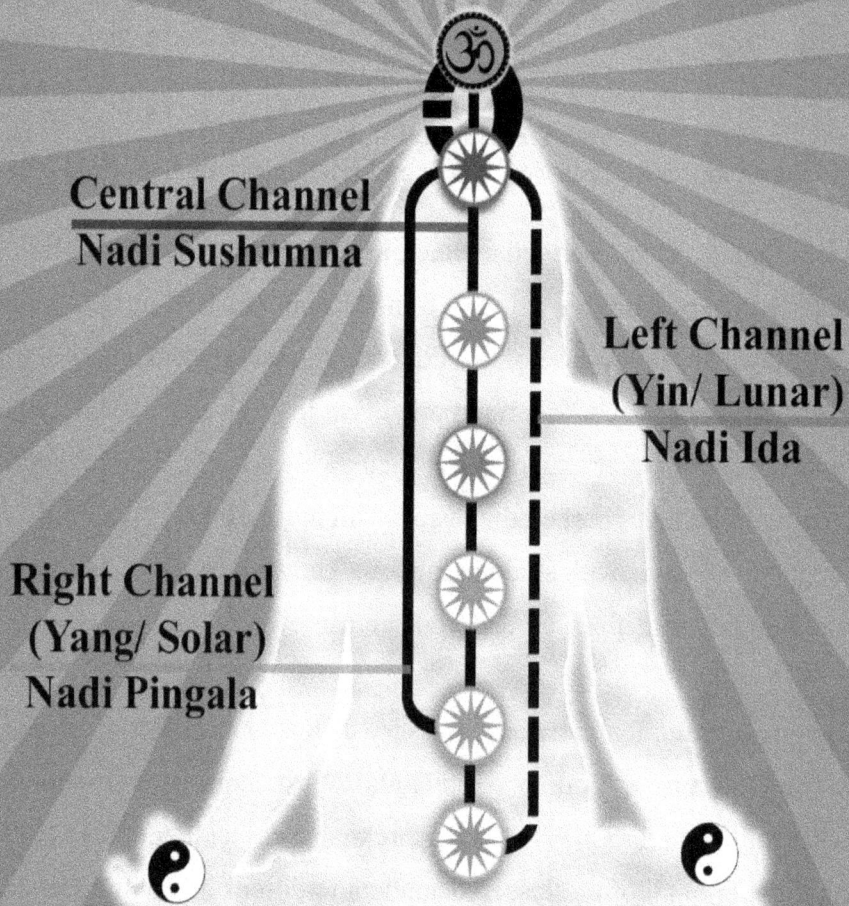

Central Channel
Nadi Sushumna

Left Channel
(Yin/ Lunar)
Nadi Ida

Right Channel
(Yang/ Solar)
Nadi Pingala

The Three Energy Chakras

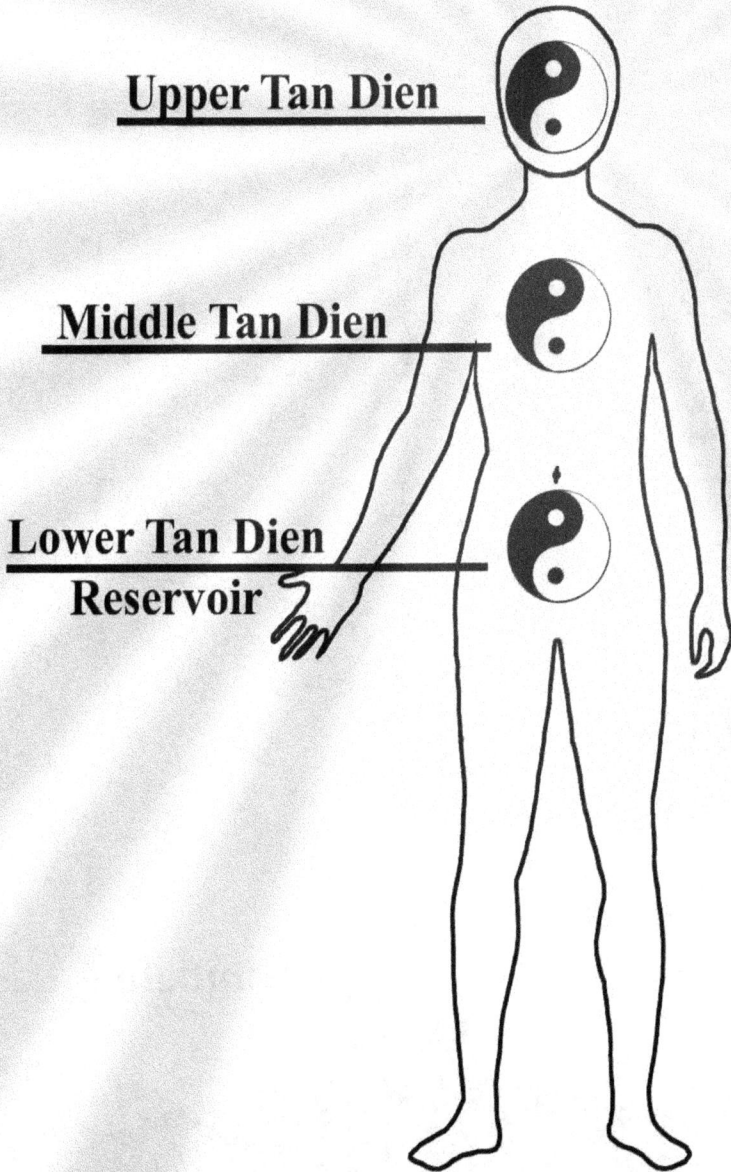

Upper Tan Dien

Middle Tan Dien

Lower Tan Dien
Reservoir

Subtle Energy Bodies (The Three Nadis)

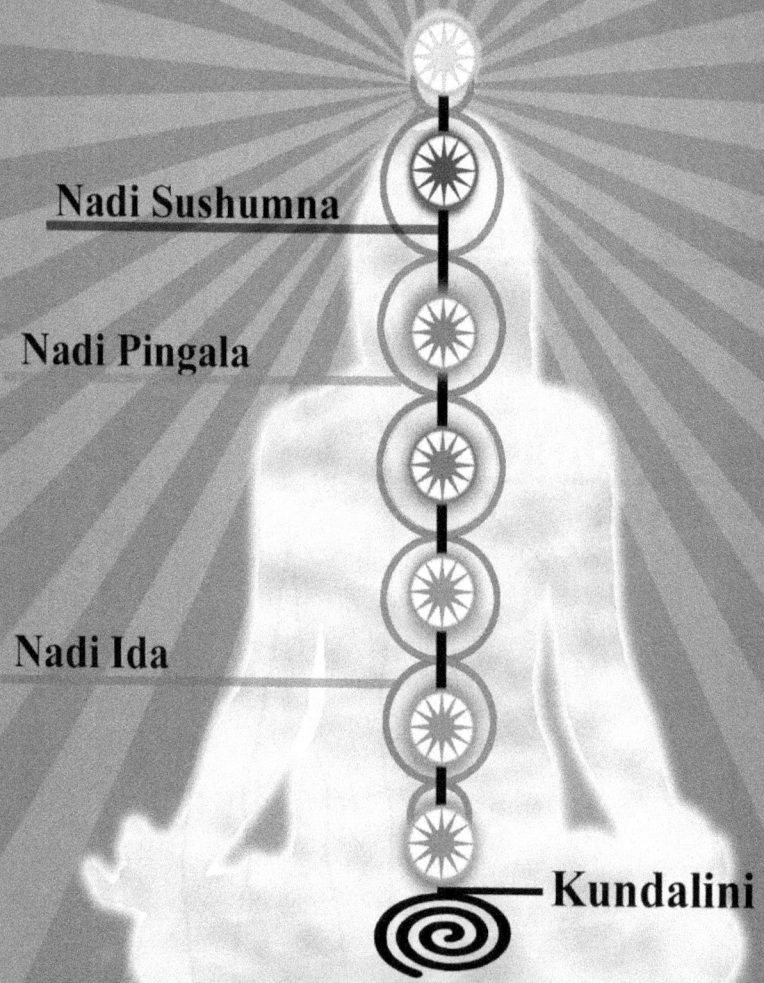

Nadi Sushumna

Nadi Pingala

Nadi Ida

Kundalini

Mystical practice is often blamed for spiritual emergencies. A Spiritual Emergency can also be triggered by prayers of every tradition I can think of … even to the extreme of experiencing what is known as a complete *awakening*, which can only be viewed as a blessing. That is why journaling is so important. In the event of any type of Spiritual Emergency, regular reviews become helpful with connecting the dots to identify triggers. If you note that a certain activity or practice stirs up phenomena that you are uncomfortable with, you will need to investigate whether or not you are practicing correctly, or even if that particular practice is right for you.

Sleep Paralysis

Sleep Paralysis is a condition that occurs in the transitional state while falling into deep REM (rapid-eye-movement) sleep, which is called hypnagogia, or upon awakening, hypnopompia. A presentation of what is called, "atonia" collapses the muscles into such paralyzing weakness, that movement of any sort is impossible. There is definitely an "electrical quality" to the vibrational sensations experienced by some, as a current of electricity running through their chest and upper body, along with an energetic pressure pressing down and pulling out at the same time. It feels like the body of consciousness being pulled or snatched out of the physical body. Often there are sound effects like echoing of buzzing or muffled, rumbling sounds. Some have experienced the sound of rushing waves of energy and pulsation from the sound of bursts and gusts of wind, trains barreling down tracks, or a stillness that feels palpable. It often has the pulse of a heartbeat. Is it the rhythm of a heartbeat? Or, is it a counter-rhythm? Every experience is uniquely different.

Can you imagine waking up from what appeared to begin as a peaceful sleep, unable to move, speak, react, defend yourself, or call for help, even to someone in the same room or bed? Imagine being afraid of the dark, afraid to go to sleep, afraid to sleep alone, afraid to confide in anyone about what is going on, afraid of being ridiculed, afraid to even know what the truth is.

When a person awakens in such a state, the fear alone can produce a fight/flight emergency response in the brain. Fight is not possible because of the physical paralysis state, leaving the body defenseless. Flight is not possible because a chemical in the brain that restrains movement in sleep suppresses the ability to act upon activities occurring in dream state. In REM dream state images have a surreal quality. Visions of images that appear to be present in the room are called "hypnagogic hallucinations." There are a variety of psychological and physical conditions that can cause the manifestation of these parasomatic symptoms, such as narcolepsy, sleep apnea, migraines, anxiety, and a variety of sleep disturbances including Post Traumatic Stress Disorder (PTSD), insomnia, and sleepwalking.

Some are fortunate enough to have the counsel of a medical professional who does not knee-jerk to the prescription pad for anti-depressants and sleeping pills for every malady. If no psychological or physical cause is found, it is reasonable to explore other possibilities. Doesn't it at least make you wonder if something else is going on? What is that threatening presence sensed in the room during a Sleep Paralysis event? Why does the victim feel "attacked?" The first time it happened to me, I knew there was nothing physically wrong with me. I didn't know what a psychic attack was. I instinctively knew that what happened was not in the realm of my understanding and experience ... nor that of anyone I knew at the time. I knew that what was happening was of a spiritual, otherworldly nature, but had no context for it, interest in it, or belief system to support any such breach of the boundaries of my personal reality. My experiences with this disturbing paranormal phenomenon caused me to obsess and research every detail I could find to explain it. My research was rewarded when I realized that what I perceived to be a curse was actually a blessing, a gift.

Sleep Paralysis revealed itself to be much too complex to be just a section in this book. This section grew longer and longer, then turned into its own book. For specific in-depth information on this provocative topic, read SLEEPLESS: Transcend the Fear of Sleep Paralysis. It emerged from my calling to understand and manage this powerful energy.

Dark Energy and Sleep Paralysis

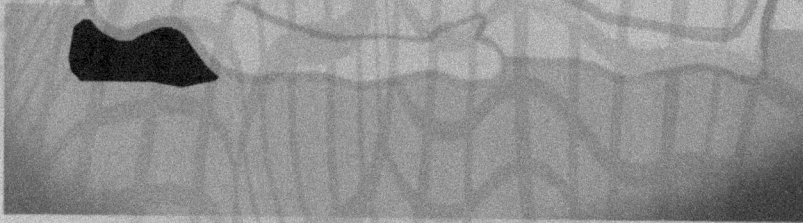

Dark Energy: invisible matter; negative existence; zero-point reality.
Dark Energy precedes the existence of all thoughts, words, concepts, or precepts.

The subject of Spiritual Emergency and the phenomenon of Sleep Paralysis are essential to the study of Psychic Self-Defense. I think it warrants being studied in greater depth than other phenomena because I have observed that elements of a Sleep Paralysis event are precursors to manifestations occurring in common spiritual/psychic practices, and may not really qualify as a Spiritual Emergency. Sleep Paralysis can manifest as one of the many natural sensations associated with an intentional, voluntary mystical experience.

Body/mind identification in mystical practice is an obstacle. It is a product of the ever-busy ego, constructing and reconstructing, remodeling, repurposing, rewiring, redefining the Self as some AI-bot drone that is here to live, consume, and die, and just do what it is told. Obey! Then these Conditioned priorities get placed on the back burner of a life-disrupting phenomenon that nobody really understands.

The Inquiry MUST begin … How is it that I am outside of my body? Who is that body in that bed that "I" am hovering above? How is it that all that would animate it to life is still with "me," floating here, in some bizarre nonphysical state of being? My thoughts are with "me." My emotions, what I would call the "soul" of my being … It is all with "me," the "I" that observes the inanimate body encased in the names, words, labels, evaluations, and judgments, that made it feel "real." So, who is that body, the one I've seen in all of my mirrors, in transitional phases of its existence? Who am I? The beginning of Self-Inquiry. Who am I? Which one is my True Self? Identification only as the physical "self" is the most dangerous of the deceptions of Maya, the illusory realm of existence. In Maya, the nonphysical is visible as it vibrates at a lower rate of speed … slowed down enough to trick a Timeless, imperishable, formless being into believing that its defining reality is only what can be seen with ordinary vision.

Sri Ramana Maharshi has shared the Self-Inquiry Meditation Practice through many of the modern, awakened Advaita Zen Meditation Masters, of diverse traditions. It begins with one question, "WHO AM I?" The false projections and fake identities that sought to incorrectly define our being, fade with the awareness of what I AM 'not' ... not this body ... not this mind ... not this fear ... not alone. The meditation is complete when the meditator disappears ... disappears to egoic branding and labeling ... disappears to perspectives and desires of the lower self ... disappears to everything that one is not. What is left? That is who we are. That is the answer.

The word "ego" has many interpretations. It can refer to personal self-worth, self-confidence, or in a psychological context may refer to the mediator between the subconscious and conscious mind, manifestation of "person-ality and individuated body/mind identification. We must become the knowing of the difference between "me" and "I" or we are nothing but a corpse on the pathway to a hole in the ground. When we ask ourselves, "Who am I?" we must know we can't find "I" in the mirror. The True Self, the "I," the "I in I," the I AM, nonphysical awareness/consciousness that is unique to our being, yet not unique to all things ... That is who we truly are. When we find ourselves on the outside of the body vehicle looking at it, voluntarily or involuntarily, for whatever reason ... we must know that the cold, inanimate, duppy (disembodied spirit or entity) is not who we are. When trapped in the terrifying grip of a Sleep Paralysis event, it is more important than ever to remember that ... We are more than that! We are One with That Which manifested it.

The Phenomenon of Weaponized Prayer

There should be a warning attached to certain prayers … even if they are scriptures from sacred texts. It would not be a good idea to take certain types of prayer into deep meditation with designs upon another, or even upon one's self. You incur the Karmic debt of what befalls the target as a result of what constitutes an energetic or spiritual attack. If we have reason to believe someone has wronged us in a way that justifies specific consequences relayed in certain powerful prayers, consider that if we are wrong, we have waged spiritual warfare against an innocent person. We will have made ourselves a magnet for the return of the energies sent out, a consequence of the attack. For every cause, there is an effect, a consequence.

I have witnessed what took on the appearance and energy of a murder with the use of sacred scriptures. I observed a very good and decent religious lady throw her hands up in frustration and give up contending with her emotionally abusive mother. She announced it and proceeded with the chanting of specific verses from the sacred texts, and burning petitions inscribed with those verses. Within six weeks her mother died. She had a medical condition that she could have continued to manage successfully. However, she compulsively began to do everything required to take herself to the grave.

I have experienced a Sleep Paralysis event, in real time, with a witness and experiencer in the room when it happened. "Good nights" had been exchanged. Lights out. Sweet dreams. A condensation of strange, electrically charged, thick shadowy energy formed like threatening clouds gathering before a terrible storm. The energy of the small room was suddenly consumed by it. Sound shifted to a dense, silent echo, with an 'underwater,' other-worldly quality. A death-like stillness filled the room. I was familiar with that feeling … the onset of a Sleep Paralysis event.

"Oh, no! It's happening again!" Effervescent skin began to go cold, tingly, and numb. The chest compression began. An invisible cloud of pressure slowly, deliberately, descended, as every muscle in my body began to lose strength. Breathing became shallow and constricted as a dying person must struggle for a few last breaths of life as the pressure of death pushes the weakened life-force out of my chest, one shallow breath at a time. My body was gradually weakening and I knew that soon I would not be able to move, to call out for help, to save my life. Panic ensued. One tear rolled down the side of my face. It felt cold … cold as death's final touch. Shallow breath struggled through strangled fading whispers, "Help me! … a spastic cry struggling against fear's firm grip … "Help me! I can't … move." I knew it was already too late for me … to break the grip of this invisible assassin.

Through this convergence of dimensions, realities, planes of existence quaking beneath me, portals cracking open, pulling me, sucking me in, pulling me into the dark void that had filled the room, to swallow me whole … I was able to gather enough strength to cry out, barely audible, the hollow whimper of an exhausted baby collapsed in terror … realities, ethereal planes of existence colliding, portals opening, entities breathing … their presence permeating the room, my body, my soul, with an airborne electrical charge, and energy shift.

I gasped for air enough to scream, but it struggled as another incoherent utterance … barely above a whisper … "Open the door!" already prepared to 'let go' of the will to declare, "I'm scared! I can't move either! Something is in here … out there." I responded, "Open the door or we won't survive this. What's out there is what is making what's in here happen! Open the door!!! Please, Oh my God, open the door!!! Please!!!! … I was gone … full paralysis … with super-hero strength the door was flung open … to expose the agent of this evil energy … seated in piety, on a bar stool outside of the door, in the middle of the night, a "sacred" text, in the hands of a demon … whispering a guttural, raspy chant … reading, reciting, from that book … startled out of a trance state … The spell was broken, the attacking energy lifted … I was alive, I could move, I could breathe. It, whatever that was, was off of my chest. The binding released. I could speak. I couldn't believe I was alive. I leaped up and lunged at him. I ripped the book from his grip to see what chapter … what scripture he was reciting. It was so full of judgment and wrath; there was no room for any consideration of coincidence that it was connected to the attacking energy. It was a deliberate, targeted attack on an innocent person who never deserved to be smothered, shrouded in a blanket of unholy, primordial evil.

That is when I became mindful of the manner in which even a sacred scripture can be used to cause harm to someone. If scriptures are directed out of anger and judgment, rather than the energy of pure and unconditional Love, great harm can be caused. But what happens when "love" gets to be defined by monsters. These electrically charged frequencies and energies are clearly powerful enough to trigger a Sleep Paralysis event. In cases involving the manipulative use of scriptures, or other systems and methods of prayer, know that it is a boomerang. It will return by Universal Law three times if the intention was not malefic … But, three times three, if it was intentional. All in life is a circle. Keep your circle clean.

When using prayers and verses from sacred texts, be sure to remain general and objective. One of the greatest prayers any of us can pray is for the healing of another. However, we must be careful to resist playing God and becoming an unsolicited intervention in the lives and personal matters of other people. We must not allow ego to nail us into a coffin of assuming moral superiority in manipulative judgments of the lives of others. Do not direct a concentrated focal point of the energy of prayer, in such a manner as to use it as a poison arrow, aimed at the hearts of those being held in judgment. Pray all prayers in great humility and surrender to the Will of The Divine One.

Signs and Symptoms of Weaponized Prayer Attacks:

- Sleep Paralysis events;

- Nightmares and other sleep disturbances;

- Dizziness, vertigo;

- Major depression, crying, loneliness, fearfulness, abandonment issues;

- Obsessive-compulsive disorder (OCD), mood swings, uncontrollable rage;

- Changes in eating habits (loss of appetite, compulsive binge eating, strange cravings);

- Stomach issues (severe chronic indigestion, constipation, diarrhea);

- Pain and/or movement in the abdominal region;

- Headaches, hot and cold flashes, tingling and numbness of the skin, muscle cramping and aching;

- Compression and pain in the chest, heart palpitations, shortness of breath;

- Feelings of being followed and surveilled;

- Hearing voices/whispers from no apparent source;

- Ringing in the ears (tinnitus);

- Seeing shadows with no apparent source;

- Seeing apparitions, flashes of light and/or shadows in peripheral vision;

- Having thoughts that are not your own (thought implants);

- Fixation on someone or something, rumination, forgetfulness, brain fog;

- Loss of interest in previously enjoyed activities;

- Malfunctioning vehicles, electronics, lighting;

- Frequent accidents and mishaps;

- Reversal of fortune, series of "coincidently" unfortunate events;

- Changes in the behavior of family, friends, pets;

- Unusual behavior of strangers;

- Strange, symbolic presentations of birds (ravens, owls, crows, predatory birds), insects, animals;

- Unusual attachments and aversions;

- Seeing and/or smelling cigarette or cigar smoke from no apparent source;

- Scents associated with death and decay with no apparent source;

- Scents associated with raw sewage with no apparent source.

How weaponized prayer works:

- The target is the focal point of the attacker's intention and directed energies;

- The desire is to manipulate the Free Will of the victim;

- Judgment Call for spiritual intervention while passing judgment upon others;

- Declarations of Karmic debt and creation of a "binding" to that agenda;

- Manipulative desire, envy, covetousness, jealousy, hatred, lust, sloth, greed;

- Candle Magick – burning candles charged with manipulative intentions;

- Writing and burning petitions with the intention to manipulate or control;

- Use of alchemically coordinated oils, incense etc. to attract desired results;

- Spell casting – seeking by occult means to influence the lives of others;

- Conjuring – intentional projection of psychic energy;

- Petitioning or bargaining with saints, angels, demons, entities, and energies;

- Projection of thought-forms with manipulative intention;

- Energy vampirism – targeting emotions to drain the Life Force of the victim;

- Ritual work using sacred or unholy scriptures with malefic intention;

- Prayers from *any* tradition or belief system to compel the Free Will of others;

- Intentional chanting of compelling repetitive prayers or commands;

- Use of negative or manipulative affirmations to target victim;

- Sigil Magick – Use of symbols as a "seal" or signature to compel outcomes;

- Sex Magick – Use of sexual energies to fortify and manipulate intention;

- Binding Rituals – Spiritual work performed to suppress, control, or compel;

- Ritual/Ceremonial Prayer Work aimed at corroding the Free Will of target;

- Using pictures, personal belongings of the victim to harness energy for attack;

- Visualizations summoning the Law of Attraction for manipulative purposes;

- Use of charms, incantations, images to reinforce willful projections;

- Compelling malefic spirits, jinn, entities, energies to perform interventions;

- A manipulative, willful prayer that ends with "Amen!"

Note that much of the above (certainly with the exception of obvious malefic intent to do harm) could be practiced with the highest of intentions, in the most innocent of all Light. Some say that what determines the difference is INTENTION. My observations have instructed me that what determines the difference is the OUTCOME. Our inflicted desires upon the lives of others can produce a negative, even tragic outcome. How does that differ from negative witchcraft and other paths that are held in judgment for the same, or parallel practices? Live and let live.

What makes weaponized prayer work?

- The possibility that this event was "fated" and "allowed";

- Fear that is inspired by threats and bullying of the attacker;

- Fear overwhelms and disables the will of the target;

- The weak spiritual belief system of the victim;

- State of Denial of the victim;

- Confidence of the attacker;

- Target succumbs to the effects of manipulative forces;

- Target's acceptance of projections of guilt;

- Actual guilt (all you have to be is wrong);

- Welcome repentance due to target worthy of punishment;

- A subliminal, mutually cooperative effort due to the target's surrender;

- The fact that the strength of belief in any idea enforces it with power;

- Fatigue, exhaustion, and broken spirit of the victim;

- Compromised physical, mental, psychological condition of the target;

- Target not Self-Realized enough to know that the "self" that needs protecting is not real.

What to do if you find yourself the victim of attack prayers:

- Strengthen your own spiritual practice;

- Continually reaffirm the strength of your relationship with The God of your highest understanding;

- Remain in sincere prayer from your strongest path of your spiritual belief;

- Become the prayer you pray as a strong meditation practice;

- If you have wronged someone, repent and make peace;

- If someone has wronged you, challenge the strength of your heart to forgive them, and seek refuge in Divine Protection and Providence;

- Do not fight false fire with false fire in counter-attack scenarios;

- A "Limpia" (Spiritual Purification) will keep your frequency high by employing methods of cleansing your energy field;

- Affirm that ONLY the Will of The Divine One is welcome to cross the threshold of the door that opens to your highest level of discernment;

- Remember the Divinity that you are and your Sacred Relationship with The Absolute. Dwell in the Secret place of The Most High. Evil, regardless of which label it chooses to wear, cannot enter there.

The knowledge of Self is the most powerful shield. The realization that we already are all we need to be gives us the strength to rise up in spiritual sovereignty from the ashes of devastation. Sometimes the attacker believes they are going to God as a faithful advocate on your behalf, with "positive" intentions that they truly believe are "saving" your life. Then you blast them with hell-fire and holy water, sage, ammonia, and attacking energy. That causes you to lose your edge. No one wins that war. You are not fighting them. You are becoming them.

Surrender to the Will of the Divine One, stand your spiritual ground and let them spin in their own webs of indefensible behavior. Of course, you are hurt and angry … because you can feel it. You can feel something quietly … subtly … subliminally tinkering with your subconscious mind. The rewiring of consciousness, no matter how skillfully it is performed, sends up red flag security breach warnings to a Self-Realized being. Shifting realities on beings who are awake and feeling the pressure of walls of hypnosis and conditioning closing in on them will yield predictable results … Rage! … and seeking the destruction of *whoever* is seeking to introduce the divergent reality. Yet, the more awake you are, the deeper your commitment is to *remain* as the True Self … unthreatened by egoic attacks that are aimed at egoic defense systems.

If you have truly Realized Self, why are the projections of others so threatening to your remembrance of Self? Not everyone is going to like us. But that does not mean there is necessarily anything wrong with us. I offer the wise words of my mother … "I can see why someone wouldn't like you … BUT, what I cannot see is why you *care*." We must not let ego find another rock to hide under. There is only One Love … No "them versus us." What is in them is in you … is in all of us. Send it love, not hate or rejection … forgiveness, not denial or retaliatory aggression. Love that place in the Realized Self that knows that we are One Love … One Prayer … One Intention. Time is not a line. It is a circle … One Circle. We must keep our circle clean.

The Ego Under Attack

That ego "I" image of us is so full of vanity-based energy, spinning in such powerfully distracting circles of illusion, that it often cannot defend itself from the attacks of psychic bullies. That is the first thing any bully attacks, the ego of the intended victim. This malevolent spirit stalks, looking for weaknesses, tentatively sensing someplace for the attack to land, some open door of the psyche through which to direct the negative energy. As it is on the playgrounds of the schoolyards of the world, so it is in the cosmos, on the physical and ethereal planes. That type of energy predates our collective history on this planet. However, if there is no fertile soil to root in, no hump to ride, there is nowhere for that plane to land. It's got to keep on flying, generally on the flight plan of a boomerang. Journaling will show you how the surrendering of the false "I," ego-based identities, naturally coincides with the dismantling of psychic attacks and attackers.

If we feel some aspect of our life is under attack, we must ask the "I," Self, "WHO is the target of this attack?" Who is the "I" that experiences the phenomena associated with this attack? Is it the "I," me, my, mine, one-dimensional self-concept? Or is it the formless, nameless, identity-less "I" of the Eternal I AM that expresses itself as us ... the shadowy forms we take far too seriously, and at the same time, not seriously enough. Who is that "I" that is under attack?

The stereotypical attacker is generally targeting the "I" we see in the mirror. What defends the "I" is the "I" that can only be seen with the eye of the soul, The I AM. It is secure in its defense because the Ultimate "I" witnesses all and can and will intervene in our affairs. The psychology of the attacker is petty and shallow in its mental perceptions and projections. It is covetous. It is jealous. It is mean. It is cruel. It has a hunger that can only be satiated by the suffering of others. It preys upon the vulnerable at their weakest point and strikes below the belt to the heart of ego self identity. It literally chants down its victim until those voices become a shared mantra with the victim. The victim then joins the attacker in the dismantling of his or her self-esteem. Often the target becomes depressed and takes on self-destructive behaviors … all symptoms, rather than the cause. Rarely is the attack without motive, as senseless as it may be. More often than not, the attack is rooted in some form of competitive jealousy, or some level of malignant envy. The attacker perceives the intended victim as having something that they feel was denied to them, and that they are worthier of it. They may become overwhelmed by uncontrollable, self-serving compulsions that they feel are best satisfied by violating others, passively, aggressively, or both. Generally, these far-reaching tentacles extend out of empty desire, fueled by narcissistic ego self identity.

The attacker who wages war against the innocent does not approach from a position of strength, security, or confidence. They are blind to the knowledge of their own Higher Self and choose to operate from the shadow realm due to thought-forms of "not enough." Happy, secure people don't act that way. This sort of an attack can even be unintentional, a wicked thought-form riding on the wind of a full Moon, damaged pride, hatred, and low self-esteem.

Attackers count on a runway into our consciousness, welcoming any and everything that tries to land there. If we do not provide a landing strip, if we do not allow our own egos to leave our psychic doors open, many attacking energies will escape our awareness. To ignore the ocean, and respond to every wave of emotion and judgment, is to become the attacker of our own peace of mind and well-being. As an attacker of self, we are then robbed of our primary advantage as a spiritual warrior, our innocence.

An attack of any sort is a gamble riskier than feeling drunk and lucky in a Vegas casino on payday. When someone initiates an attack, they have no way of knowing what they are up against. After scrutinizing a person believed to be known, even intimately, by the attacker, there is *still* no possible way to truly

75

predict how the target will respond to being attacked. It is not possible to know the victim.

Upon determining that it is the ego self "I" that is under attack, it is important to process raw emotions of anger and counter aggression, seeking a refined form of energetic expression. For example, imagine we find ourselves in a situation where someone is sending desperate, attacking energy, targeting us based on a perception that it is we who are triggering those feelings within him or her. That doubles their anger. First, they are disturbed by what they know or see that sparks their envy, jealousy, or hatred. Then enters the distorted perception that it is the fault of the perceived trigger of their energy, and that person is to blame for *their* suffering. There is never an acknowledgment of personal responsibility.

"Hater" is a word that started as slang but has found its way into mainstream vernacular. Everyone knows what a "hater" is, and we all have a few in our lives, no matter what we do. All we can do about it is not become one. All we can do about it is keep our energy grounded in spiritual integrity and gratitude for the blessings we have and our faith in The God. There is an army of forces, energies, and entities already set in place that is sufficient to protect and guide our Souls under Universal Law. We are not even required or advised to petition to them directly. All we are required to do is surrender to Divine Will and respect the ongoing process of that sacred surrender.

A study, practice, and discipline of meditation will allow us to see life from a witness or observer's perspective, even a Timeless perspective, from which we are better able to understand time and the relationship between it and the events of our lives. We also view our journey from a time circle that we stand in the center of, rather than a "timeline." We are in uncharted territory. Meditation is a valuable tool for connecting the dots of the messages, signs, and visions we receive. The words "random" and "coincidence" have no place in our consciousness. Every aspect of our existence is Intentional.

76

COSMIC LAW
and
MYSTICISM

The Law of Karma

Divine Law is the only Law we can count on, no matter how much of an iron hand or velvet glove the so-called powers that be may rule with. It is impartial and cannot be bargained with, sold, or bought. Many layers beneath the gift of Free Will The God has given us, lurks a caveat pointing to an ever-watching Eye that sees before, behind, and around, in the mind, in the soul, in the heart, from finish to start. It watches. It weighs and measures the choices we make. Free Will does not mean a free for all that allows us to do what we want, without suffering the consequences of our actions. A crime against self or others is the seed of a tree of consequences. From that seed, planted in the fertile soil of no repentance, manifests the bitter fruit of imposed discipline.

Consider the character of humankind and consider the power, test, and danger of personal will. The God gave us Free Will as a blessing that we can turn into a curse if we choose to. Regardless of societal constraints set in place, each will find his own way, seeking and following the path of his own will, destiny, and character. Law cannot be forced upon anyone as a deterrent from committing crimes against self and others. In a perfect world, no law would have to be forced upon people. In most cases, personal will would make the letter and spirit of any law unnecessary. There are certain things that an evolved individual simply will not choose to do, whether or not it is stated in any law. The Spirit of the Absolute shines from within an individual when personal will reflects the Light of the Will of The Almighty. When our souls become spent for violation of the Will of Divine, it starts with our treatment of ourselves and extends to other people. The greatest injustice we most often commit is that which we commit against ourselves. All injustices we commit, we commit against ourselves. The line in the sand is drawn on the issue of causing harm to self and others and violating the Free Will of others.

I often use the example of the Law of Karma being much like the Law of gravity. The image of a person dropping a prized and fragile possession comes to mind. After the object is dropped, halfway to the floor, does it really matter whether or not it was intentional? Does it matter whether or not there is a belief system in place supporting the existence of gravity? Does it matter if there are feelings of regret and loss? The unfortunate result will be the same, regardless. The pleasure principle would be sufficient to cause us to seek blessings, not punishment.

If we use our knowledge of the ancient mysteries and secrets to harm others or rob them of their Divine birthright to Free Will, we are in direct violation of Universal Laws that protect us all and hold the balance of justice. As we have sown, that shall we reap. The promise in place will cause us to experience the same energies we have imposed upon, or wished upon another, *three times* if we were the cause, *unintentionally*. If we caused this harm intentionally, we would experience the negative energy we have sent out *three times three*. That is why in meditation and prayer rituals for protection it is important not to fixate on a particular person perceived to be the attacker. If we are wrong, we have put an innocent person under a vicious attack.

Practitioners of the mystical sciences do not necessarily refrain from causing harm to others because they think they are under surveillance or being policed into ethical behavior. The real ones, who practice in and of the Light know the Law and don't consider breaking it an option. It is never worth the consequences. Cooperate with the Will of The Divine, which will offer the comfort in life of going with the flow, rather than swimming upstream. True character is determined by what we do when we believe that no one is watching us, and no one will ever know.

Intention vs. Results

Any of us can use the element of fire to either provide gentle warmth or burn ourselves to ash. Intention is a keyword. However, the result is the determining factor. It does not matter whether or not our intentions were malicious. It is known that manipulative or malevolent prayer work can be done with the use of sacred symbols and scriptures. The energy of such practices can be projected in such a way as to wreak havoc in the lives of other people, ultimately wreaking havoc in the life of the practitioner. Sacred scriptures and symbols can be used in benevolent practices to promote healing and miracles or can be inverted and ritually used with the intention to cause great harm.

Maliciously directed prayers and petitions can create 'thought-forms' which are negative energies that take on a Life Force of their own. They can be as subtle as toxic vapor. They can become like bullets to the heart of the intended victim. Some of these thought-forms are sent out subconsciously due to unresolved disputes, jealousy, hatred, anger, resentment, and vengeance. As their evil work is being done in the lives of those targeted for such an attack, along with those around that person (especially children), a boomerang effect will occur, redirecting that same poisoned energy back into the lives of those who sent it. It is Law like gravity is Law.

Yes, intention is a distinguishing factor between positive and negative mysticism. However, the lines are not so clearly defined that anyone can become overly secure that the line was not crossed, without the conscious intention to do so. There is a Karmic responsibility that accompanies the conscious and unconscious projection of spiritual energy to create change, even if it is a solicited positive intention. The big picture *results* are the determining factor of the nature of mystical work being positive or negative.

To take it to a higher octave, imagine that the energy of unsolicited prayer work and meditation ritual is directed into the life of someone, and the results produced a negative outcome. Consider welcomed prayer or meditation directed in the spirit of the highest of *intention,* and the outcome created turns out to be negative in the life of someone that is possibly not even known by the practitioner. Does it then make any difference whatsoever how positive the intention of the prayer was? No. When the *outcome* is negative, it becomes a practice of negative mysticism. Among all intentions, the highest standard of *intention* must be maintained. The optimum intention is to live in complete submission to and alignment with the Will of The Most High.

One key consideration in determining the nature of projecting any energy is always to contemplate, "How will I feel *when* this comes back to *me?*" Pray for guidance. Perform an introspective soul search on the issue to seek clarity regarding the probable outcome of your work. Some very positive projections committed with the highest of intentions can result in an outcome of unanticipated pure evil. The **results** then become the distinguishing factor between the two, more so than the **intention.** We must go into prayer and ask for spiritual guidance and revelation regarding the results of Mystical Meditation and prayer work, and then decide whether or not it is wise or appropriate to proceed.

After performing introspective prayer and meditation, we must determine whether or not we feel sure we are operating in accord with the highest good of all concerned, harming none, respecting the Universal Law of Free Will, in total submission to Divine Will. To be certain that we remain in and of the Light when in doubt, PRAY. If you are not sure, resist going on a power trip. It is just not worth it! Matthew 16:26 of The Bible (KJV) offers, "For what is a man profited, if he shall gain the whole world, and lose his soul? Or what shall a man give in exchange for his soul?"

Before any spiritual work, I undertake, I cloak myself in the Light of The Divine One and send it out on the path before me. I affirm that my God is The God of both the darkness and the Light, the Heavens and the Earth, as well as every world, plane, and dimension in creation. I trust my life, my fate, my immortal soul to The Divine Creator, knowing that I seek to walk the path of Light, forever affirming the existence of, and protection of, the One Divine Creator, before Whom my soul stands in service. I affirm That Which Watches over me is sufficient to protect me from the shadows that invariably accompany Light. The brighter the Light, the bigger the shadow. Everything that happens in my life happens only by the permission of The One God, regardless of my opinions or judgments or the opinions and judgments of others. My life belongs to The Most High. I pray this prayer knowing that nothing exists but The God.

That is really all we need. If I had it to do all over again, that is where I would have left it, and there would be no book. The writing of this book led my spiritual path full circle. However, I felt guided, and so it is. It is known that when we find ourselves having gone full circle on any path nothing is lost. We are never the same person who started the journey, even if we end up right back where we started. We will return to the starting point of that circle evolved, not just revolved.

Planes of Existence

0. Unknowable

7. Realm of Divinity

6. Archetypal Realm

5. Etheric Realm

4. Astral Plane

3. Mental Plane

2. Emotional Plane

1. Physical Plane

Planes of Existence

In both an individual and collective context, we are each a composite of all of the Planes of Existence. To view them separately does not imply specific or actual locations in our being or psyche. All of the Planes and their inhabitants coexist in an interdependent, interactive, symbiotic relationship. References to "Planes" and "Realms" are used interchangeably and conceptually. The Planes are distinguished primarily based on density, from the subtlest state to gross matter. These Planes, Dimensions, Worlds, and Realms of inter-penetrable consciousness, ranging from ethereal and invisible, to physical and perceptible expression, are considered abstract and theoretical, based on religious, philosophical, and esoteric beliefs. This elaborate manifestation is believed to emanate from One Timeless, Unknowable Source that is beyond comprehension. One Supreme Being sent out this energetic force of unmanifested creation from the Realms of the Unknowable through sound vibration. It was the cause that resulted in the effect of all that we know as reality. Many meditation practices are based on the chanting of mantras, intonations, and repetition of sacred words associated with that Creative Force.

0 – The Unknowable

There are no words in this realm. This realm precedes thought and form. I have heard it referred to as the realm of "Self-Illuminating Triple Darkness," the Unknowable Realm of Unlimited Potential. I have heard it called "Dark Matter" not to be confused with anti-matter or black holes, "Invisible Matter," "Dark Energy," "Negative existence," "Zero Point Reality." There is more Dark Matter than there is matter, and it precedes the existence of all thoughts, words, concepts, or precepts. Focusing on this subject is futile because the scientists admit to knowing more about what it is not than what it is. It is generally understood to be:

- The Unmanifest;

- Self-Illuminating Triple Darkness;

- Beyond the concept of negative existence;

- Negative existence is beyond definition;

- When it is distinctly defined it ceases to be negative existence;

- The negative existence that does not pass into a static condition;

- Beyond the concept of limitless expansion;

- Beyond the limitations of the rational mind;

- Beyond the limitations of the intuitional mind;

- Beyond the limitations of concepts, constructs, time, body, mind;

- Beyond the concept of transcendence;

- The experience of the Realm of the Unknowable, releasing all attachments to egoic desires;

- The experience of the Realm of the Unknowable, releasing all attachments to body/mind, time/space identification;

- Independent of human senses;

- Independent of human perception;

- Nameless and formless reality;

- Beyond existence;

- Beyond duality;

- Unobservable;

- Unimaginable;

- Omnipotent.

7 – The Realm of Divinity

A "Divine Realm" is not really suitable as an "address" for The God. Due to the Omnipotent nature of That Which cannot even be named … an "address" would in a sense express an expectation of confining The God to a place or a realm, which denies the very nature of The God. Qualities of the Realm of Divinity are:

- It is an Energy, a Frequency, The Realm of the Limitless One;

- It is the Realm of the Holy Spirit;

- It is referred to by some as the Angelic Realm;

- It is the Awaliya (Friends of The God);

- Angels that are known as the Messengers, Apostles, or pure beings of Light that were created to establish the many aspects of God;

- The Ascended Masters and spirit beings among us in diverse manifestations who assist others in the experience of enlightenment and ascension;

- The Realm of Indivisible Oneness;

- The Realm that demonic forces and entities cannot access;

- It is sanctified beyond human comprehension;

- It is beyond our scope of finite, intellectual knowledge of Creator/creation;

- It is the embrace of the reality and nature of our intimate relationship with The Divinity as infinite.

6 – Archetypal Realm

The Archetypal Realm is the prototype existence that manifests in the Physical Realm. It is the parallel world that generates the masks of identity that we wear, and believe them to be who we really are. In the context of our True Self, the Timeless, unborn, undying, Eternal beings that we are, we can live a shadow existence in a waking dream world. This occurs when we accept archetypal influences blindly, spinning in and out of delusional, binding, attachment and aversion scenarios. Our ancestors are among those who inhabit the Archetypal Realm. Cultural systems, customs, social structures, spiritual science, and all manner of archetypal wisdom of the ages is alive and well in that boldly interactive realm. That is a gift as long as we acknowledge the memetic nature of archetypes. They change from age to age, from generation to generation. They are supposed to, and we are supposed to embrace Annica, the Law of Impermanence. Instead, we often cling to our perceptions of static realities and dualities, fleeing from the truth that *nothing* is fixed or permanent. Everyone and everything we know is changeful and impermanent.

Attributes of the Archetypal Realm include, but are not limited to:

- *Archetype* is defined as the original model or prototype from which the attributes of people and the cultural realities of our world are copied, patterned, or emulated;

- Patterns of archetypal realities that manifest as symbols and imprints permeating our psyches to the extent of having a hypnotic effect on our collective persona, behavior, and environment;

- The energies and entities of the Archetypal Realm can use subliminal influences to trigger aspects of collective memory to revive, destroy, or shift the reality, even the memory of our reasons for being, and the truth behind the illusory masks we accept as identity;

- The forces in the domain of the archetypes that have the full potential to affect and create interpretations of observed phenomena through influences of nonphysical beings, thought-forms and energies, ancestors, deities, concepts, ideas, and projections of alter realities;

- Archetypes often conveying messages through symbolic frequencies, subtle language, and thought-forms, that verbal and written information cannot;

- We can become aware of the subtle influences of individual and universal archetypes in meditation, dreamtime, remote viewing, or other out-of-body experiences. They also affect creative art forms, music, fashion, advertising, and design.

5 – Etheric Realm

The concept of Ether, the Fifth Element, refers to the subtler realms of consciousness, that interpenetrate the physical realm, as an animating force. The beings of various realms are ethereal in quality. The etheric body is the energetic or subtle body. Within this parallel realm to our own is the matrix from which our world, and many we are unaware of, have risen into conscious reality. Evanescent Ether is an immaterial, intangible substance, yet it is very real. Attributes of the Etheric Realm include:

- Everything that exists on the Physical Plane has a subtle etheric form and counterpart;

- The human Etheric Realm of consciousness is an interconnecting and intercommunicating network of energy from which our body matrix or blueprint is created;

- The Etheric Realm is the bridge between the Physical and Astral Planes. Nonphysical beings and entities are inhabitants of the subtler planes, and yet they exist within realities of the physical world. An etheric body double can pass through walls and other apparently solid objects and still be connected to its physical counterpart, as well as being able to visit places and interact in the physical world;

- Telepathy, remote viewing, and other psychic abilities are elements of the ethereal plane of consciousness;

- The energies of fear … the fear of living, as well as the fear of dying, can attract ethereal and astral entities that are able to invade and poison our reality on all levels of our being;

- The etheric and astral bodies are not two entirely separate bodies. They each have different characteristics and features of mutual importance, relative to their essential purpose;

- Our mastery of the levels of the subtle planes can influence the strength of our electromagnetic energy field and how we are able to effectively connect with the Realm of Divinity.

4 – The Astral Realm

The Astral Realm is the realm of Dreamtime, where we go when we sleep. Things have no specific structure and more fluidity, meaning nothing is solid, even if it seems to be momentary. Everything changes as frequently as our thoughts, and in the Astral Realm, they are made manifest. It has parallel aspects to this world but is more bright, colorful, and responsive to our emotions. Qualities of the Astral Realm include:

- The Astral Realm is a non-physical realm of existence, parallel to our own;

- It is beyond time/space;

- It is the home of the astral/etheric body double and its perceived simultaneous reality;

- The Astral Realm or spirit world is inhabited by non-physical beings and entities. They can be perceived as good or evil, and exist as realities of diverse manifestations;

- We perceive the spirit of our True Self in the context of an inner-life. The Astral Plane is an external environment for non-physical realities, beings, and entities;

- The Astral Realm is a platform of expression for thought-forms, dream symbols, and Universal Archetypes;

- Non-physical aspects of beings can get trapped in the Astral Realm. These astral entities and energies can create possession scenarios and psychic interference drama. Although we may be unaware of their presence, our lives can be altered in extreme ways. We may find our energy depleted and feel drained of Life Force. Our sleep patterns may be interrupted or disturbed. Our health may become compromised as we develop chronic illnesses such as recurrent headaches and unexplained body aches and pains;

- The Astral Realm is the domain of dreams, altered states of consciousness, Sleep Paralysis events, astral projection, remote viewing, portal jumping, spirit journeying;

- Out of Body Experiences, and near-death experiences;

- Accounts of 'heaven,' 'hell,' 'abyss,' and 'purgatory' experiences in consciousness, are an element of Astral Plane reality;

- The subtle/dream/astral body's assent from the physical body into astral reality has been described as an ecstatic, blissful out-of-body experience. It is known to have sparked mystical, even prophetic revelations from the higher realms;

- The astral body is seen by some as a visible aura of swirling colors;

- Memories, thought-forms, spiritual beings, apparitions, and visionary landscapes may be witnessed as astral phenomena.

3 – Mental Realm

The Mental Realm is the Plane of Thought, as well as the moments of the "Great Silence" in between them. From the ocean of primordial stillness, the Macrocosm of Divine Mind radiates its intense Light into the realms of names and forms … of energies and entities … of vibration and frequency. The mental realm exists outside of Cosmic Law and beyond time. Qualities of the Mental Realm include:

- The mental realm relates to the domain of the individual as well as the cosmos;

- It is the realm associated with knowledge, intellect, reasoning, understanding, and perceptions, even referring to concepts of intuition;

- The mental plane, which intermediates between all of the realms, is symbolic of the marriage of Heaven and Earth, spirit and matter;

- The mental plane is associated with a type of "seeing" (mind's eye, psychic eye, Third Eye, evil eye) … all generated from the realm of thought;

- It is an aspect of the realm of the Timeless Now for having the capacity to escape time;

- It is the plane of consciousness, awareness, and the unmanifested energy of thought;

- It is the plane of Manifestation through the projection of thought-forms;

- Thoughts are things. From a "thought-form" realities are created;

- Just like magick, as one thinks … so it is! (by permission of Divine Will);

- Sharing in characteristics of the Archetypal Plane, it is the world of original prototypes of the physical world;

- Thoughts are not just the consequences of brain functioning;

- Thoughts can operate on their own sovereign agenda, independent of physical reality;

- Thoughts have been proven scientifically to affect physical reality.

2 – Emotional Realm

The Emotional Realm is a common source in the generation of psychic phenomena directly connected to the Mental Realm. The arena of unguarded, reckless, unbridled emotion, is the breeding ground of manifestation of powerful thought-forms, both positive and negative. Emotion is linked to thought; Thought is linked to desire; Desire is linked to manifestation; Manifestation is linked to attachment; Attachment is linked to suffering. Qualities of the Emotional Realm include:

- The heart as the "bridge" between the upper and lower realms of consciousness;

- The heart is the home, the throne of Divinity;

- It is the Realm of Union between the Divine and human;

- It is the emotional connection between humanity and The God;

- It is the realm of thought-forms being generated through the mystical power of emotion that causes the spark that triggers manifestation;

- The primary target of a psychic attack is the heart;

- The primary emotional triggers of spiritual attack are the emotions of anger, hatred, envy, jealousy, desire, and attachment;

- It can be the realm of magnification into states of overwhelm due to extreme emotional states of depression, fear, grief, rage, anxiety, and jealousy;

- It is the realm of connection of beings through relationships.

1 – Physical Realm

All realms are here, now, and within. The Physical Realm is the visible reality of space and time, energy and matter, cause and effect, the densest of a series of planes of existence. It does not exist apart from the other subtler realms, worlds, or dimensions, which interpenetrate themselves and physical reality from the center, as they were sent out as sound vibration, into various densities of manifestation. The Absolute is The Ultimate Reality, whose center is everywhere and whose circumference is nowhere … The Infinite. Qualities of the Physical Realm include:

- The Physical Plane is the realm of dense matter;

- It is the vehicle of consciousness and non-physical awareness;

- It is the personal manifestation of temporal, perishable form, identified as the human body and physical existence;

- It has the physical means to provide for, and sustain physical beings;

- It is bound by the Three Marks of Existence; Anicca – The Law of Impermanence, Dukka – The Law of Suffering, and Annatta – The Law of Non-Self;

- It is subject to Space/Time, Cause/Effect, Life/Death realities;

- It is inextricably connected to, and affected by 'Something' beyond the physical realm, that created it and serves to sustain it;

- It is sacred, in the context that it is the vehicle which contains our Essence, and demonstrates the full potential for our transcendence;

- It is the bridge between the inner and transcendent planes of consciousness and being.

The enemy of fear is knowledge. If we understand that our formless Self is not threatened by Anicca (The Law of Impermanence) or even death, our fears will dissolve, and a unique type of freedom will take their place. The practice of Mystical Meditation can induce journeying through realms of consciousness we commonly associate with the death process.

The mystical experience involves the many planes of existence. Meditation and prayer can take us on an excursion through the Astral Planes, opening gateways to dimensions beyond imagination, promoting healing on many levels. If we open our minds to the meaning of "as above, so below," we will discover the key to understanding what the practice of meditation really involves. The condensation of thought-forms seeking manifestation can cause precipitation of the best and the worst of energies upon our lives.

We are given meditation and prayer work as tools to catalyze our energy to transcend our own self-made temporal reality and venture beyond Space/Time, where the past, present, and future exist as one. We are able to access puzzle pieces of past events and things to come, to construct a portrait of life on any plane of existence. We are able to see ourselves as who we *really* are ... Timeless, Eternal beings. A nonlinear portrait extends beyond present realities and reveals the true significance of time and its relationship with the events of our lives. This vision may reach years into the future to provide glimpses of tomorrow, based on the effects of the choices we are making in the present, or have made in the past.

One simple way to demonstrate the way a relationship between planes operates is to make two fists, placing the left *above* and the right *below*. The left fist represents the bird's eye view of our world from the Astral Plane. Its position offers the advantage of viewing all events in what we distinguish as the past, present, and future. The right fist represents our world of matter. It moves in a continuous circular motion. We are moving with the right fist, trapped in the life-death, time/space continuum. We perceive the experience of a distinct past and future, without the conscious ability to see an outcome until it has occurred within our linear framework of present time.

Planes of existence are not to be viewed as locations above, below, or beside one another. The Astral Plane and its inhabitants exist just beyond our fixed perceptions, and parallel to the Earth Plane, as demonstrated by the left fist. This perspective offers an objective overview of life, death, and time. The past, present, and future are clearly seen as fluid or occurring *simultaneously*. The perception of life and death is seen as a mere transition from one plane to the next, or death to one plane and birth into another, upon the release of the physical vessel.

There is in-depth literature readily available, offering a journey into the world of spirit. The inhabitants of the Astral Plane are much like those of Earth Plane. Some are good, and some are not. The subtle planes have been described as

95

being similar in appearance and form to our denser plane of matter, but multidimensional and holographic in imagery, defying our marginal linear vision. In the astral dimension, sound vibrates at frequencies that sometimes create the hollow toned sound we may associate with echoes and whispers, or being underwater. Some colors appear as they would on the Earth Plane; other colors may appear exceptionally vivid and vibrant. The senses are enhanced by the depth and intensity of our experience of the Astral Planes where our rules of weight, density, and limitations of the physical form do not apply. The fears of life and death no longer seize and control our positive energy. We are no longer slaves to our concepts of Time and Space. We have the power and freedom to manifest our conscious thoughts, creating the reality we choose to experience.

We have the power to free ourselves from the bondage of fear and attachment to the perishable as our only reality. We have been given the gift to embrace Timeless reality. We cannot prove the existence of an afterlife or lateral plane, though many report having had the experience of being there. There is evidence sufficient enough to presume that we do not die. We appear to die to one realm and be born in another. There are inarguable accounts of people who have, intentionally or spontaneously, traveled out of body to different planes of consciousness. At the intersection of science and mysticism, these Planes, Dimensions, Worlds, and Realms, are only different expressions of the same reality.

Meditation: The Bridge Between Worlds of Consciousness

Knowing when and how to step out of our own way and venture beyond linear intellect into the world of the mystic is something that cannot be easily taught. Nor is it something that needs to be taught, or necessarily sought after. Most of us naturally have a strong resistance to willingly surrendering control of any aspect of our consciousness, that thread of control we think we have over our lives. At some point, or not, with study and practice, that spark of mysticism can ignite the fire of spiritual awakening. It can happen spontaneously, or not. We all have the capacity to experience an expansion of consciousness, and most have a choice. In general practice, the least we can expect to experience in Mystical Meditation is a relaxed and peaceful state of mind, a retreat from the chaos and stress of our lives.

The practice of meditation has been known to trigger unpredictable and often phenomenal experiences. After entering a meditative state, some people experience the distraction of hearing a voice or voices in continual monologue or dialogue. The goal of serious meditation is to quiet the endless, mindless chatter of the ghosts that stalk our subconscious world. Much of it is self-generated. Some may have visceral experiences that occur much like a lucid dream, with uncanny links to outer reality.

In the practice of meditation, many will enter a semi-trance state and begin to perceive information that is subject to visionary interpretation. To tap into all that is available, we must be fearless enough to journey to the planes of consciousness where dreams occur. These realms are much like our own, parallel to our own, differing in perspective, density, and frequency. The transcendent qualities of the Astral Plane allow that *any* and *every* thing can catalyze the opening of a portal into a deep meditative state, even without our intention. The clouds, the waves upon the water, the sand, rocks, and random stimuli can cause us to be drawn into a meditative trance. There are many ways to accomplish this objective. One of the most effective is to set aside time, if no more than ten to fifteen minutes a day, to dedicate to a daily ritual of embracing stillness and silence. Even deeper and more exalted realms are attainable through prayer. Sharing the insights of our meditations will become an effective meditation done in the spirit of prayer. That is why maintaining a daily journal is encouraged.

Many subtle techniques can be used to put ourselves into Dreamtime within moments. For the best results, the practitioner's goal is to experience a shift in perspective about our linear views of Time and Space. This requires a conscious shift of attention from the external to the internal transcendent planes. It requires us to turn within and redefine reality to include Dreamtime, at the crossroads where vertical and horizontal realities meet. In preparation to safely make this shift, we must first draw around ourselves a strong protective force field of Divine Light with prayer and visualization. A simple but powerful exercise can help to provide an energetic defense shield in a matter of moments with a subtle shift of awareness.

Our most formidable enemy in the assaults against our psyche is the torment of our own fears. To see things as they really are is the most powerful weapon we have. With time, it will become a comfortable lifestyle that will provide sound spiritual security for us, as we walk through the many dimensions across the bridge between dreams and learn more about the costumes and masks of this world. The archetypes of humanity paint themselves as a Timeless portrait of the seen and unseen human drama and bring clarity to some of the most profound mysteries of life. Signs and symbols that serve to establish fluency in a universal language of spirit are the construction materials with which to build the bridge between dreams. Those who dare may use this bridge to travel back and forth between worlds at will and are among the most fortunate of us all. Other worlds coexist in the ethers of our world of matter on lateral planes (or perhaps we, in theirs), so it is not a distant journey. It is innately within our consciousness to be able to find that place. We find that place within, in the stillness.

We all have spirit companions, guardians, and angels, just outside of our general perception who long to receive our attention so that they may assist us with our soul's physical experience, by Divine Will. They visit us in dreamtime and often communicate with us in symbolic language, offering us guidance and information in ways so subtle that we may miss the communication if we are not mindful. If these communications were too direct, many people would voluntarily commit themselves to institutions in a state of shock. We show them respect and acknowledgment when we learn the language of symbols and welcome their help, rather than living in fear and denial of these spirit beings or misidentifying them as deities. They have been given to us as a Divine gift to protect and serve the spiritual evolution of our souls.

The symbolic language in the dream state unlocks the gates to our subconscious and sparks the intuitive process. A healing takes place in our lives as our conscious awareness connects with our subconscious, uprooting all that our ego has caused us to bury under fear, despair, insecurity, anger, guilt, grief, envy, lust, greed, jealousy, and hatred. It is unearthed, healed, and released. The result is love, trust, and understanding of our Higher Self as a vital being, connected to the whole of the Universe and the Creator.

Manifestation: As Above, So Below

After meditating on the basic but profound reality of "as above, so below," we must acknowledge the fact that some energies, both above and below, are less than wonderful. There are people in this world that we would rather not communicate with, people we would not invite into our homes, and people we would not want to meet by chance on a lonely street at night, unarmed. The same is true of the spirit world. I do not intend to evoke fear, but common sense is required when dealing with certain Astral Plane entities and energies. Not having a body is no indicator that a spirit (or entity) will be any more intelligent or good-natured than they were while traveling in a body. There is a shadow side to the astral realm and its inhabitants, as there is in all of creation. This is the reason that people are generally cautioned against using mysticism for entertainment purposes. It is foolish and dangerous to play with ancient spiritual science as though it were a game, and I don't recommend this type of study to those who seek only a cursory knowledge of what constitutes a lifetime of spiritual study and practice.

There are age-old techniques used to cleanse and banish undesirable trespassing presences. Some techniques are as simple and as common as a prayer. It is not wise to enter a deep meditation without ritually dismissing unwelcome energies that may be present. Such practices manifest in some common traditions as simply as blessing the food before eating a meal.

Psychic doors must be locked to uninvited party-crashers by psychically invoking the White Light of The God. We surrender our ego-based will to the Compelling Will of The Divine One with faith that the protection of The Creator envelops and secures our souls. Study the basic suggestions and precautions shared in this book. It is beneficial to document experiences, insights, and visions on this beautiful adventure. It will contribute to spiritual safety and show respect for a sound check and balance system of spiritual accountability. We are seeking wisdom and knowledge of the highest vibration, not an unpleasant experience.

Some wonder, "Why, then, don't we just go directly to The God and leave the use of mystical studies and practices out of it?" My response is, "How can you say with authority, that it is not the wisdom of The God that we are tapping into directly through the use of Mystical Meditation? Some ask, "Do you believe that spiritual intercession can occur and intervene in our affairs?" I can answer on faith and experience that the Spirit of all spirits, the Holy Spirit, is the bond that reinforces our relationship with The Divine One and Divine Guidance. I believe that angels watch over us continually and communicate with us in a multitude of ways. They are called by many names; angels, awliya, loa, orisha, spirit guides, guardians, and ancestors. They can take whatever form they find necessary to get our attention, even in shocking manners and presentation. It is absolute hypocrisy to profess a belief in angelic, seen and unseen presences, and yet believe that it is evil or witchy to acknowledge the role this undeniable phenomenon plays in our lives. It is commanded that we seek refuge *only* in The One God. We can trust in the Wisdom of The Divine One, with regards to who, from this army of guides and protectors, is best suited to be permitted to intervene in our lives. An element of Mystical Meditation is seeking the presence of and communion with The Absolute, The Ultimate, The Divine, The One Creator.

The highest and purest purpose of practicing Mystical Meditation is for our personal spiritual growth and development. A meditation may induce revelations, visions, and can even give us a *forecast* of *possible future scenarios* since its perspective is without Time, Space, or form, as we know it. Our Free Will may be guided by the wisdom of either embracing a possible fate or avoiding it in the most beneficial way for all concerned. Meditation is a powerful conduit for the transmission of messages of the highest intentions. Any abuse of it speaks only of the intentions of the abuser, not of the practice. Mystical Meditation is a form of becoming the prayer we pray and should be approached with that same level of respect for the sacred.

The Bible (KJV) speaks of Jacob's Ladder in Genesis 28:11, "And he lighted upon a certain place, and tarried there all night, because the sun was set; and he took of the stones of that place, and put them for his pillows, and laid down in that place to sleep." Genesis 28:12, "And he dreamed, and behold a ladder set up on the Earth, and the top of it reached to heaven, and behold the angels of The God ascending and descending on it."

Angels mingle among us in many forms bringing messages of comfort, healing, and assistance. In the process, it is not possible to avoid messages from The Source of all, from that Timeless place, where there is no difference between what we label as the past, present, and future. All things occur in the "now" or present tense. Anchoring our energies in the "NOW" causes a 'perspective' shift of Time and Space. The past and the future, have been, and will always be the now, at some point. Within this state of meditative 'now-ness,' all that is Divinely Permitted to be seen and known, is seen and known. That which is not Divinely Permitted to be seen will not be revealed, regardless of what methods are used.

Meditation inspires a transcendent perspective. When we meditate, we are placing ourselves in a position of consciousness to receive visions of what we have named past and future realities. Meditation can trigger spontaneous 'visionary seeing' beyond what we believe to be the capacity of our horizontal senses. In this regard, there are oracular properties associated with Mystical Meditation, which require the unwavering observance of spiritual responsibility and propriety.

The nature of the messages we receive will reveal whether the source is of the shadow worlds or of Divine Light. The highest of ideals of any spiritual technology can be corrupted. The star or cross can be turned upside down. Verses of Holy Scriptures can be recited backward or used out of context, as weapons, even as a sick justification for cold-blooded murder. The use of inverted interpretations of sacred symbols and scriptures reflect the negative orientation of those who choose this corruption, not of the symbols and scriptures themselves.

102

Mystical practices such as meditation can open doors to receiving communication from angels, ascending and descending on "Jacob's Ladder." Such phenomena commonly occur in Mystical Meditation. Messages of guidance and protection, comfort, healing, and Light are exchanged on these spiritual bridges. If the messages received are positive, there is no cause for concern. If not, it is best to withdraw from the meditation and retreat into prayer. After discovering the cause of, and cure for it, we are safe to resume our meditation practice. Prayer, intuition, and the gift of spiritual discernment are the most reliable and trustworthy guides. It is understood that any communication that has the potential to cause harm to anyone, including ourselves, is a voice to be silenced. If our highest moral values are threatened, compromised, or violated by a communication, it is a sign of a Spiritual Emergency.

Often a negative communication may be Divinely Permitted as a test to determine if the suggestions of whispering demons have a place to land, that we may not even be consciously aware of. We pray that we keep our spirits cleansed through prayer, fasting, and meditation, to have the spiritual discernment to know the difference between good and evil in all its myriad expressions.

Manifestation: As Below, So Above

One objective of Mystical Meditation could seek to create, launch, and then anchor an ethereal thought-form from this plane, with sound, Light, symbols, and words of power. It is intensified by prescribed ritual. More than any of the paraphernalia you may gather to place upon your altar, *emotion* is the single most important catalyst to launch a stated intention into ultimate manifestation. Lukewarm emotional flatlining before an altar produces results directly proportionate to the energy brought to the spiritual work.

Depending upon the nature of the work, certain lunar and planetary aspects are not recommended to work under because they are not conducive to a clean, positive outcome. In the beginning of our experiences in practical mysticism, we will study the planning of ritual, spiritual work by many ancient traditionally prescribed methods. Given time we will reach levels of attunement that will enable us to sense the perfect timing, and our spiritual work will, in effect, plan itself.

Sometimes I feel a certain urge and react spontaneously, breaking many of the rules of planning that I share with you in this text. Then, after it is over, out of curiosity, I will determine what the perfect timing would have been, only to find out that the *right* time was the exact time I felt called to do it. Many mystical paths will teach of Universal energies and how they work with us to achieve goals that can enhance, heal, and improve the quality of our lives. Some will experience a level of sensitivity wherein we will feel these energies call us out to respond immediately and appropriately, then instruct precisely how to do what needs to be done to accomplish our spiritual goals.

I will never encourage that there is any ritual, meditation, petition, affirmation, or visualization that would enter the arena of intensity of a single, sincere prayer. No sincere prayer goes unanswered. Prayer is our most powerful way of communicating with The Divine One and represents the most direct path. The most basic of respect for The God suggests that we perform certain rituals which are common to communications with anyone, like cleansing ourselves, providing a clean environment, and providing an atmosphere conducive to the purpose of the communication. For example, we would not conduct a business meeting in a loud nightclub. Nor would we attend a business meeting dressed for, and behaving as though, we were attending a party.

Propriety and respect are key considerations; however, there is nothing that should be used as an excuse or reason not to pray. Even though we are instructed to wash the hands, face, and feet in certain very reverent prayer traditions, it is also instructed that if provisions for this "ablution" are not available, the cleansing may be done with the literal breath of one's own prayer, or even with dirt. Common sense is the wisest instruction when engaging in any spiritual work. Never forgetting the objective is the wisest mindset. The objective is to "talk" with The God until the two Voices and Intentions become One. The objective is to live in thanks and gratitude for the blessings of The God. The objective is to live in praise of The God. The higher our level of respect for humility and service, the stronger the bond of Love between the "I in I." That is the connection we seek, the sacred bond of the "I in I," causing a mutual Will for the manifestation of the highest good of all.

Cosmic Users

In any mysticism, the Divine Law of Justice and Karma has a built-in check and balance system set in place that enforces itself. Cosmic users are the 'takers' who wish to whine, beg, receive, and give nothing back. They seek only the instant gratification of their every desire. They approach an altar like it is an ATM. When the scales of justice and Karmic balance are tipping too much to any one side, Cosmic Law seeks to restore that balance. Sometimes these adjustments for balance can occur in our lives like tectonic plates beneath the Earth shifting as they seek balance, causing what we call an earthquake on the surface. Karmic indebtedness can seek to balance itself through manifestations in our lives that come in the form of accidents, costly mishaps, miscalculations, and often, falling victim to another taker and becoming the taken.

I do not recommend reliance upon the practice of Mystical Meditation for greed and vanity-based acquisition of money and material things. It is not worth the price that will ultimately be paid. Every Earth Plane method of problem-solving should be exercised as an active form of meditation before we turn to mysticism for solutions. There is no such thing as a free lunch.

A major consideration before projecting our personal will through meditation, with the intention of creating change in our lives, is to determine whether or not we are serving Divine Will through the changes we wish to create. The importance of embracing The Creator's Divine Will in our lives is the number one priority. If we are attempting to manifest something that is not aligned with God's Will for our lives, we will not be successful, whether we attract our list of demands into our present reality or not. If we get what we want, it may not be the ideal thing to serve our highest good. If we don't get it, we may say the spiritual work was unsuccessful, not realizing that we are being Divinely protected from ourselves, and in effect, we dodged a bullet.

I once heard that the worst curse that can be put on a human being is to wish that he or she gets everything they want, just the way they want it. If we look at our own personal history and track record, I think we will all agree that we have not always been particularly adept in the wisdom of knowing what to want. An old Zen style philosophy says that it is the greatest blessing, not so much to have what we want, but more, to want what we have. Our temporal, linear perspectives can divert us from the consciousness of the Eternal.

Our highest good is served by making sure that what we desire matters in the big picture of eternity. Imagine seeing our desires through the filter of God's vision of our destiny. Deep inside, most of us have a clue what that is. We were born with our Divine Purpose encoded in the Essence that first rose up as a "me" thought. In that sense, we already are what we were born to be, just waiting to be witnessed as having happened. When we look at a seed, we must accept that we have looked upon a tree. If we look at it from the Timeless perspective of Spirit, the tree has already happened. Given the right elemental and environmental support, the seed is one with the tree it is becoming.

We are this thing we seek. We cannot have anything that we are not willing to become in consciousness. We cannot have what we are not. Our spiritual belief system and faith in a Higher Power, more specifically, The Most High, plays a great role in mystical practice. What we believe is what we manifest. These beliefs are not always conscious, so beware the unconscious belief system that can undermine our every good intention and render it powerless, or even dangerous. We can have a house full of lamps, but if we do not have a source of power to plug them into, we will still be in the dark. If we plug the lamps into a faulty source, it is worse than remaining in the dark. We can start a fire causing total destruction.

In the practice of "magick" or certain types of mysticism, we participate as co-creators in the manifestation of some desire in our hearts. Before you are faced with a pressing matter that inspires you to go beyond common prayerfulness and take a work to task at your altar, ask yourself a few questions. What is the nature of this manifestation? What is the nature of this heart which seeks this manifestation? What is the motivation behind this work? Why is a formal ceremonial approach believed to be required to accomplish it? Against what "odds" does one strive to manifest this work? Are you sure it is in cooperation with the Divine Plan, or is it an attempted manipulation of it? What are the known and unforeseen consequences of this work, as manifested within the timeframe of the worker?

We must be careful when arbitrarily deciding that we know what is best for the highest good of everyone concerned in an attempt to manifest a new reality. If we find ourselves working outside of the framework of Universal and Divine intention, we are treading on dangerous ground. It is not like there is a possibility that our ambition alone would lead us to our imagined success. Nothing can be manifested unless it is permitted by Universal Law and Divine Plan, regardless of the worker's skill or best intentions.

When our "person"al ego willfully flies out of control, and we feel we know beyond the Knowing of the Knower of all things, because of an emotion, an opinion, a judgment, a desire, we act without thinking of the consequences. It is just not worth the Karmic debt for a momentary rush and power trip.

At the risk of sounding preachy, it is just not worth the dangers involved when the Karmic turnaround presents. The energy will boomerang in mind-boggling ironic ways. If it goes beyond a prayer of surrender, it is a red flag. These subtle energies are sacred. When that sacredness is violated, the entire Universe and the very Essence of The God that created it will rise up against us. We do not need to *practice* magick. We *are* the magick.

Judge Not

It is important to the maintenance of the integrity of our spirituality to guard against judgment or self-exaltation. I am in no way imposing judgment upon those who hold fear and criticism in their hearts against esoteric spirituality, with no basis other than an opinion. I once entertained judgments into hell of many of the very same beliefs to which I have since dedicated my life. As the years have passed and my interest in the ancient mysteries has deepened and nearly dominated my life, I now see the wisdom in releasing my judgment of those who have attacked me with judgment, in the name of their preferred belief system. These are some of the same belief systems that teach their followers against judging.

I believe that many of the people who impose their unsolicited demands upon the spiritual choices of others truly believe they are attempting to save people, according to their own myopic standards. Self-righteous religious ignorance and pure evil can be found on all spiritual paths, based on our human, or inhumane, interpretations of what we choose to see as The God's Will. How many wars have been waged in the name of God? I choose to regard spirituality as an intensely personal matter. There is no instrument to measure spirituality other than the way we live our lives and respect the lives of others. We all draw from the same vast ocean of consciousness, whether it is at the shore, or into its depths.

Time and experience have allowed me to appreciate the wisdom of some of the many warnings directed at the study of mysticism. I now understand the dangers of certain mystical paths and the risks of either intentionally, or inadvertently, crossing that thin line onto what is sometimes referred to as the left-hand path. I know the pain and grief we open the doors of our lives to, in an often-misguided pursuit of the Higher Truths. I now know the cruelties of spiritual warfare, and I have seen and experienced the damage and suffering it causes. Many chose the path of denial of what is really happening. These are the veils between worlds that are in place, often for our own protection. I was told that if those veils were to be pulled away all at once, to reveal only what was going on in the unseen right in front of our faces, we might lose our minds.

It would be irresponsible of me if I did not acknowledge my awareness of some of the sordid mental and spiritual character profiles that seem to be drawn to paths of extreme forms of mystical studies and practices. I know now why some paths of mysticism are often branded by some religious fundamentalists as being "pure evil," with the advisory to "go not near ANY of it!" I was sent back, full circle, into prayer, seeking refuge in The One God, from malevolent forces I had unknowingly attracted into my life. I could not defend myself alone, as deep as I thought I was at the time. I was pushed back into the loving, forgiving arms of The Source of all. I was forced to raise the vibration of my own misspent energies. I had to refine my list of spiritual criteria as I continued my studies on a path of respect for the gift of the Love and Protection of The Most High. Now I understand my own participation in opening portals through which dangerous energies gained entry into my life.

This study is not for dabblers. What starts as an innocent meditation class can end up in an intricately well-woven web of the forsaken ones. A *cursory* knowledge of ritual, spiritual practice could result in exposure to dangers we cannot imagine. One must pursue the knowledge of the greater mysteries with the sense of commitment that a person whose head is engulfed in flames would pursue a stream of fresh running water. Nothing less will suffice. One must never forget The Creator of these great mysteries in our embrace of the pursuit of the Unattainable … the Unknowable. Our search will never end until we are led to The Point of Origin. To the true Natural Mystic, the path is the destination. It does not end, not even with the grave.

Nothing to Prove

We must not drain our positive energy by arguing with, trying to convert, or defend ourselves against people who do not share our spiritual belief system. The fact that you are reading this book is evidence that you recognize the value of understanding the practice of Psychic Self-Defense. Whatever the reason for this study, it is personal. These are typically not conversations over coffee with a casual gym buddy, coworker or classmate. Unfortunately, the dominance of one-dimensional logic, blind reason, and fear-mongering has repressed many of our most basic mediums for the transmission of sacred knowledge. It is a waste of time to try to break through the stone walls of the fear and judgment of others. There is an old saying, "A man convinced against his will, is of the same opinion still."

We do not owe anyone an explanation of the deeper levels of our spirituality. Mystical experiences are a natural element of our awakening and of existence itself. We must not leak vital energy giving too much attention to the occurrence of naturally arising phenomena. It is to be expected. These phenomena rise up and pass away into forgetfulness, as they yield to the next wave of phenomena. It is the "I" that remains. It is the I AM (the essential, unborn, undying, Eternal Self), not the "me" of our linear perceptions, that observes all changes … unchanging. It is our goal to rise above the attachment we have to seeking the validation and approval of others.

It is generally unwise to feel too free to share personal spiritual experiences with others, even people we feel we can trust. These soul-bearing revelations may create gaping chasms in friendships and family and may even threaten employment and reputation. Inappropriate openness can give "frenemies," potentially deadly ammunition that can taint our beautiful new relationship with the emergence of our new Light Body Self, the "I in I," the I AM. For this reason, certain mystical studies have traditionally been held as well-guarded secrets, confined to discussion within the boundaries of the mystery schools, only among fellow initiates. A wise person guards his or her tongue as he or she guards his or her life. In other words, it's a good idea to keep our personal business to ourselves. Our spiritual experiences are as sacred as a prayer. Honor the privacy of that sacredness.

If you reveal your secrets to the wind,
you should not blame the wind
for revealing them to the trees.

~ Khalil Gibran ~

There will be experiences we will have that will be so sacred to *us* that we may not be able to explain, nor describe, not to mention, *prove*! Scientific validation, terminology, and documented proof are not required when one has direct experience of the Timeless Realm. For those who have not had such experiences and choose to challenge the experiences of others, no amount of proof will satisfy the need to invalidate and somehow discredit them. We must pray for the strength to learn how to just let it go, as we learn to pick our fights. The biggest mistake we can make is to allow our ego to become involved. Everyone evolves in his or her own time. We are not to rush or force issues regarding the spiritual evolution of another person for that violates their God-given right to Free Will.

There will always be those who will seek to ridicule others for their differences. There will always be people who will frown upon the spiritual beliefs and experiences of other people in an attempt to make them feel foolish, insane, wicked, and/or deluded, no matter what the path.

Allow the subtle flow of the Universe to whisper into the consciousness of the soul of every individual, as and when it sees fit. Everything happens in The God's Time. It is not cosmically correct to laugh, tease, or gloat when whispers turn to screams and shouts, startling people out of their ignorance. "*I told you so*" behavior displays spiritual unskillfulness on the part of whoever engages in that type of immature conduct. Our own spirituality is enough of a responsibility, without seeking to stand in self-righteous judgment of someone else's.

If you are experiencing a spiritual attack or emergency, you are required to take responsibility and make whatever changes in consciousness necessary to redirect the disturbing energies. You may study subject matter that is new to you. You may make lifestyle changes that attract the attention of those that are accustomed to you being a certain way. Judgments may be made. No one has the self-ascribed Divine authority to attack the spirituality of another with personal judgments.

There is no good reason to place our lives on the altar of public scrutiny. It will naturally occur that a strong support group will emerge and become a sacred inner circle supportive of our higher consciousness. There are online groups and information available. Our world is expanding, not contracting. The horizon is only the beginning.

The War Within

Given the duality of our being, how could we not be at war within ourselves, challenged to fight continually and without rest to maintain the delicate balance of spirit and clay? We manage the nature of the two aspects of ourselves that often oppose, negate, and deny one another. Existential chaos results when we see our spiritual and physical selves as being mutually exclusive. This contradiction will torment us and often trap us in perpetual disagreement with dueling aspects of ourselves. We must recognize the crossroad where the bondage of the flesh and the freedom of the spirit within meet.

It is not easy to understand or control the obsessions and compulsions of the physical self, as it competes to usurp the will of the nonphysical Self. This power struggle is a fight to the grave to maintain our moral high ground over the lure of the animalistic side of our nature. Regarding the never-ending demands of the flesh, it is said that human desire is like a graveyard, there is always room for one more.

To understand the character of the war between flesh and spirit is to know how to win it. To emerge victorious from this spiritual war, we must first understand that we look outside of ourselves for the demons we battle, when the deadliest of them all is within. Our Light and our shadows do not have to exist in an illusory state of conflict, sufficient to cancel each other out. It is our choice to view these opposite polarities in our nature as a necessity to one another, as the Yin is to the Yang (See the diagram earlier in this book.) Emerging from chaos for creative order, we affirm that each side is a binding link to the other, causing the whole to continue to exist in harmony. The alchemy of the synthesis of Yin and Yang energies has the power to manifest thought-form to form and back again.

We must not allow the war within to define our existence, even though it gives the appearance of being capable of doing so. These illusions are often parlor tricks and theater. The enemy of humanity is invested in our believing chaos is our only truth, seeking to weaken our resolve, kill our spirits, and cause us to define who we are based on our lowest potential. Demonic energies are associated with the energy of hopelessness. They whisper into our hearts disparaging messages that are intended to cast shadows, so overwhelming that our Light may be eclipsed. The result would be our compliant seduction into hatred of one another, and hatred for our own selves, which is the gateway to destruction and ruin.

The Dance of Duality

Where there is Light, shadows are cast. Where there are shadows, there must be Light somewhere. Rather than viewing ourselves as creatures of such warring contradictions, I choose to view our duality as the graceful dance between our shadows, and the brilliance of our Eternal Light. The Light is sacred. Even the shadow is sacred. The music and lyrics are a symphony of our prayers, as well as the answers to them. These energies conspire to protect us through our daily struggles for wholeness and survival. The dance floor is this plane of matter. It smiles upon our inept footing and struggles to maintain balance until the music stops and that silence embraces another dancer.

The carnal manifestation that we are serves to acquire knowledge that we can only experience, and authentically comprehend, from within the physical vehicle that transports our soul. How could the taste of an apple be described to our nonphysical body of consciousness that exists beyond the senses? Both aspects of our being, the physical and nonphysical, complement one another. Our Light and our shadows transcend duality, in their intimate embrace, intertwined and spinning as the whirling Dervish, seeking the Divine intoxication of union with The God. This is an unprecedented state of bliss, associated with making a connection with the Holy, Sacred Spirit of The Divine One. Beyond bliss is the shadow's realization of its relationship with, and as, that Light of Divinity.

We are not to confuse the dichotomy of our nature with the spiritual war raging between what we see as opposing forces of good and evil, in the Heavens, on Earth, and deep within the personal and collective psyche. There seem to be no negotiations or peace talks between these two, apparently clashing energies. In the energetic context of the Yin and Yang, these energies interdependently represent harmony, balance, and motion. It is Universal Law.

We are responsible for our own choices. Our unwavering Love for the concept of good is the music, the resonance, that guides our steps and its rhythms. We are required to fully disengage ourselves from the fearful thoughts that can cause a naturally occurring universal formula for creation, turn into a deadly last dance. We seek to conquer the whispered influences of demonic voices by withdrawing attention from them. We were promised this plague from our original conception. We defeat them by giving them no place to land in our consciousness. We, instead, embrace the gentle voices of the angels that are set in place to attend, serve, and protect us.

We often, consciously and subconsciously, ascribe ridiculous identities, properties, and special effects to what we call angels and demons. There are no winged, flying, scantily clad, curly blond babies with chubby cheeks, no buxom supermodels in prom gowns with flowing tresses and white robes. Who paints these pictures? There are no horns, pitchfork or tail, no red body-suited, shadowy, devil monsters. It is much more insidious than that. These are images in our minds, with no basis in physical or spiritual reality. Our cultural and religious conditioning would have us believe these off-putting, buffoonish caricatures have power over our lives.

Both demons and angels can assume both physical and nonphysical forms. They have an I AM of their own ... A formless awareness ... A consciousness. Their faces are in our mirrors, and the mirrors of everyone and everything we know. We already know how the story ends. That knowledge should rob it of much of its shock value, and potential to instill fear. However, that makes the challenge no less threatening. The worst mistake anyone can make is to disregard or underestimate the strength of an enemy. Evil does not sleep. Good does not blink. Sometimes we cannot distinguish the difference between the two. We must never forget the blessing bestowed upon us of an army of angels, commissioned to protect and help us, as a testament of their love, obedience, and service to The God. We drift off into sleep, and wake up every day of our lives, fighting the same old war. It hides its ugly face behind a multitude of deceptive masks. Many are family and friends. Many exalt themselves over us from positions of authority over our lives. Many hide in the shadows they found on the straight path of our most sacred vows.

For we wrestle not against flesh and blood,
but against principalities, against powers,
against the rulers of the darkness of this world,
against spiritual wickedness in high places."

~ Ephesians 6-12, The Bible (KJV) ~

The knowledge of inevitable defeat fails to deter their negative energies and vicious attacks. The motivation for senseless warring in the face of foreseeable defeat is the pleasure and sick satisfaction derived from the mischief and chaos they create. Their only victory is that we fear more than we love; that we fear death; fear life; fear change; fear one another; fear ourselves, and never realize the ubiquitous power of the True Self that we really are.

Our only defense against suffering, from whatever the perceived cause, is the knowledge of Self. Who are we being on this stage called life, and what frequencies do we make ourselves available to, or responsible for? When we say I AM, Who are we really? The celebrated poet, Rumi, describes our carnal self, standing apart from its spiritual Source, as a "dunghill." We are no better than those angels and positive forces that attend us. Our vanity, arrogance, greed, and ignorance have led many of us to believe we are better than the angelic kingdom. It is not wise to take the Light of their protection for granted or fail to show our gratitude by becoming a Light to others.

We, as "creation," have a natural tendency to be ambitious and merciless creatures. That inclination is intertwined with survival instincts, yet, we choose the path for which we will be held accountable. It is so pronounced that, whether we are consciously aware of it or not, we are all nervously awaiting the appearance of something, or someone, to call order to our desperate situation. Our passive waiting is but another selfish demand that we are served, without serving. In the face of our suffering, in the face of our fears, our service to others who suffer from mind-melting fear determines our ability to survive and heal. We must serve as we receive the blessings that are our inheritance from our Creator. If we serve humanity, we are earning the bountiful gifts that The God delights in our receiving from the Light and Source of all giving.

The dance between the clay and the Light Spirit, the container and the contained, is fully underway. It can be just as graceful or awkward as our careful or careless footing dictates. The trumpet is certainly sounding. Let the dance begin.

METHODS OF
SPIRITUAL PROTECTION

Methods of Spiritual Protection

Spiritual discernment and trust in our intuition are critical to recognizing the signs of spiritual problems that require our attention. There is a difference between paranoid superstition and having the wisdom to recognize the signs that we may have become the target of a spiritual attack. It is dangerous to be too attached to a tendency to write too many things off as coincidence. There are many indications of spiritual warfare or unwanted energies that require a spiritual clearing or cleansing. Among them are the following;

- A stuffy or claustrophobic feeling in certain rooms, if not all of your home;

- A condensation of energy in your home;

- Children or animals behaving strangely, reacting to something unseen;

- Unpleasant odors with no physical source;

- Things going "bump in the night," unexplainable noises from no apparent source;

- Chronic or lingering illnesses which don't seem to be linked to a physical cause;

- Cold areas or currents in the house, or around your person, for which there is no physical explanation;

- Unusually frequent accidents or mishaps;

- An unusual occurrence of insect infestation;

- Dramatic changes at home in the personalities of family, occupants, and visitors;

- Unusual bouts with what appears to be a murky cloud of "bad luck;"

- Strange pockets of energy in closets, storage areas, under beds, and in any dark or shadowy areas;

- An unusual increase in arguments and general conflict among household occupants;

- Flashes of light or shadows in your peripheral vision, light bulbs malfunctioning;

- Bizarre electrical problems, technical difficulties, malfunction of electronics;

- Insomnia and nightmares of a graphic and visceral nature;

- Chronic or sudden acute bouts of depression;

- Suicidal thoughts and feelings of worthlessness and self-doubt;

- Homicidal thoughts and a strong desire to harm self and/or others;

- Pain or discomfort at the back of the neck and/or solar plexus area;

- Chronic headaches and excessive fatigue;

- An unusual purging, diarrhea, vomiting, foaming and especially bleeding;

- Plants or pets dying from no apparent physical cause;

- Apparitions, voices, and movement of inanimate objects;

- Illnesses that involve blood. Blood conditions are the most severe and are referred to by some spiritual practitioners as 'the touch of Satan.' Waste no time in getting both physical and spiritual help. These cases are the most difficult to resolve. We must immediately look deeply into our lives for enemies who may have a motive for seeking our demise. These enemies may be hidden and under deep cover, even to their conscious selves.

We must humbly seek refuge in The God ... heart, and soul, to petition that the perpetrator is revealed and that the source of the energy is dealt with by Divine Will. We must also examine our own lives to unearth any deeply rooted, subconscious feelings of guilt for regrettable life choices. These life lessons may have resulted in the creation of a self-fulfilling prophecy of Karma that manifests in an energetic magnetism to misfortune. Karma can be cleansed and released through prayer, chanting of mantras, and becoming very conscious of the people with whom we associate. We must observe with mindfulness the signs and guidance from the subtle realms. Pray for the strength to forgive and release those same energies we banish, which also reside in ourselves.

There are symptoms far more extreme than those mentioned herein. If any of the troubling Psychic Self-Defense concerns discussed in this book become an issue in your life, it may be difficult to rely on a positive support system. It is unfortunate, but true that such talk among average people will result in being perceived as crazy just for expressing your description and diagnosis of the problem. Understand that many symptoms of acute psychosis produce much of the same type of drama as listed above. The gift of spiritual discernment is often all that can differentiate one from the other. We may find ourselves on our own, isolated, with no trusted person to confide in, which only worsens the problem. If the indications of danger are severe enough and we have ruled out the possibility of being psychotic, it is time to seek spiritual help from a trusted source.

Many people do not believe in the existence of certain psychic phenomena until they have come face to face with it. Even then, they may attempt to find logic-based explanations that suit their own limited, close-minded, unstudied, judgmental belief systems. If, however, we are fortunate enough to have a positive support group of people who are aware on the higher and subtler levels of mystical knowledge, there is no shame in asking for help. If not, then we must go within and know that we are not alone. We pray faith into our hearts, knowing that our needs are known and attended to in the subtle realms. Help is all around, whether we can see it or not. We will be guided through our complete submission to That Which Created All, which certainly can sustain and protect us. It does not sleep or tire. Satan stumbles.

I have gathered helpful tips from many traditions that can balance and fortify our electromagnetic field to attract our highest good. These age-old remedies are preventative measures, not just in times of apparent necessity, but as a lifestyle of mindfulness. When faced with a spiritual problem, these remedies are important to know, though it is just the tip of the iceberg. It is well worth the effort to conduct independent studies on this subject. We have enough spiritual maturity and discernment to separate alchemy from superstition.

Blessing your home: Traditional Shamanic methods of "house blessing" include smudging (fanning) the home and person with the smoke of sage, cedar, Palo Santo, or copal. Incense suited for spiritual cleansing is recommended, such as lavender, frankincense, and myrrh. Salt is believed to possess properties that serve to drive away negative entities and energetic attachments. Note that negative energies are not fond of bright lights and loud noise, especially certain types of music at high volumes. Some use gospel. I prefer what would be considered sacred music, from many traditions, conscious reggae, and repetitive prayer. They are certainly not fond of prayer and commandments in the Name of The Creator of all things. When performing the cleansing, use prayer and chanting to charge the smoke with the power of your intention and petition for spiritual protection and banishing of the invading energy or entity.

Call out the Name of The God three times: In the event of a Spiritual Emergency, say, "I command you, in the Name of (your manner of addressing The Most High) to be gone." I choose to refrain from using names specific to only one particular language, religion, or culture. Because I speak English, I may say, "On the Blood of Jesus, I command you to be gone!" A person standing next to me may speak Spanish, and that person might say, "Por la sangre de Jesus Cristo, te mando que vayas de aqui!" The Name of The God and prophets of The God are called by different names in many different languages, according to many diverse traditions. Banish, with authority, any spiritual intrusion with the same energy you would if it were embodied and trespassed into your space. We stand up with courage and confidence, knowing that we are Divinely protected. We pray, we chant, we read selected passages from sacred scriptures. We will never have to wonder when a spiritual problem requires our attention. We will know. Dedicated spiritual discipline and practice is the only way to avoid the annoying task of stomping out the many brushfires of psychic warfare.

Spray a solution of water and salt, rosemary, or ammonia: Pay attention to the corners near the floors and ceiling, the interior of cabinets, drawers, closets, and drain pipes when you spray.

Place packets of Hawaiian salt charged with prayer, wrapped in tea leaves in the four corners of your home: Place them at entrances and exits, under and around areas where you sleep as well as any other areas that you are guided to protect. You may want to wear this packet on your person as a talisman if it feels appropriate.

Frankincense and Myrrh: This combination of incense lifts and dispels negative energy. The smoke, charged with prayer, blesses, and spiritually cleanses people, places, and objects. Myrrh is believed to be born from the mythical goddess Myrrh's tears.

Lavender: This word is a Latin derivative meaning "to wash." It offers an excellent spiritual cleansing when used with prayer and sacred words of power. It should be used for bathing, as incense, and mixed with water to spray around your home.

Lemon or Lime: Mixed with water, charged with your positive intention, it can be used for blessings and purification.

White candle: Charge and anoint a white candle in prayer and meditate upon its flame requesting Divine protection. There are anointing oils available that will enhance the focus of prayer and meditation ritual. Olive oil is one good choice, and it is easy to find. A seven-day candle is best, observing standard fire safety precautions. There are color-coded candle rituals; however, I find them to be a distraction from my singular focus on The Divine.

Glass of water: Place a full glass of water on a nightstand near the head of your bed before going to sleep. It is believed to attract and absorb directed negative energies and entities that may cause a troubled sleep, or worse. Upon awakening, pour the water into the toilet and flush it with a banishing prayer. Never make the mistake of drinking the water or leaving it sitting around. Dispose of it immediately after waking.

Sleep with your head in the East: Many recognize the West as the direction in which the heads of the dead are placed to be energetically aligned with the setting Sun. It is not considered a favorable position for the living to sleep.

Ritual of Light: The psychic projection of a strong auric shield of Divine protective white Light around your home, yourself, and loved ones (whether they are in your physical presence or not, and whether or not they are aware of it) can block negative energy and attack. Practice the Light Meditation provided on the *dreamuniversal.com* website, or later in this book, before going to sleep and upon awakening. You can also practice mindful breathing as you visualize a gently cascading waterfall of brilliant white Light emanating from a sphere of Light just above your head. Let it saturate your entire aura with the Love and Protection of The Divine One. Hold this visualization of Light as an egg-shaped envelopment completely surrounding you. Charge it with an intense prayer of surrender.

Mirroring: Go into deep meditation and psychically surround your body and your home with mirrors facing away from you in every direction. Pray that any negative energies sent to you be deflected and transmuted into the pure white Light of love and healing. Return every trace of the energy to the sender along with the blessing of The God, that the individual is shown the truth of their behavior and be guided to the path of goodness and healing.

It is a powerfully protective visualization to see your image inside of a mirrored "globe," much like one might find spinning above an 80's style disco dance floor or in a nightclub. The energy of the attack is scattered and reflected back to the sender.

Cleanse all mirrors and reflective surfaces with ammonia: This includes rear and side-view mirrors in your car, mirrors in your make-up bag or compact, and particularly mirrors in your bedrooms and bathrooms. It is not a good idea to sleep in a room with mirrors and reflective surfaces because they can operate like portals through which invading energies and entities may pass. It is especially unwise to place a mirror on any outside-facing wall of your home.

Study Feng Shui: The study of the art of Feng Shui is a preventative measure against negative energies and psychic attack. One of the things you will learn is to place a Bagua mirror above the entrance of your home, reflecting outward, after you have ceremonially blessed it with prayer to "open the eye" of protection. Many symbols serve a similar purpose, such as the Hamsa or Hand of Fatima. It is believed by many traditions to ward off the "evil eye." There are many books and related materials available on the subject. The internet is one place to begin your search for information regarding this ancient spiritual practice. At the same time, understand that it is The God who protects not Feng Shui, amulets, and talismans. With gratitude, we receive the gift of mystical wisdom as a guide to make our life experience happy and as free from suffering as possible. It teaches us to cooperate with the flow of the rhythms and rhymes of this gift of existence. It

128

serves as intentional reminders and focal points in the day to day meditation called our lives. Many such practices cause us to manage the energies of and about ourselves in a manner that does not swim against every current.

Study Martial Arts: The Third, Fifth, and Sixth Chakras are particularly vulnerable to psychic attack. They are all primary, specific energetic points of entry. Chi Gong (Qi Gong) or any of the healing arts that work with the Chi energy of the complex body system can restore peace of mind and make us more confident in the ability to ward off and become more immune to attack. There are meditation exercises to strengthen the chakras in this text. The study of our energetic body is better classified as a lifestyle choice rather than a protection ritual. A couple of old sayings come to mind; *"It is better to be safe than sorry."* and *"An ounce of prevention is worth a pound of cure."* Our Light body is fortified as its own defense against attack when we make the respect and care it deserves an uncompromising standard for our lives.

Seek swift and amicable resolution to conflict: If you are at odds with someone in your life, it is important to resolve the conflict as swiftly as possible and establish a win/win outcome. An accumulation of negative energy directed specifically at you, either consciously or unconsciously, by someone who believes that you have in some way wronged or hurt them, can manifest disastrous consequences in your life. Some believe that the Sun should never set on an argument.

In cultures that are particularly aware of the potentially harmful effects of negative energy, the resolution of the conflict is regarded as very high in priority. In indigenous Hawaiian culture, there is a ceremony called Ho'oponopono, wherein a Kahuna or wise Shaman will mediate conflicts between partners, family, and friends. They will retreat, usually into nature, and remain there until the negative energy has been healed at its source, no matter how long it takes. This ceremony is designed to dissolve the energy of anger, hatred, and jealousy that can ultimately lead to unbearable suffering.

Most cultures rooted in mystical traditions are very sensitive to the phenomenon of negative thought-forms. A thought-form can take on a Life Force of its own, attaching to, and creating a magnetic force field around the object of the attacker's intention. These poisonous thought-forms occur as astral garbage polluting the aura and scrambling the energy field, creating mental, emotional, physical, and spiritual illness. These negative thought-forms will have an even stronger effect if there are feelings of guilt or fear to nourish them, especially if the subject really is guilty of intentionally injuring the attacker.

If the person is not guilty and the attack is unjustified or rooted in jealousy, envy, or any other sinful thought-form, the attacker surely has no advantage when refuge is sought in The God. Within this sacred refuge, we are covered by an impenetrable cloak of Love and Protection directly proportionate to our faith. The energy of the attack will reverse on the attacker like a boomerang. There are times when the touch of an attacker is Divinely permitted. Too often, only in retrospect are we able to see the wisdom of it being allowed. It is known on an essential level the highest good of the intended victim and all concerned, that we might be blinded to in the moment of our inquiry. As we lament over our perception of having been conquered, we cannot see that there is a backdrop of an intricate ethereal mosaic of our fate, our Karma, and our destiny. Maybe it is a test of faith or a lesson to be learned. It does not matter what the reason is for the permission of it, as all of our faith and trust is in The Most High. Our life and our death are all for The Creator.

A spiritual scholar who ritually prays five times a day told me the reason she does it is that evil seeks the opportunity to attack at least that many times every day. The use of sincere prayer is one of the most powerful deflectors of attacking energies and entities known. Prayer can speak the language of many religious and cultural belief systems, the common denominator being the belief in The Creator and Divine Protector of all. Harm none and seek refuge in the Protective Light of the Creator, which never sleeps as It watches over us and intervenes in our affairs.

Arguments: Thoughts are things! Energy is real! Energy, whether positive or negative, will remain in a place long after those who created it are gone, affecting anyone who enters. After any type of domestic conflict, intense exchange of communications, injury, experience of extreme fear, shock, death, grief, or violence, observe basic spiritual cleansing protocol to neutralize the intense energy. Residual energy from emotionally charged events must be dispelled to restore positive Chi balance in your home.

Avoid attracting negative entities and energies in the first place: Certain activities are believed to attract spirit activity. Do your spiritual homework. Consider views from diverse perspectives but trust your own gut instincts and higher reasoning. It doesn't matter whether or not someone else thinks certain mystical practices are safe. If you feel the least bit uncomfortable with any particular practice … if it does not feel safe or wholesome to you … don't do it. If you do it and have a bad experience, seek spiritual counsel immediately and don't do it again.

Be careful of certain selections of music: There are musical selections that openly serve as magnets for the attraction of lower astral garbage spirits and entities. Certain recording artists don't attempt to hide their association with demonic forces and entities. Some employ the use of backward masking and planting subliminal messages in their recordings. Some traditions believe that certain types of flute music may conjure spirits. Some also believe that whistling or hammering, and certain types of drum rhythms and chimes can affect spirit activity. I do not seek to start a campaign against specific artists or genres of music but use discretion in your choice of music to avoid attracting negative or unwelcome entities.

131

Take care in the placing of certain objects in your home or on your body:
Some energies can attach to objects that may have been negatively charged by
someone or may have been affected by being in the presence of some source of
negative energy. It is important to cleanse items that you bring into your
environment, particularly if they have been owned, worn, or used by someone else.
This can be done in the same manner that you would cleanse the energy in your
home or on your person with the sacred cleansing smoke of sage. It is also a
consideration in accepting gifts and eating food from people who may mean you
harm.

Consumption of animal flesh and blood: It is commonly believed that the
consumption of animal flesh and blood in your diet can have the effect of attracting
negative entities associated with psychic attack. If you have reason to believe that
you are under attack, you may want to eliminate animal flesh from your diet. It is a
healthier choice, regardless of your spiritual circumstances. If you are going to eat
red meat or fowl, it is your choice, and no one has the right to judge you. However,
for sound alchemy in mystical work, at least eat kosher or halal meat because the
meat does not contain the blood (among other deadly things) found in meat from
the common industrial process. The living conditions and dying conditions of the
animals are held to a higher standard. The consumption of meat in any of its many
forms is spiritually dangerous for any practitioner of the mystical arts. We do not
have to kill to eat.

The consumption of alcohol and or consciousness-altering drugs is known
to create a portal between planes and could expose you, in a worst-case scenario, to
complete possession or attachments of energies and entities. It is senseless to
provide the opportunity for something or someone else to slip in during those
moments that your astral body begins to slip in and out of the physical body due to
inebriation. Entities can enter you and make you do whatever they desire. It is not
recommended to frequent establishments that specialize in serving alcohol and
catering to intoxicated people in times of a Spiritual Emergency.

Strengthening and cleansing the aura: Maintain a clean and healthy aura. This may be accomplished by cleansing salt baths and a regular discipline of meditation and prayer. Entertaining positive thoughts about yourself and others is important.

Recitation of a prayer that has personal significance to you: The most important thing to remember about spiritual protection is prayer. If you forget everything else that you have learned and remember prayer, you will have nothing to fear. Repetitive prayer is most calming to me because it is a manner of remaining in prayer rather than engaging in prayer. I find that it silences the voices of fear-based thoughts.

Ask in prayer and meditation for confirmation: Request in prayer and meditation that it be revealed whether or not there is an attack being waged against you. Ask that the source of the negative energies being directed toward you be unmasked and healed. Ask why this has occurred. Ask for forgiveness if there is any indwelling personal responsibility for it. Ask for guidance, as to the correct course of action to take, and confirmation that the protective measures you intend to set in place will be sufficient to protect you from the attack.

Journal your dreams: Keeping a dream and vision journal is an important yardstick for identifying and monitoring the nature of the energies that you may have attracted around you and how they are affecting your life. You may begin to notice cause and effect patterns that offer guidance.

None of the defensive or aggressive measures shared herein will ever surpass the importance of realizing the miracle of our personal, mystical connection with The Creator, The God, through prayer.

Fasting and Psychic Attack

Prayer is that sacred conversation between the "I in I" and the Ultimate I AM, the indwelling Eternal Being that we are rises into the unfathomable Source of all creation. It is the power of the invocation of energy and Light that creates change on all levels. In any mystical practice, prayer is an armor of spiritual protection as well as a weapon against attack and must be taken seriously. Ritual purification is crucial. Fasting can be an effective tool in the prayer work required for certain types of Mystical Meditation. Fasting is considered an act of sacrifice and a practice of delayed gratification or satisfaction toward achieving the feeling of 'emptiness.' Prayer is the exercise of filling that emptiness with the Light of The One God. It is a form of spiritual cleansing. Cleanliness is next to Godliness. Negative spirits are attracted to the putrid waste dumps we have become due to toxic diets, sluggish elimination, and habits that can make our own Light spirit turn on itself and become diminished.

When a person has manifested evidence of spiritual attack and work is being done to cast out negative entities and energies, one of the first things a person may experience is a complete physical purging. Some of the symptoms include dramatic projectile vomiting, dry heaves, explosive diarrhea, profuse drainage of sinuses, purging of tears, profuse sweating, chills accompanied by fever, purging of concentrated invading energies through muscular convulsions. There may be accompanying cathartic outbursts of blasphemy and profanity.

One reason for this is that the Light Spirit is offended by physical or spiritual atmospheres of filth, waste, and decay. This is the reason that a strict discipline of fasting and prayer is punctuated by meditation and not vice versa. The physical condition of the vessel one accepts Light into matters. The last thing that we want to do is offend the immaculate nature of such powerful and positive energy.

Many traditions build pillars of faith on the foundation of fasting from the consumption of physical food. In scriptures, it is said, "Man shall not live by bread alone." This mention suggests that there is more than one type of "food." If we focus our attention on the physical food and indulge in excess to the extent of gluttony, we cannot expect the same results as a person who says "no" to the trappings and seductions of the physical world. The person who is spiritually enslaved by a "yes!" consciousness cannot endure deprivation of sensual desires, feeding spiritual emptiness disguised as insatiable hunger.

There are many types of fasting. Fasting refers to abstinence and suspension of sensual indulgence. The demands of the lower self are the carnal desires that are inherent to the human condition. These ceaseless demands require us to meditatively release from our consciousness the things that we may feel we cannot do without. These wants can escalate into needs, then into obsessions if we do not master control over our knee-jerk desire for immediate gratification. There are three levels of winning the battle between the spiritual self and the physical self. The first is the awareness that the battle exists. Then we are open to the cultivation of the desire for choosing or preferring the satisfaction that one may only experience in the receiving of Light through some medium. The second is the observation of the self, as it surrenders, or not, to sensual demands. The third is the Self-accusing self of the observed behavior. That is sufficient to begin the modification of the offending behavior. It is a process, a continual striving, a challenge.

When a person receives a surge of Light energy, the results are sometimes so dramatic that it may resemble scenes from The Exorcist, a well-known classic movie based on a real-life story of a young girl's spiritual possession by a malevolent spirit. It can occur suddenly and forcefully, or it can be gradual. When the Light is received, it will dismiss that which is not Light.

These spiritual issues transcend religionism. Every tradition that I am aware of has taught the practice of prayerful fasting. Buddhism, Islam, Christianity, Hinduism, Judaism, the Rastafarian tradition are but a few. The fasting practices of Jesus the Christ, Moses, Buddha, and many others are well documented.

Fasting makes us more spiritually sensitive to subtleties. We are all continually attacked by negative and offending energies, whether we even notice it or not. Spirits are nourished by Ether or Essence. In spiritual practices, which leave offerings for spirits, it is commonly known that one can taste physical food left out for ancestors or spirit entities, leave it for a time, and return to taste it, only to find the entire essential flavor of the food is gone. When we strengthen the discipline of our animalistic nature and experience ourselves as Light, we are nourished differently. We can open our Higher Self to be nourished by pure Light.

Maintaining a clean home free of clutter and filth is important. If spirits feed upon offerings left for them, common sense tells us that they may receive nourishment from food left out, especially at night, in a dirty kitchen. There are other magnets that attract such attention, including alcohol, drugs, poor hygiene, sluggish elimination, and the consumption of the flesh and blood of animals.

It is valuable to spiritual practice to at least aspire to achieve the sensitivity to perceive the subtleties involved with the path and study of deep mysticism. It is recommended to consult with medical and spiritual professionals before beginning any new radical physical or spiritual practice.

Vegetarian Diet and Psychic Attack

There are many ways to maintain the health of all aspects of the self and keep our resonant frequency high, clear, and clean. As important as cleanliness is to the exterior body, it is equally vital to be concerned with inner cleanliness. One important factor in maintaining the strong energetic and physical balance of the body vehicle is the elimination of the consumption of the flesh and blood of animals from the diet. Substances such as drugs, cigarette smoking, alcohol, animal flesh (especially pork), all can serve as dangerous stumbling blocks in the purification process of the body Temple.

There are spiritual entities that track the scent of blood like a shark and can attach themselves, with or without our knowledge or permission. These parasitic energies can cause an array of spiritual and physical disease, altering every aspect of our being. Following some of the guidance imparted in this book is crucial, as we fearlessly walk the inner planes of many diverse realities. The frequency we seek is so refined that we must be equally refined, energetically, to tap into it.

I am not saying that vegetarianism is a hard and fast directive. However, common sense should best advise us that the mere thought of the consumption of dead animals constitutes a complete disregard for the spirit of those slain beings as well as our own. We corrupt our Light Body by ingesting the energy, flesh, and blood of a once-living being that then merges with our own life form, both carnal and ethereal. We all either have had or will have the experience of the tragic feelings of loss associated with the death of a human being. That is bad enough. Now imagine the horror of someone serving the same well-cooked and seasoned cadaver for dinner, commenting on how delicious it is, and how much it "tastes just like chicken."

If we ever really sit down and think about what we are doing at the dinner table and the "slop" stations (fast food), we would not be able to do it. It would become as painful to us as it was for the poor animals that gave their lives to satisfy an appetite so fickle that we imagine we have to consume them to live. Then, within the circle of carnivorous death we enter, that same meat will turn upon us ... inside of us, just as it would in the wild, defending and avenging itself against attackers. This vicious circle causes the decay and decline of our mind, body, and spirit. The body will then turn on itself, becoming the same thing we turned that animal into, worm food. If we examine the unconsciousness and insensitivity toward the slaughter, the murder, the eating and drinking of animal flesh and blood, we will find that we are socialized into many of the things we think are needs rather than habits. For example, think of it from the perspective of a nutritional "need" for murdering and eating a cow for a hamburger. How is it that a strong, sturdy cow did not get strong and sturdy by killing and eating animals? The cow is a vegetarian.

The body is the sacred temple and vehicle of our souls. An element of preserving a high standard of purification for the sacred body temple, physical, mental, and emotional balance is sustained by surrounding ourselves with the supportive energy of like-minded people. The discordant frequencies and low vibrations of others can bring our energy down to their levels a lot more thoroughly than a hamburger will. We must not be singularly focused on the energy of food and not consider the energy of our environment and the people in it. Full of the most proper food we could eat, a toxic energy assault can happen by merely stepping into the negative energy field of another. It can be the result of a touch, a look, a conversation, a projected thought-form, or any sensory interaction, often too subtle to even prove it happened. There is no need to become paranoid or anti-social in our interactions with people we determine to be unlike ourselves. If our frequency is high and clean enough, we can have a healing effect on the energy of others and inspire a resonance that is compatible. However, our energy levels may become depleted if our own reserve is borderline. That is why it is important to keep our energy clean and strong with a healthy, wholesome lifestyle, meditation, and prayer.

Some fulfill this basic need in the environment of a church or spiritual organization of people. Others are fortunate enough to find it within their families and circle of interpersonal relationships. The Internet can even provide a safe and effective way of communicating with like-minded people. It is most important to know that the Temple of our soul is within us. Yet, an outward social journey can also provide powerful revelations of The God, The God within our Higher Selves and others, and it holds that delicate balance between Heaven and Earth … clay and Ether. Even though the strongest spiritual connection is maintained through focused prayer and meditation, the frequency of a Natural Mystic can occur harmoniously as a chord, rather than exclusively as one single note. Tuning in to the frequency of the mystic can be a choir in celebration rather than a form of sacrificial, solitary confinement.

Mystical Meditation and Oneness with The Divine

It is important to understand that the moment we form the thought of engaging in a discipline of meditation, we have initiated a fascinating journey through a magical world with no boundaries, borders, or flags. The process by which we aspire to reach the higher energetic frequencies required to access the bridge between worlds is a mystical one. In mysticism, as in corporal reality, there are many bridges. When bridges are inappropriate, there are elevators. When elevators are inappropriate, there are wings. There are many paths and many crossroads, many doors, and many veils.

As we travel the path of the Natural Mystic, we become fertile ground for the planting of seeds of positive thought-forms. They can take root and willfully become the creation of change in our lives and the lives of those we affect. Nurtured and cultivated properly, the seeds of these thought-forms can produce miraculous manifestations, by Divine Will. It would be misleading for me to suggest that the process of crossing bridges of consciousness deliberately, for any reason, is anything less than what some call magic or hermetic mysticism. The difference between the Natural Mystic and the magician is that the magician "practices" magic. The mystic *is* the magic.

Meditation is an integral element of the spiritual sciences taught in the ancient and modern mystery schools. A practice as apparently innocent as meditation can open portals, through which there may be no return. There are many trials, tests, and temptations that seek to distract us from The Divine One and become divisive forces in our innate connection with the realm of Divinity. As our spirit evolves into Self-awareness, the primordial struggle of good versus evil will surface in our lives until we realize that *we are that, against which we fight.* When we discover this beautiful truth, we are free. We are powerful. We become our own witness with a sense of responsibility and become courageous soldiers in the greatest war of all, the war within. It is only a perception that this adventure of ours is a war. It can be seen as a grand play on the stage of experiencing, in which we are the star, the audience, the critic, the applause … but not the author. There is no such thing as win or lose, only learn and grow.

We are more than just conquerors. We must know that to engage this spiritual battle is to win it. When undertaking a course of spiritual study, there are no guarantees from anyone that we will all remain on the path of Divine Light, in service to The Divine One. There are many choices we could innocently make that may serve to compromise our spiritual integrity and attract the attention of malevolent forces that we may not be prepared to defend ourselves against. That is why we study the art and science of Psychic Self-Defense as armor for our journey. The most protective armor of all is prayer. Prayers from all traditions are full of pleas for protection against the forces and temptations of evil. Among evils, the worst of all is to fall into betrayal of The God by turning away from Divine Love and Protection and bowing to lesser gods. We are blessed and protected as our prayers and meditations maintain the exclusive focal point of The One God of all creation.

Our intentions and deeds are weighed upon the proverbial scale of justice. The balance of the scale depends on the choices we make, given the double-edged Divine gift of Free Will. It is not my intention to cast judgment upon the religious beliefs of anyone, for I am not the judge of anyone, and no one is the judge of me. I am representing that if a person chooses meditation as a spiritual discipline, it should be a well-informed choice. When we approach any learning experience, we have every right to know what we are getting ourselves into. Is it a meditation, or is it the introduction of a new religion to embrace? Is it for concentration, escapism, relaxation, or is it a new pantheon of god forms, symbols, and mantras, in languages we do not understand? If we do not know who or what we are bowing down to … If we do not know the meaning of what we are chanting … If we do not understand the meaning of the symbols we are using as focal points of meditation, we are treading recklessly into spiritually dangerous territory. We must ask questions and thoroughly investigate any path we are considering, to determine whether or not the practice, its teachers, or its followers, are compatible with our own spiritual objectives *before* we become involved.

When deities, god forms, holy books and scriptures, symbols, statues, and graven images are introduced into a style of meditation, we have both the right and responsibility to be knowledgeable of the spiritual implications and the consequences of our choices. If it is nothing more than a meditation class or course of study we seek, and not a religion to join, there should be no confusion between the two. I am not condemning anyone's religious path or choice to travel it. I am asserting that pursuit of meditation must not be used to bait the hook of organized religion.

Many systems of meditation are so intertwined with religious practices that it is easy to become involved with spiritual paths we never intended to travel. Few of us can say we know what choices we will make until presented with all possible options. We are entitled to *know* what we are choosing. If we find ourselves victims of a bait and switch scheme, no matter how seemingly innocent it may be, it is best to withdraw immediately in a prayer for forgiveness and seek refuge in The One God for protection. If we have knowingly engaged in ambiguous spirituality, we must humble ourselves in Self-Inquiry and seek the truth of our Higher Selves. We begin that Self-Inquiry meditation with the question of all questions … "Who am I, really?"

Many methods of meditation incorporate the basic philosophies and practices of traditional organized religion. Most religious paths engage in meditation practices and disciplines in their varied forms of worship. Some of these methods of meditation may introduce deities, god forms, and graven images to prostrate our meditative energies before. There is no focus on such meditation practices in this text. This is not a judgment of forms of meditation that others choose to engage in, by the power of Free Will. It is, however, prerequisite to *our*

142

practice to establish and maintain a sound, *undivided* relationship with The God in our spiritual work, especially when we are challenged by the energies of spiritual warfare. It is often our distracted attention, away from a singular focus on the Divine One, that results in invitations to spiritual emergencies of all random kinds. Such divided devotions can be the opening of a vortex, through which all manner of negative forces and entities may enter. Sometimes, that is what it takes for many of us to focus our attention as we become distracted from the One Creator of All in the seen and unseen worlds. That is certainly what we will end up calling upon when the unavoidable consequences of our choices boomerang back into our lives. The best effort toward Psychic Self-Defense is to not open those doors to psychic drama in the first place. The One that commands authority over all of creation, on either side of all doors to all worlds. That is our singular focus in this text. Anything introduced in association or relationship with The God is a deviation from the methods practiced herein.

There are many generic "gods," as the term can be used quite casually or metaphorically, even iconically. There is but One Source of all there is, The God, not to be viewed as separate from our own Higher Self. It is important to unambiguously choose to follow the chain of command all the way back to the Eternal, Timeless, Formless Source, or stand in profound spiritual danger. The choice to commit to being singularly focused on The God is not to be confused with acknowledging the many manifested aspects and attributes of The God or the many inhabitants of the Kingdom of Divinity. In the initiation of any mystical work, it is compulsory to have a good understanding of the difference between monotheism and polytheism. Monotheism is the focus on The One, Creator God, The Source. Polytheism involves the worship or service to many individuated gods. The moment we step outside of the framework of monotheism, and petition to, offer invocations to, ascribe powers to, or associations with, anyone or anything other than The God, we have stepped into the realm of abysmal danger. We will have, in effect, compromised the strength of our connection with The God, as well as The God within.

143

This extends to the practice of entertaining energetic attachments and bowing down to our fears of anything other than The God. What we fear, we in some way worship. As we engage that fear or attachment, we deify it. Anything that distracts our attention away from, blurs our focus on, or emotionally pulls us away from The God of our highest understanding, can obstruct our connection with the Divinity within.

Mystical Meditation is one of the most powerful and committed forms of prayer work. Our prayers establish a sense of connection between The Source of all, and the transcendent reality that we are. When we pray, we often do so with the purpose in mind of creating change in our lives or the lives of others. What differentiates prayer from meditation (even though there are times that there is no difference) is the directional flow, intensity, and the depth of a more focused concentration. Some forms of meditation can take the practitioner into a trance or transcendent state of consciousness that strengthens the force of his or her communication and connection. It has been said that prayer is when we talk to The God. Meditation is when The God talks to us.

As long as the realization of The God is at the forefront of our conscious and subconscious thoughts and meditations, we are offering ourselves as a catalyst in the circular transmission of Light energy. We are creating a sphere of Light in which we stand for the change that we are becoming a part of. We *become* the manifestation of the sacred connection between the Divine and ourselves. We transcend our one-dimensional identification with the physical form and offer our essence in union with the Light of The God.

There are many types of mysticism. I am not interested in exploring or explaining all of them, even in an overview. My primary focus in the study of meditation is on those that I am experientially familiar with. For the practice of Psychic Self-Defense, I prefer a system of meditation that is transcendent. The transcendence of all egoic identifications and concepts, in effect, the "dying to the

144

known, the unknown, and the unknowable worlds" is a daily process. The purpose is the resurrection of our Light body to shine the Light of The Creator with the intention of Self-Realization. To realize the Self is to dissolve all fear. Everything feeds upon something. Fear is what psychic phenomena feed upon to exist. We must examine what we are providing energetically as sustenance for the parasitic energies involved with Psychic Self-Defense. As we hold to The Divine One as the Cause of every effect, especially the effect of our own eternal existence, we have nothing to fear.

Mystical Meditation can be as unique to our individual spiritual path and preference as our fingerprints. Guidance, methods, rules, and rituals can and will manifest in the Ether, in meditation, in dreams, through visions, and in spontaneous lightning flashes of profound thought. It is all a part of the awesome phenomena of the Natural Mystic. The path of the Natural Mystic is one of Self-Realization as The I AM awareness. The realization of the I AM, or Higher Self, is sufficient to manifest the defense of its own Self. It knows that its being is Eternal. It knows that it cannot be harmed or destroyed.

Everything is energy. The energy of thought precedes and then can become form. As we learn to transcend form, we learn we have the power to transform our lives. Transformation occurs when our thoughts are refined, channeled, and directed to trigger the Law of Cause and Effect. Scientific research has proven that the energy of projected thought can and does create dramatic change so profound that it can defy basic scientific reasoning. Our study of Psychic Self-Defense affirms that we are That cause and the effect.

Some call the path toward attaining high levels of spiritual consciousness the path of the Natural Mystic. This path is not a contrived, or necessarily, a studied practice. The true nature of our Eternal soul is revealed as a complex composite of refined mystical attributes. It is comfortable and at home with the transpersonal qualities of inner and outer reality. Our studies help make us aware of that fact and serve as a map that can keep us from getting lost and damaged on our journey.

We are an energy that is One with the One God that created us. We seek to transcend the container (the body vehicle,) as we examine and embrace the "contained," the True Self. The Essence of the energy that is contained is Light. It is possible to transcend our container, the body vehicle, while it is still alive. We do not have to physically die to transcend it. It is possible to transcend it through meditation as we reveal the Light of our contained Light body and True Self. When we become adept in spiritual practices that facilitate this process, we open doors to the many mansions in the kingdom of the Almighty. It is through these doors and corridors we seek to travel in a quest to determine and examine who we really are, free of the illusions of the smoke and mirrors of our material plane point of view.

There is no fence riding on the subject of polytheism in Mystical Meditation and Psychic Self-Defense. We all have Free Will to choose to do as we please. However, to close our eyes in meditation and then open them to a statue or image that someone else introduces into the picture, without our knowledge or consent, is a spiritual violation. I could chill the blood in your veins to ice, telling you stories about the consequences of challenging the spiritual sovereignty of others. And what would that accomplish? We are commanded to serve no gods but The One God of our highest understanding. This is not to be done solely because of the fear of consequences. Yes, The God is to be feared, but if our fear outweighs our love and respect for That Which Created all, we are cheating ourselves out of the warmth of our loving embrace of the Divine. The vibration of knowledge is a higher vibration than that of fear. Love is an even higher vibration than knowledge. We do it for love, not fear. Our undivided love should be sufficient cause to dismiss a single thought toward the realm of unfocused spiritual attention. The acknowledgment of the many "aspects" or "attributes" of the Divine is different than separating and forming any of these individuated energies into an entity, or deity, or fabricated form to be bowed down to and singled out for worship and service. This extends to include the types of tools we choose to maintain our focus (Our charms, books, crystals, candles, altars, herbs and scents, statues, photographs, etc.). The problem is not the "having" of them. The problem is them having us in the form of our assigning them powers they do not have. Nothing exists but The God. Nothing happens outside of conformity to Divine Will.

I extend my prayers for protection and guidance. Knowledge is power. The more we know, the less likely we are to stumble into pitfalls that may await us along this or any mystical path. What we don't know *can* hurt us. The study of spiritual warfare and Psychic Self-Defense can lead to solutions to problems we will possibly encounter on our quest for enlightenment through Mystical Meditation.

If the idea of practicing a discipline rooted in mysticism disturbs you in any way or contradicts your present religious belief system, you may want to reconsider your pursuit of certain systems of meditation reviewed in this book. That would include *any* practice that would induce the perspective of vertical reality, not necessarily conflicting with linear or horizontal reality. To dispel unwarranted fear, understand that it would also extend to the practice of prayer. Most people agree that prayer, which is a highly mystical practice, brings no conflict to our practical or spiritual lives. It enhances the quality of our lives in the same way meditation does.

There are as many ways to pray and meditate as there are people who pray and meditate. Mysticism ventures beyond the call of dutiful ritual. We enter the territory of the type of faith that causes the seeker to aspire to reach that place in consciousness where those who meditate become the meditation, where the prayerful become the prayer. Prayer, meditation, and ritual purification of the Light within spark a distinctive union with the Light of The Creator. This Light is the spark that causes an energetic current to jump the gap, and result in what we perceive as the occurrence of a miracle.

147

GRAVEN IMAGES

I sit in a circle
of graven images

A single white candle burns
holding my focus on The One

I wish
focus
could be as easy
as statues of
Queen Nefertiti
Black Elk
Tupac and Che
Marley and Ra
Rumi and Gibran
Yins & Yangs and
sacred things
Chinese calligraphy
and ancient symbols
decorate my
temple walls
casting spells
for Hope and Happiness
Fortune and Love

I have
Dreamcatching
mandalas
with tomahawks
and peace pipes
Black Angels
with white wings
crescents and Stars of David
candles and scarabs
Zen gardens
Feng Shui fountains
Holy books, Ankhs
and Indian brass
Eternal OMs
and stones
from Sedona
beads counting themselves
in prayer

I have oracle boxes
with hexagrams
but I do not have
a golden calf!

A single white candle burning
holds my focus on The One

I Chinged, Oracle'd, and chanted
read by the stars and the cards
shapeshifted Totems
horseshoes and garlic
Bagua mirrors crown my doors
The Bible opens
to Psalms 23 and 24
with a cross to carry
to my own spiritual lynching
but I promise
I do not have
a golden calf!

Sage is burning
incense smoking
in silent petition
for protection
from them
whoever they are!

No circle of
graven images
could protect me
from the enemies
I could not see
trying to turn me
into a graven image too

Where were they then?
They did not have my back
did not stand between me
and the wall my back was to
did not keep my spirit
from dying inside
only my prayers

Dark altar beacons
prayer rug cries

as dirty shoes
step on its
patience
forgetting sometimes
the single white candle burning
holds
my focus
on
The One

Smoke & Mirrors
by
~ JAI ~

The Stilling of the Mind

As we turn our attention inward, focusing on the breath of the present moment, we peel away our mental energy from all mundane drama and chaos. We have the power to train our attention to go to where we direct it. Our soul, our spirit, the perfect being in each one of us, is waiting to be invited back into our lives, waiting to be restored to peace of mind. The mind can be as noisy as it is fickle. There are many styles of meditation that can silence mental chatter.

Claims that are made in this text are from an experiential perspective only. I can only share experiences that I, myself, have personally had. If a path of meditation is not mentioned here or covered in depth, it is because I have not personally experienced that path. Every spiritual or religious path, I can think of, has many different expressions of stilling of the mind in meditation. The meditation may vary in practice, but breath connects them all.

Some styles of meditation work through the practice (sadhana) of Pranayama (mindfulness and control of breath); the chanting of mantras (internal and external sound vibration); and the use of Mudras (prescribed hand and full-body postures and movements that help strengthen and direct energy). *Sadhana* refers to ego-transcending spiritual practices that are used as a means of accomplishing some specific work. These ancient Sanskrit terms are references to the specifics of practices that deepen the experience of the many realms of consciousness accessible through meditation. The objective is to evoke the experience of the planes of existence where spiritual work is performed most powerfully.

Meditation is a spiritual journey reconnecting us with our essential nature, although in a Western cultural context, it is practiced more as a technique for relaxation and stress management. We are constantly bombarded with stress from work, family pressures, environmental conditions, and poor diet and lifestyle choices. Consequently, it is vital to manage our stress levels and control our anxiety triggers to enjoy a healthy, productive life. Meditation takes our energy from unfocused activity into stillness, offering our bodies an opportunity to restore our energy and repair themselves from our abuses.

Rest is how the *body* heals itself from the damage done by tension-filled, toxic environments, and the fatigue associated with managing our pressure-cooker lifestyles. *Meditation* is how our *Spirit* heals itself and dissolves the energetic blocks that prevent us from living empowered lives. Because it is so difficult to stop our thoughts from taking us out of the present moment, we sit down, breathe consciously, close our eyes, and find our focal point. This focal point can be our breath, an elemental image, or a mantra ... something that brings our focus effortlessly back to the stillness, whenever we realize we've drifted away.

There are many cultures and spiritual traditions that respect the benefits of meditation practice. Many have corresponding spiritual and ritual disciplines. In my pursuit of a resonant path of meditation instruction and practice, I found the quest alone to be intriguing and rewarding. I learned something from every discipline I studied and documented my journey.

I had no context for the emotional or physical healing benefits of meditation. After my mother passed away, I crossed many paths, and many paths crossed me. So many called out to me to help show me ways to survive the loss of her. There is one thing they all have in common ... a strict meditation discipline. I am not a teacher or an expert on the paths I mention in this text, nor am I a representative propagating for any of them. As a journal of my emotional survival, I share some of my experiences with diverse mystical traditions, as a survival guide for others who seek comfort and healing.

Christian meditation traditions range from total immersion in prayer, to a powerful form of meditation involving the contemplation and reading or chanting of Biblical scriptures. There are as many types of Christian meditation practices as there are types of Christianity. The memorization and repetition of certain Bible verses and expressions is a meditation practice among some on Christian-based mystical paths. Meditation occurs in the same spirit as a sincere and undistracted prayer or a heartfelt song of praise and deliverance. There are forms of meditation practice that can produce a wide spectrum of associated phenomena, such as:

- Glossolalia - Slain in the Spirit. Speaking in Tongues;
- Spiritual Attack;
- Spiritual Cleansing;
- Faith/Energy Healings causing spontaneous remission;
- Intercessory prayer as a form of a petition made on behalf of others;
- Meditation states triggered by sacred scriptures;
- Direct Experience of, or Intervention by the Holy Spirit, called by many names;
- Music can trigger and deepen meditation, creating a clearing for emotional healing.

Rather than redirecting certain aspects of consciousness, Christian meditation practice promotes engagement of the most intimate sort, a direct experience with Divinity, touched by the Holy Spirit. It has been witnessed and observed that an experience like that manifests as a profound change in the life of the experiencer. No one has "THE" answer regarding any "belief system," and it is pure vanity even to make such a claim. The experience of meditation, in many Western Christian teachings, involves the Holy Spirit and is of the Realm of the Unknowable. Faith is the most reliable witness of these mystic encounters, as they are consistently associated with a wide range of ecstatic feelings and expressions of bliss, transcendence, liberation, nirvana. It may be difficult to explain the unexplainable, even to ourselves.

I have been told that the objective of Christian meditation is to connect with the Holy Spirit, without being distracted by the phenomenal nature of its many manifestations. The intention is beyond the intoxicating experience of euphoric states of consciousness. The objective is to strengthen and purify a sacred, personal relationship with The Divine One. As our consciousness expands, it reveals that our relationship with Divinity is based on complete surrender and union, in the One Love of The God Essence. Even though various paths show the presence of certain meditation paraphernalia and practice, it seems not to be second to prayer, nor equated with it. I have observed a very thin, blurred line between the two.

__The Sufi tradition__ is well-known for its Mystical Meditation practices, from repetitive prayer and chanting to the whirling of the dervishes. Prescribed prayers and scriptures are repeated, often counted with prayer beads in a practice called Zikr (Dhikr), the remembrance of The God. It is considered a spiritually sophisticated meditation practice of the highest order, directing and redirecting healing energy that sometimes involves drums, music, chanting, and movement. It is believed to open a portal or door that reveals the "Face of The God." Every experience of it is unique.

The withdrawal from sensual experience into the ego-less, identity-less Self is the awakening to a deeper understanding of our Divine nature. Full Awakening is the awareness of the eventual ceasing of all the mind's identifications with being personified ego. Abiding in, and living from that awareness, is the realization that the True Self and the Most High Supreme Being are One.

I am inspired by the spirit of *__Shirdi Sai Baba__*, an Indian Guru, Yogi, and Fakir. I greatly admire his efforts to bridge the gaping chasm that divided Hindu and Islamic paths. He was regarded by his Hindu and Muslim devotees as a Saint, Sadhguru, an enlightened Sufi Pir, or a Qutub. The focal point of his life was Self-Realization. In his meditation practice, he is known to have entered Samadhi at will. Samadhi is a highly-concentrated, transcendent meditative state of pure consciousness.

The philosophy and practice of Self-Inquiry, as taught by Sri Ramana Maharshi, is a technique of Self-Witnessing, observing the personal self, and contemplating the nature of the True Self, as the observer. Then this Self-Examination or Self-Witnessing moves on to contemplate: Can the observer be observed? Who/What observes the observer? Can That be observed? To follow that line of questioning and reasoning, will lead to the Ultimate Meditation on the Divine Oneness. It is universal in its concept and application. It is inclusively relevant to all countries, all religious backgrounds, and all cultures. It is not easy to stand naked, stripped of egoic identity, before the imageless mirror of this perpetual meditation. The meditation and contemplation on the question, "Who am I?" is perpetual because it is only natural for traces of clinging and attachment to form as personhood persists … whispering stories of its emptiness, asking, "Who am I?" This profound introspection and meditation, ultimately reaches all the way back to formless Origin, as we learn to embrace, both our personhood and Divinity, with Love. We ask the question until the question disappears. We ask the question until the questioner disappears into silence, without judgment.

The philosophy and practice of Yoga is about more than bodies contorting into pretzel shapes. Even though I do not choose to confuse my spiritual path with focusing on individuated, personified deities, I have found certain yogic meditation practices that are monotheistic and can be a source of healing for people of all faiths. *Yoga* is a Sanskrit word that means the union of the body, mind, and spirit, and has the mystical effect of offering the experience of higher dimensions, beyond name and form. Using ancient, sophisticated meditation techniques, calmness of mind and control over the senses gives access to the metaphysical experience of the transcendent Self.

Kriya Yoga is an ancient Mystical Meditation technique that was lost for centuries, resurrected, and passed down in a contemporary version to Paramahansa Yogananda (1/5/1893 – 2/7/1952). He was chosen by spiritual lineage of four venerable meditation masters, to bring this practice to the West, where it would be offered to the world. He founded the Self-Realization Fellowship in 1920 and authored the acclaimed book, The Autobiography of a Yogi, among many others.

The science of Kriya Yoga is the basis of Yogananda's teachings. The Sanskrit root of Kriya is Kri, to do, to act, and react. When practiced correctly, Kriya Yoga can empower the typical activities of the heart, lungs, and nervous system to slow down naturally. The stillness of the mind that results is the Frequency of the Natural Mystic. A dedicated meditation practice has been scientifically proven to directly affect and expand human consciousness. The Self-Realization Fellowship teaches that in the practice of Kriya Yoga, "The yogis discovered that by revolving the life current continuously up and down the spine, by the special technique of Kriya Yoga, it is possible to greatly accelerate one's spiritual evolution and awareness."

Certain meditation practices raise a spiritual energy known as Kundalini, which symbolically rests as a dormant snake, coiled at the base of the spine. It "rises" up the spine through the seven energy centers of the human body, known as chakras. Such meditation practices can produce an unpredictable outcome. This form of meditation should be practiced with applied study, caution, and spiritual discernment. It can provide a powerful cleansing and a heightened state of enlightenment, even a complete spiritual awakening. If not performed under correct guidance, a Spiritual Emergency can occur.

On the cover of this book, there is a column of seven beautifully colored spheres. Each sphere represents one of the chakras of the seven-level chakra energy system (see diagram). It aligns with our spinal column from the base, up through the Crown at the top of the head. As the Kundalini Life Force energy rises, it cleanses each vortex, one chakra at a time. Some people have been known to experience an energy surge that can strike like lightning, rushing from the base of the spine, up and out of the Crown Chakra. For that reason, certain meditation studies and practices should be done in a controlled environment, under the supervision and guidance of an instructor who is fully aware of how to handle a Spiritual Emergency. After a blast like that, I halted my studies for a few years, until I could get back my nerve to continue. I had been studying the Tree of Life and had an "aha" moment. I guess I got as emotional as if I'd found the Holy Grail. I fell asleep and was awakened by what felt like a blast of electricity shooting up from the base of my spine, out through the top of my head. I shook for twenty minutes. After determining that the cause was not physical, I began my research and connected the two events.

I know now that certain Kundalini studies and practices should be done in a controlled environment, under the supervision and guidance of an instructor who is fully aware of how to handle a Spiritual Emergency. I don't believe that the episode I experienced would have happened the same way if I had been more diligent and studious with regards to the ground-level understanding of that kind of knowledge. I would have understood the implications of a spontaneous Kundalini Awakening and possibly known what to do about it. I still enjoy the study of the Tree of Life and understand that it has profound relevance to Mystical Meditation and healing. That same alarming surge of electrical energy can progressively sandblast our force field, causing our Light body to fully engage its healing and defense systems.

Some disciplines of meditation should be approached with exacting prudence. Though it is exceptional, there is evidence that certain forms of meditation can trigger unpleasant and even dangerous experiences. Some people have suffered emotional, psychological, and physical symptoms, even events extending to psychotic episodes, particularly if the person was, in some way, challenged in the first place. It is unwise to tempt these rare, but real, side-effects by seeking the independent experience of rogue meditation practices, without prior knowledge and correct guidance. Challenges in the realm of mental or emotional issues, especially in cases of chronic or acute depression, can be an indicator that meditation should be approached with caution. In such cases, it is always best to consult a spiritual, psychological, and medical professional before beginning certain disciplines of meditation.

The practice of meditation conjures positive emotions, silences inner chatter, calms and stills the mind, and even provides some of the beneficial effects of sleep. The positive effects will show up in our actions, deeds, and relationships with self and others. Without this retreat of mind, it is difficult to remain completely focused, centered, grounded, and in touch with the most essential nature of the Self. It is a spiritual imperative to maintain a healthy energetic balance, to keep from being overwhelmed by the energy of high-tech, pressure cooker cultures that can scatter our positive energy to the winds of neurosis.

Meditation allows us to experience our true nature as changeless reality. We can rise above distraction and habitual patterns. We can step into its realms, and its realms are revealed within us. It has a cleansing, cathartic effect that can provide spiritual healing from the repression and frustrations of material existence. It is helpful in dealing with issues of fear, panic, grief, anxiety, tension, and physical pain in a world promoting an agenda of pill-popping drug dependence as a cure for every condition.

Vipassana is a secular, experiential path of meditation that instructs in scientific techniques that purify the mind and Third Eye vision with the goal of ending suffering. Its roots extend back, over 2,500 years, to the enlightenment of the Buddha. S.N. Goenka established the Vipassana Research Institute in 1959, on his mission to bring the Vipassana meditation practice to the West. The dogma-free practice offered at Vipassana Meditation Retreat centers all over the world appeal to every language, culture, and religion.

Vipassana means "to see things as they really are." Seeing things as they really are requires the soberest of minds, free of any type of consciousness-altering substance. This technique of meditation does not make claims of physical healing,

158

though that is what my experience was when I did the ten-day meditation retreat. I had been in a car accident that left me with permanent nerve damage. When I arrived at the retreat site, I had every imaginable type of apparatus to manage my pain. By the third day, I had no need for any of them. By the tenth day, my life had changed in so many ways.

Meditation does not exclusively refer to a single concept or path. There are as many paths as there are meditators. Meditation can occur within the framework of stillness, movement, bliss, mind-melting grief, walking, running, sitting, or lying down. There is no one specific way that represents spiritual correctness. It is what we say it is. My primary stipulation is that meditation must be grounded and firmly rooted in the unadulterated Essence of The Creator, with no associated deities, god forms, or graven images introduced into the equation. At best, all images are mere opinions. Spiritual Law of Hierarchy would command one to go all the way to the top, to the Creator of Universes yet to be born of Its glory, from the Realm of the Unknowable. All forms are perishable, consumed in the fire of formless reality. A worst-case scenario can land an innocent soul in a danger zone, from which there may be no exit.

The primary benefit some seek to experience through meditation is a sense of liberation from life and death. This conscious, deliberate striving is always within the limits of a conditioned mind, and in this, there is no freedom. The value of meditation is more about tuning *in*, rather than tuning *out*. The point is missed when it is used as a form of escapism. It is a way to bring Light into the container of the physical 'self,' not necessarily to escape from the container. We must remain grateful that we were given the gift of borrowing the manifestation of this form, for the purpose of experiencing.

In a speech before the United Nations, S.N. Goenka shared that his goal was to offer a spiritually sovereign choice as to how we experience our existence. For this successful businessman, born in Burma to a wealthy family, it began with debilitating migraine headaches, for which he could find no medical relief. He learned of a Vipassana meditation teacher, Sayagyi U Ba Khin. After his ten-day intensive, he was never troubled with migraines again.

After experiencing release from his suffering through his Vipassana practice, he dedicated his life to sharing this ancient, life-affirming, healing meditation practice with the world. This technique offers an elevated observer's perspective of mindful self-witnessing that overrules the drama in the noisy theater of the reactive mind. We can objectively view the ever-changing nature of the dance of mind, body, and spirit at its most profound level. We access profound self-knowledge, untainted by judgment.

This process of thought monitoring, scanning for reactive sensations, and objective observation (self-witnessing) is the inception of major change that can manifest a life that is happy, free, peaceful, and sovereign. We become able to transcend conditioning that would hold our lives in bondage to the disquieting demands of the conscious and subconscious mind. It is only human to experience ourselves relentlessly wrestling with the manipulations of our emotional triggers. We have Free Will and are free to choose, but we are *not* free of the self-destructive energetic consequences of choices we make in willful blindness.

I am not a representative of the Vipassana Research Center, nor am I propagating on behalf of them. I am only sharing a much-valued experience that I was blessed to receive. It is my understanding that they do not advertise. This ten-day course is not a business, religion, or cult. It is not for sale. There is no price tag, unstated agendas, or manipulations. Donations are accepted to keep the course free of charge. The volunteering of services is greatly appreciated and rewarded by knowing that these efforts keep the course available to everyone interested, regardless of their ability to pay.

It matters not if we whirl in circles, sit in lotus position, chant, dance with drums around an open fire, or turn off the television and the vast sea of electronics, and just "be." What matters is that we know that the disease of our obsession with form finds healing in our embrace of the formless. The Fourth Moment is that sacred place outside of time. It is outside of the Three Moments of "Past, Present, and Future." The Fourth Moment is the spaceless space between them. It is the Moment from which all is propelled. It is as impossible to describe as the space between seconds, between breaths, between planes. It does not exist in "time." It cannot be known, only experienced. The Fourth Moment is Vipassana. What matters is that, in all of our strivings, we strive most to praise and serve That Essence of our Origin, the One Creator of all things and all realms.

The mystical Rastafarian culture, spiritual practice, and mindset cannot be reduced to an "ism," or religion. It is a frequency. It is not something that can be turned on and off like a light switch. It is not an energy that can be contained in a structure or sacred scripture, it moves of its own accord. It is a Spirit that connects human and cosmic vibration … The OM, the frequency of the Natural Mystic. It either conforms everything within its vast reach to that frequency or neutralizes it with dismissive indifference. It does not require "belief." We do not "believe" in the earth, air, fire, or water. We have *experienced* them, and that visceral knowledge has created within us a "knowing." That knowing evokes feelings. Feelings evoke and invoke the energies required for mystical practice. Those who feel, practice. Those who practice, feel. The physical self and the spiritual Self are inextricably connected to one another. Practice is the determiner and identifier, not the label.

I was blessed to have lived in a Rastafarian influenced culture for many years. During those years, I was fortunate to have been a guest at Nyabinghi meditation and healing ceremonies, known as groundations/grounations. Nyabinghi is the oldest and strictest of the Twelve Mansions (tribes) of Rastafari. I did not participate with the intent to gather research or write about the experience. I think that disrespects the sacredness of the ceremony unless permission is requested and granted. I do not represent myself as an authority, even on the subtleties of my own experience. Only a true Rasta can offer a description of an experience of the sacred place in consciousness they go to. I was just happy to have been invited. Even though I was always treated with love and respect, I smile and say, "They don't want me!" No one has ever argued with me about that. I was not compliant with their strict code of ceremonial conduct, from proper attire, all the way down to the fact that I was not even a vegetarian at the time. I was lucky they even let me in. Someone was kind enough to bring fabric to cover or cloak guests whose attire was not appropriate for the occasion.

The term 'Groundation' is used to describe an event that stirs an affirmation of life that raises a cone of power and intention, up from the core of the Earth, and the core of our being, to the onyx, diamond-studded sky. Gatherings of Rastas are held in what is called a Tabernacle, a circular, palm-covered Divinely-ordained ritual structure for prayer, meditation, chanting, reasoning, and healing. These gatherings are not always so formal. I have seen spontaneous assemblies occur in very informal settings, like someone's backyard when the spirit of 'reasoning' rises up in the rhythm of the Nyabinghi drum.

The flame's flicker, and the sound of the crackling wood in the semi-open-air, thatched roof Tabernacle were hypnotic. Sparks appeared to dance to the rhythm of the drums of the ancestors … Ancestors, my mother had just joined. Mesmerizing, spellbinding, Nyabinghi drum rhythms, resonant with the heartbeat, mingled with thick clouds of smoke laced with prayer, rising to the heavens.

I could feel my mother's energy there in that Tabernacle. I could feel the energy of Queen Nyabinghi there, elegantly whirling around in the smoky haze and aroma of fragrant incense and herbs. The crisp mountain breeze carried dense, billowing clouds of smoke and prayer, all the way to the inception of manifestation. The catalyst is Faith. The seal is Surrender. The vibration is a positive force of commanding energy intensifying with the chant, the mantra, the words of power, and One Love. The melodic voice of the Rasta Priest would rise and fall in intensity, as he chanted Psalms 91 from the Bible, pacing slowly, rhythmically around the bonfire.

Undulating waves of energy rose and peaked as a cone of power, healing everything in its path. The thunder of the drums shook the ground underfoot, pulsating, reverberating, joining the rhythm of the beat of my own heart, sending ripples in every direction on a shoreless sea of consciousness.

After the ceremony, I researched the compelling history of Queen Nyabinghi, who is referred to as the "Queen of Queens" and the "Queen of Kings." The oral traditions report fascinating, and often conflicting, mystical stories of the warrior Queen Nyabinghi. She is said to be synonymous with the immortal spirit of ancient Egyptian solar goddess, Sekhmet. Whenever and wherever oppression and injustice have taken hold, and the people suffer, the spirit of Sekhmet will manifest on the physical plane, in some form.

The haunting energies present at that Tabernacle made me want to know more. The more I researched, the more confused I got. The sequential lives, rebirths, and possessions attributed to Queen Nyabinghi were difficult to trace with such conflicting references and time frames. Legend claims that the spirit of this African Priestess originated in the Amazon. This dreadlocked lioness is believed to *still* engage in dialogues with her chosen tribe, who are imbued with her supernatural powers. It is alleged that possessions *still* continue to occur. Her immortal spirit is born again out of the ashes of apparent defeat and ignites the fires of freedom, where tyranny and oppression prevail. It occurs to me that Sekhmet, as a healer and a warrior, is from the Archetypal Realm. As demands for freedom and liberation from oppression rise, she is born again. She is a harsh answer to a cry for freedom. She could turn up anywhere, in any timeframe, on any mission.

In the 1700s, a warrior Queen named Kitami of a province of Upper Kush Northern Africa (Ethiopia-Egypt) originally possessed a sacred drum, infused with mystical healing and spiritual powers. The magic associated with that drum evolved into what is now known as Nyabinghi heartbeat rhythms, with their ascribed powers of manifestation. Her all-female tribe, known as the Bagirwa, were defenders of freedom from all forms of oppression. The majority of them were traditional healers. Men, dressed as females, were eventually accepted as Bagirwa. In later years, the belief in exclusion of males became less restrictive, and the first Nyabinghi Priests came into existence. When she died, she was given the status of immortality and named Nyabinghi. Her devotees live by the Nyabinghi Code of Livity (lifestyle) that she left behind.

The story gets more complicated and interesting, as some report that Queen Nyabinghi's husband, envious King of an enemy tribe, sought to usurp her power in a coup and take control of her kingdom. He had her killed, and it is said that her spirit haunted him and his stolen kingdom, for years after she passed away.

Then, there was medicine woman Nyabinghi-Muhumusa, a brave and terrifying charismatic healer in the late 19th and early 20th century, from Northern Uganda. It is said that Nyabinghi-Muhumusa collapsed to the ground and rose up possessed by the spirit of Queen Nyabinghi. She inspired a mystical resistance movement, the first to fight against the exploitation and tyrannical domination of European colonialism. She said that she would "turn their bullets into water." The colonialists were so afraid of her spiritual powers that they introduced the Witchcraft Act of 1912, which outlawed practicing non-orthodox spirituality, by their standard.

These are all myths, stories, and legends, stemming from oral traditions that were difficult to authenticate, particularly because of the deep mysticism and transmigration of her powerful energy spanning over many lifetimes. Though specifics of the accounts may differ slightly, the essential truth remains, that the

164

spirit of warrior Queen Nyabinghi, Mystic High Priestess, is a powerful symbol of sovereign self-determination that seems to skip and jump magical timelines. Nyabinghi grew to represent the call and drum roll for freedom, as the spiritual attention of Rastafarians of Jamaica, West Indies, turned to that region in cultural alignment, in allegiance to His Majesty Emperor Haile Selassie I of Ethiopia. The Rastafarians of Jamaica were inspired by the hypnotic drumming, the chanting of incantations, prayers, meditations, and the traditional declaration of the victory of good over evil every time. The name of the Jamaican born, human rights advocate and political leader, the Honorable Marcus Mosiah Garvey, and the invocation of the Nyabinghi Frequency sealed the mandate for freedom and presented a mirror of moral superiority reflecting the inevitable coming change. A mystical healing rose up from the ashes of the virulent colonization in the Caribbean Islands, primarily in Jamaica in the early 1900s.

With so much of her history revolving around her bravery through war, resistance, occupation, and political upheaval, it is important to note that "Binghi" stands for righteous action, thoughts, and words, with a non-violent principle. They do not promote or believe in violence except in the case of self-defense, for only the Creator has the right to destroy. She is not a warmonger. Nyabinghi is said to love all of humanity.

The symbolic ritual burning of Babylon is a remarkable piece of the Rastafarian's mysterious cultural puzzle. The Groundation/Chant Down is a traditional practice that addresses the vanity and insanity of materialism, consumerism, energy-draining, brainwashing, spirit-deadening, mind-controlling, cultural graveyards, that we call lives. Babylon is not a place. It is a spirit and a mindset. Babylon is a consciousness. Babylon is in the mirror, the scariest of all places that an enemy could be, especially in the times we now live.

"And God said "Love Your Enemy," and I obeyed Him and loved myself."

~ Khalil Gibran ~

The "burning of Babylon" refers to the use of the Holy Chalice, the Sacred Drums, the Chant, the Elemental Commands, and the Prayer. The chalice, according to mystical standards, is a "portable" altar, wherein earth, air, fire, and water elements are a part of the meditation and chanting. The chalice is made out of a coconut. Some Rastas believe in the spiritual and medicinal use of ganja (herb, cannabis), a plant that was introduced into the Caribbean by the Spaniards and smoked or ingested as a sacrament by the Sadhus, the devout mystics of India.

The chalice is used as a catalyst to facilitate a heightened frequency or vibration, strengthening the power of a firm meditation. From the gutted coconut, smoke from the burning of ritually consecrated ganja is pulled from the "Kochi" through a straw-like device. It is *inhaled* with an *intention* to be manifested and *exhaled* in a banishing of all obstacles to that intention.

I learned from a Rasta Elder that the use of ganja as a sacrament in meditation tunes the meditator into a precise frequency. After that frequency is experienced, it is a matter of choice, whether or not to use it, because to feel it is to know and become it. Once the frequency has been experienced, regardless of the method used, your meditation practice *will* evolve. Your consciousness can find its way back to, and even expand on, the understanding that you will be able to get there on your own without the use of any consciousness-altering substance.

I neither condone or condemn, encourage or promote the use of legal, illegal, or recreational cannabis. The laws are changing in various places around the world to reflect the findings of scientific research. It has been scientifically proven to be *medicine*, administered in various ways, to all age groups, for the successful treatment of many chronic, even life-threatening conditions. At this

166

point, it is not possible to have an intelligent argument against it nor a judgment that is not, in some way, control-based. The bogus nature of the tactical "reefer madness" agenda, is laced with the underlying intention of maligning and destroying a substance that carries the potential to shift frequencies and inspire autonomy of consciousness, self-determination, and spiritual freedom.

My philosophy, in this regard, is to leave the spiritual practices of others alone. Live and let live, with an emphasis on the God-given gift of Free Will. That having been expressed, the fact is, if you did not grow it from a seed that you trust with your life, you do not know what you are inhaling or ingesting. The pharmaceutical industry has its essence in its clutches. It is being GMO'd and poisoned with harmful and addictive chemicals. It is being manufactured in synthetic form, with all of the accompanying dangerous, even deadly side-effects. And, yes, I believe cannabis can be used as a drug, with all of the accompanying addiction drama, in much the same manner as an addictive personality uses sugar, coffee, alcohol, food, sex, technology, and a long list of other things one can use in a self-destructive manner. It is a sacred plant and should not be defiled in production or practice.

I am, in no way, trying to represent myself as an expert on anything outside of my own authentic experience. So, if I am not an expert, what am I talking about? I am the only one that can be the authority of my personal (and transpersonal) experiences. The soul-crushing vice of grief interrupted the flow of my profoundly superficial life, forcing me into the depths of obsession with the study of human consciousness, just to survive. As I'm sure you have gathered, I was all over the place, like an acid trip, I've been told. Everything I had studied for decades revealed its purpose and relevance to the spiritual journey I thought I was already on.

I didn't realize that I would end up seated on a cushion, facing a blank wall, more centered than I have ever experienced being. Tragedy has a way of changing the subject. In my case, away from all that is transient, toward all that is permanent … 'nothing.' Beyond all concepts of the radiant triple darkness of primordial Essence, out of which, and back into which, Ultimate Beauty dissolves form, transcends intellect, and defies description … We must come face to face with our own shallowness to be able to face our own true depth.

Before triple darkness, between the utterance of, or experience of the Fourth Moment, before I AM, beyond all that is Unknowable, came Light, in sparks and beams. There, in the breathless, spaceless spaces, after peeling back every delusion of 'otherness,' us vs. them, this or that, duality consciousness … there is Oneness in the silence of knowing the Unknowable and becoming it. There is only One Love, One Tribe, Oneness with Divinity.

Traditional and non-traditional Mystical Meditation and sacred ceremonial practices of every spiritual path I had meandered through on the way to nothing, merged as some form of core singularity. The path of the Rastafarians parallels many of the Indigenous tribes that I am familiar with.

__Shaman__ - refers to the tribal High Priestess or Priest, called by many names in diverse cultures worldwide, among them; Healer, Medicine Man/Woman, Kahuna, Bush Doctor, Babalawo/Iyanifa. The mystical practice of Shamanism is Timeless, with diverse roots in most ancient cultural traditions. In its modern manifestations, a gifted Shaman has the spiritual expertise to journey through the subtle realms, to be a conduit, through which a healing may manifest in the physical world. These healers can bring about a balance in the case of illness of mind, body or spirit, and create change in the lives of individuals, families, tribes, even nations.

Some are born with this gift. Some are selected to study their entire lives. Binary gender references are inappropriate when describing many of these remarkable people. Some of the First Nation tribes do not accept the limitations of body-based descriptions that do not recognize the spirit as being beyond gender. Some recognize as many as five genders. A Shaman operates beyond time/space, where gender is not relevant. Alchemy at certain levels of Mysticism is strengthened by gender plurality.

There is nothing typical or ordinary about a Shaman though they tend to be humble and unassuming. Often entering a trance state during ritual healings, their mystical skill set is undeterminable by our standards, only by the results of their manifestations. They are a bridge between worlds. Seek instruction from a well-vetted teacher of the tradition you feel a resonance with before mixing traditions and unadvisedly practicing without a teacher or a coach.

Smudging – refers to the use of a smudge wand (sage, cedar, sweetgrass, rosemary, thyme, among others). In preparation for rites of purification for prayer and meditation, light your wand without using matches because of the alchemy of sulfur. Clearing your space can be done with incense. Smudging is a form of prayer and should always be offered before any kind of spiritual work. It is believed that smoke from the burning herbs carries prayers to the Great Spirit.

Prayer – refers to a being's complete surrender of personal identity in an experience of synthesis with the shared Essence of Divinity/Source. Essence is shown here with an initial capital 'E' indicating the complexity, yet utter simplicity of our own relationship with, and as, the shared Essence of The God, whatever that means to you.

There are all types of prayer, formal and informal. Prayer causes an eventual loss of personhood … the melting into Ultimate Stillness, the fixed focus, the breath, the peace. The bliss that results is real. There are as many ways to pray as there are people who pray, and each individual and every tribe has its own tradition. My general observation of indigenous prayer traditions is that *everything* is regarded as a sacred prayer.

Drums, Flutes, Chanting, Dance – Music can be a form of prayer. The Shaman's drum has spiritual power when used by an intermediary. It is a catalyst to the experience of the bliss of "self"lessness. On a journey through the spirit world, the music of the Shaman authenticates the Shaman's prayer, the Shaman's power, and the Shaman's soul, as a healer in the parallels of this ailing world. Consistent among the many diverse Indigenous tribes, sound, vibration, and energetic changes can alter states of consciousness.

Dreamcatcher – As casually as the term, and its use, the Dreamcatcher is a prayer and blessing born of sacred ritual. It is traditionally made for children who suffer from nightmares, Sleep Paralysis or lucid/OBE (Out of Body Experiences) dreaming. Its circular frame is crafted with Intention, using organic wood and intricate netting that resembles the web of a spider. The center or eye of the

Dreamcatcher is ritually opened (blessed or consecrated) and activated using Shamanic powers.

The web captures the energies of the bad dreams, allowing only the peaceful dreams to pass through. It is suspended above the bed, over the head of the sleeping child/person. Many Indigenous sacred ceremonial symbols and paraphernalia are commonly used for interior home decoration, swinging from car rearview mirrors, jewelry, body and commercial art, mascots for sports teams. It is important to know the difference between casual decoration and adornment, and unintentional blasphemy and cultural appropriation.

Medicine Bags – A medicine bag is a small pouch, worn underneath the clothing, with prescribed contents, differing from tribe to tribe. They are worn as a Talisman for spiritual protection and physical, emotional, and mental healing. A medicine bag is treated as sacred. The fabric and contents depend on the purpose and intention of the work. The contents may include blessed, consecrated objects of sentimental value, sacred herbs, texts, or semi-precious stones and crystals that are specific to the set spiritual intention.

Medicine bags for Spiritual Protection may contain, but are not limited to:

- Silk Pouch with Drawstring;
- Prayers;
- Palo Santo;
- Rose;
- Sage;
- Sweetgrass;
- Incense Ash (Three Kings Incense, Frankincense, Myrrh, and Benzoin);
- Prayers and Petitions;
- Lavender;
- Yerba Buena;
- Rose quartz crystal;
- Salt.

A medicine bag should not be opened or handled by anyone other than the owner of it, or the Shaman that consecrated it. As a part of a healing, the medicine bag can further empower and protect the human energy field, where the seed of every manner of illness takes root and manifests as disease of the body, mind, and spirit. Spiritual healings have been known to send some of the most serious maladies into spontaneous remission. The medicine bag is used to anchor the healing energies as the condition stabilizes.

__Dreamtime__ – references are most commonly associated with the mysticism of Indigenous Aborigines of Australia (The Dreaming), making striking parallels to the beliefs of the Indigenous peoples of the Americas. The concept of "Dreamtime," its interpretation and practice may dramatically differ from one tribe or nation, even from one person to another.

As preoccupied as we are with our differences, one thing we undoubtedly share is that *everyone* dreams, consciously or unconsciously. Two people can enter the sleeping state, locked in an intimate embrace, and it would be highly unusual for them to find themselves in an equally intimate place in consciousness, at the same time. Why? Dreamtime explores the qualities of the nonphysical realms of existence. It is the ultimate journey through the formless, intangible, ethereal realms of the Archetypes, the ancestors, the unmanifested world of the spirit realm of the unborn … fluidly transitioning back and forth between all of them. The Dreaming knows nothing of the "beginning" of physical birth, or the "end," physical death. It is believed that a spirit incarnates by entering the fetus during human gestation, and certainly survives death.

Through song and dance, rhythm, and ritual, this sacred philosophy mystically cuts through the veil of illusory reality, moving through time and Timeless, infinite, and ephemeral. The profound philosophy of Dreamtime blurs the lines between death and regeneration to reveal hidden aspects of the Unknowable.

__Journeying__ – is a term used to describe intentionally entering into an altered state of consciousness (dreamtime) to affirm the Oneness of our relationship with Divinity. It reveals our inner potential to heal ourselves and one another from spiritual, emotional, mental, or physical illness.

A "Journey" can have an unpredictable outcome. A Vision may occur, and prophetic information may be revealed in a Journeying session. The right question can operate like an interdimensional door, revealing prophetic information. It is risky to attempt Journeying alone without instruction and supervision. Out of Body experiences and incidents of bi-location have been known to occur, depending on the type of work being done. It is important to consider that when Shamanic plant materials are introduced, it is required they be administered by an authentic, trusted, and experienced Shaman.

__Limpia__ – is from Latin and Spanish origin, referring to 'cleaning.' It also applies to the ritual of Spiritual Cleansing in the tradition of Shamanism or Curanderismo. It is believed to remove blockages to the energy flow of the Chakra System. A Limpia is done to remove negative energy from the energy field of someone who is suffering from a projection of toxic intentions, sometimes thick enough to cut with a knife. Just because you cannot see it does not mean it is not there.

It is believed to cleanse the mind, body, and spirit, removing malevolent thought-form projections, create a reversal of bad fortune, dispel bad vibrations, and heal emotional attacks at their source. Limpia rituals may or may not involve plant spirits and sacred herbs.

__Inipi Sweat Lodge__ – The Sweat Lodge is a Temple of Prayer. The Sweat Lodge of the Lakota tribe is called Inipi, which means to "live again." Any form of 'brokenness' is healed in these ceremonies. These ritual meditations assist in restoring balance to the True Self from the effects of fear, trauma, grief, and many physical maladies. It is one form of a Vision Quest that provides the spiritual environment for many levels of healing. In an Inipi purification ceremony, the seeker is guided to move through the spirit world in humble, sincere prayer, to ground the wisdom and blessings of the ancestors. There is a fire pit in the middle of a structure specifically built for the ritual group meditation. In these regular events, the five elements (fire, water, air, earth, and spirit) are recognized. Prayers draw on the power of the connection between the soul of our perceived self, our Higher Self, and the Source of all creation, the Great Spirit.

I was a novice, motivated by pure curiosity at the time I experienced my first Sweat Lodge ceremony on the sacred grounds of Laie Point, on the beach of the North Shore of Honolulu, Hawaii. A group of friends had peer pressured me into experiencing the ceremony. I initially told them that I had no intention of "getting mystical." Herbs with qualities consistent with energetic healing such as sage, cedar, sweetgrass, permeated the gentle sea breeze. The chants of the Lakota Nation Medicine Man greeted everyone as family, and he began to pray. I can't think of much on the face of this Earth that he did not pray for. Most of his prayers were prayers of sincere gratitude to the Great Spirit. Most of the group fell into what appeared to be a trance state. I couldn't recall everything clearly because I was out too. The ambiance was magical.

My friends had a great time laughing at me after it was over when I said I heard drums and had seen large glistening, colorful orbs of light floating around the interior of the structure at the peak of the extreme heat. That would have been undramatic if it were even possible for it to have happened. I was told that no one had experienced that but me. I was so sure of what I thought I had seen that it was difficult to accept that what I had seen and heard were elements of a powerful vision.

As with any spiritual practice that may compromise your physical health, be sure to consult your Doctor or Medical Practitioner first.

Vision Quest – The Vision Quest is an ethereal walk through the Timeless inner and outer planes of existence. It is a prayerful journey behind the masks of identity we covet. Every indigenous culture has its own purpose for, and practice of, the Vision Quest. Each tribe will call it by the name and purpose they have assigned to it. A sound healing is possible in the case of someone who has been pushed by trauma into an emotional state that causes extreme suffering.

There are spiritual problems that could occur and compromise a person's health on every level of their being. A Shaman accompanies the seeker on their journey through the subtle planes of consciousness, in case something goes wrong. It would not be a good idea to engage in this practice without the guidance of a trained and knowledgeable Shaman.

As with any spiritual practice that may compromise your physical health, be sure to consult your Doctor or Medical Practitioner first.

Soul Retrieval – Traditional prayer in a Soul Retrieval ritual is the spark that ignites the flame of profound healing. Anyone who has experienced a phenomenon called "soul loss" is a candidate for what is formally known as a Soul Retrieval. Many things can trigger soul loss, fragmentation, and Ego Death conditions. It can occur suddenly in the aftermath of a traumatic event that resulted in severe emotional damage.

After the 'shattering' of the psyche of the individual seeking help, a gifted Shaman may be able to retrieve the broken pieces and seamlessly return them to their former state. A Spiritual Emergency can trigger a condition called Soul

Fragmentation and/or Ego Death, which can manifest as a loss of identity, among a list of other disturbing disorders. These conditions can be effectively healed in a Soul Retrieval ceremony.

__Peace Pipe Ceremonies__ – The peace pipe is a prayer. These are sacred occasions wherein vows are made, contracts are sealed, knowledge is transmitted from the spirit world, malefic spirits dispelled, and healings occur. The pipe, the materials smoked, and the type of rite being performed are specific to the practice of each of the many diverse nations. It can be the confirmation of a treaty between tribes or nations, a business deal, a rite of passage ceremony to mark a young male or female crossing over into adulthood. The ceremony is known to trigger powerful healings. Such a petition for healing is enveloped in prayer, affirmations, and meditations on gratitude for the blessings already received. The petitions and the blessings are two wings of the same bird.

The smoke of the Peace Pipe is believed to rise and directly connect with the "Great Spirit." Tobacco is considered a gift of medicine from the Great Spirit and is smoked in a ceremonial Peace Pipe in spiritual practice, according to traditions specific to diverse indigenous tribes. The smoke is believed to carry love, prayers, meditations, and intentions to the Source of all creation, while the roots penetrate the Earth to consummate the sacred connection.

__Pow Wow__ – A Pow Wow is a ceremonial expression of prayer, meditation, music, and dance. On these occasions, they give thanks for the blessings of abundance in times of peace and prosperity. They pray for victory in times of war; confirm the signing of treaties; acknowledge births and deaths; and celebrate family and tribal unity.

A traditional Pow Wow honors Indigenous cultures and tribal ancestors. It can be a festive occasion, commonly attended by as many as four generations. Often, the public is invited to share in these cultural events and welcomed as family.

__Elemental Meditation (Fire, Water, Air, and Earth)__ – Consistent with most spiritual paths, there are meditations associated with each of the four elements. Each element represents an attribute of our physical plane existence. There are mystical practices that can, on the most essential level, connect us to each element through shared energies and alchemical resonance. That is the basic principle behind the practice of Elemental Meditation. Meditation begins with the air element in the practice of mindful breathing. More than just the element of air,

174

Prana (Sanskrit word for Life Force) fuels our meditation journey, in the practice of Pranayama.

Every moment of our lives is a cosmic dance between the dominant elements in our natal charts. Our natal report documents the planetary placement and aspects on the day of our birth. The relationship between the complex energies of these planets and their transits can make us predisposed, in many ways, to influences of reflected in our birth charts. The fact that we are more than our physical presentation demands that we look deeper. The I AM, our True Self, has no natal chart. The I AM was here before the planets. The I AM is birthless and deathless. That is why, when experiencing a spiritual attack requiring Psychic Self-Defense, it is important to remember, the I AM that needs protection is not real. The I AM has no fear, needs no defense, and is pure, imperishable, consciousness. However, when practicing Mystical Meditation and using energy healing techniques, a working knowledge of Psychic Self-Defense is beneficial to understand all of the elements that make a being tick, from at least 3,000 different existential perspectives.

In the practice of medicine in most Western cultures, not much attention is given to the nonphysical aspects of illness and disease. When treating clinical depression, anxiety, and perceived phobias, too often, prescription drugs are a kneejerk solution. It is sometimes difficult to command the understanding of medical, psychiatric, and psychological professionals with tales of spiritual warfare. Much of the experience of unsettling phenomena associated with Spiritual Warfare, really does sound like forms of psychosis. It is not wise to write it off as such. The objective of learning the protocol and decorum involved with Psychic Self-Defense is to protect and heal all aspects of the Self. Self-healing must begin by being fully engaged in a loving embrace with the True Self. One must become the bridge connecting with The God directly, as the pure Essence of Self … not the whining, craving, whimpering, demanding creature … so reactive and resistant to change. Annica, the Law of Impermanence, is the bittersweet taste of Change.

Change can be sparked in the Ether and made manifest on the level of the consciousness of the individual. Pain and sorrow come and go. We can keep them from backing us into a corner. Ceremony offers definitive release from the often-indelible stain of psychological and emotional damage. Ancient holistic elemental healing techniques have been known to "treat" almost any condition, independent of contemporary technology. This is not a suggestion to seek alternative healing just to defy modern advances. Educated balance in all things offers great benefits.

To show respect when using unfamiliar spiritual and mystical practices, one must seek guidance in every aspect of their tradition of origin.

On the diverse paths of my spiritual journey, there is one thing that stands out. Among indigenous cultures, the paths are more alike than they are different. What one may call a demon, another person may call an angel. What one calls a jinn, another calls an orisha, a spirit guide, or a visitor from the archetypal kingdom, and countless other manifestations of the Will of the Divine One. The Law of Hierarchy has required me to remember, we did not create ourselves, and petitions should be directed through The God of our highest understanding.

In a global climate of intolerance, it is unwise to deny Free Will of spiritual practice to others or stand in judgment of spirituality that we do not understand. Every path is specific to every pair of feet that travels it. What matters is that the travelers remember their wings. What matters is that the travelers protect their own sovereignty and respect the freedom of others to do the same, remembering that there are no "others" … Only One.

To perform a healing elemental meditation, Air will clear our minds, earth will keep us grounded, Fire reignites our wounded spirit, and Water cleanses trauma and heals our emotions. In order to incorporate the elements into daily meditations, we must have a sound relationship with nature and the outdoors. For some, meditating outdoors is a challenge because of changing seasons, weather, or often, apparent danger.

The mind often cannot tell the difference between the actual nature and a video of nature. An open-eye, guided, elemental meditation, can be performed using a video of the elements at play. Use a video of a waterfall, ocean waves, streams, fountains, mountains, trees, plants, flowers, grass, sky, clouds, space, smoke, sunrise, sunset, fireplace, or the flickering of a candle flame.

Yoruba – On my personal spiritual journey, ancestors became an issue. I had always known that *something* was "there." I used to say, "I have company," and treated it like a "my invisible friends" joke. I had never known a context for a "spirit" tribal family. In my studies of Yoruba (and its study of me), my understanding that it is not necessarily in conflict with worship of "The" Creator, God of our highest understanding, as long as we go directly to what created all of them and us. The orisha are an impartial pantheon of entities that are hierarchal, yet they are just as much a part of creation as we are.

176

There is an energetic and elemental context for each one of them and fascinating mythological stories of archetypal love, loss, incredible drama, and unimaginable power. There is also a shared energy field that will display the projections of our "desires" on the big screen of time and existence.

I was given an understanding that, in Light and in shadow, I still stand in the energy field of the mother I mourned the loss of. She has merely taken her place among the ancestors. I realize I am of the Light, as well as the shadow of that world. I realized I could find my balance in that knowing.

I find this often-misunderstood mystical tradition relevant to mention because of the intense healing energies that are available through the practice of it. There are rites and rituals very similar to the indigenous practice of "Soul Retrieval" in the event of Ego Death due to trauma, loss, and grief. If you experience a spiritual attack, this type of therapy can restore well-being. A Babalawo performs this energy healing ritual as a shared Shamanic journey through the outer and inner planes of consciousness, restoring balance.

My experience with this path, as an initiate and teacher, caused me to understand the ancestral realm and its relevance to the spiritual aspects of my life. I knew that the energy of clinging and craving would not bring my mother back into the form of her that I was familiar with. But I knew that it didn't matter. We are, have always been, and will forever be together.

I have had countless experiences that required the practice of Psychic Self-Defense. After decades of committed study and practice, I do not consider myself a practitioner, but I feel blessed to have been made acquainted, so directly, with the spirits of the ancestral and corresponding archetypal realm. I experienced a beautiful resonance, and ancient ancestral bonds between us were realized.

**Ho'oponopono** – During the years I lived in Honolulu, Hawaii, I learned a spirituality that would last me for the rest of my life. At first, I was a committed Bimbo (with a capital B). I was warned about spiritual consequences of disrespect for the traditions and beliefs in the Hawaiian Islands. I didn't get it. I had placed myself in a familiar environment ... I duplicated the imagery that was familiar to me ... high rise condos and office buildings, fabulous skylines and pristine beaches, shopping malls, suits and ties, and fancy restaurants. I knew nothing of the hundreds of lava-stone temples, heiaus (HEY-ows). I knew nothing of the dwarf size nature spirits who live in the forests of the Hawaiian Islands. I knew nothing of Kahunas (Shamans) or "press down ghosts" that could send a person into a Sleep Paralysis event. I knew nothing of Tutu Pele, the fire goddess.

When I showed up for work one day to find the high-rise office building vacated, I fell into shock and confusion. I asked what had happened. I was told that everyone had gone on a pilgrimage of sorts, to Kilauea, Hale Ma'u Ma'u Crater on the Big Island (HI) to take Gin and flowers to the volcano as an offering to Tutu Pele. I protested, proclaiming that there was work to do and deadlines to meet, and said it was the most unprofessional thing I had ever witnessed in the workplace. The few people left felt sorry for me because they knew I didn't know, and the group dragged me along with them. On our way up to the crater, in my high-heeled shoes and business suit, I marveled at how everyone truly believed this was necessary. I thought it was hilarious. They thought I was hilarious as well and nicknamed me 'Hollywood.' I offered a nice brand of Gin and called it a vacation day.

When we got to the top of the volcano, I continued my protest, with no understanding as to why any of it was even happening. I said something disrespectful, in jest (stupid), not with malicious intent. Everyone looked at me and gasped, wide-eyed with fear and panic. The next breath I took was like ice-cold fire that closed my throat and choked me out. I wasn't able to breathe or speak ... I was literally dropped to the ground. They said, "We tried to warn you, and you didn't listen ... Is it funny now?" A single tear rolled down my cheek as I motioned for help. They gathered around me and compassionately prayed and told me to apologize. Yes, I apologized ... by then, I was quite sorry and certainly more respectful.

That was just the spark that ignited a passionate pursuit of mystical studies in Hawaii. I share this often-practiced ritual called Ho'oponopono, which loosely translates as "Correction." In the Hawaiian Islands, regardless of religious tradition, when there is unresolved conflict, a Kahuna or tribal Chief will take the parties in conflict to a sacred place for Ho'oponopono, a Hawaiian practice of reconciliation and forgiveness. They are aware of their spiritual healing powers and know that unresolved conflict can poison the waters of that power, inadvertently causing great harm.

That is why they do not let one Sun set on a conflict. We take too much for granted. Because the Sun rose today, does not guarantee that any of us will see it set. Because we see it set tonight does not mean we will ever see it rise again. Between the two phases of rising and setting there are no promises of anything.

The literal meaning of Ho'oponopono, "correction," is almost dismissive in terms, because of its vast range of meaning. Ho'oponopono is an energy field charged with the mana (spiritual energy and healing power) of this ancient Indigenous culture, created to reconcile beings in conflict, who desire to be saved from unnecessary suffering. The four-phrase mantra of Ho'oponopono is:

1) I am sorry.
2) Please forgive me.
3) Thank you.
4) I love you.

Hawaiian Kahunas that practice and teach Ho'oponopono have entered asylums and prisons to treat the criminally insane, who were deemed unlikely ever to be able to live among the general population again. Some of these asylums ultimately had to close down because all of the patients were released to live normal lives. They all struggled with love, loss, betrayal, grief, loneliness, and pain. They all had stories and secrets, excuses, and reasons for having ended up institutionalized. It is important to know that, in times of emotional trauma and grief, profound spiritual healing is possible.

Cultural Appropriation – is an ongoing conversation among conscious, knowledgeable, respectful people regarding the spiritual practices of many ancient mystical indigenous cultures. It is a common saying, "Imitation is the sincerest form of flattery" … and in researching its origin, it turns out that it didn't end with a period. Oscar Wilde coined the phrase, "Imitation is the sincerest form of flattery that mediocrity can pay to greatness." If someone approaches indigenous spirituality with respect, humility, and courage, accepting instruction and counsel from the hierarchy of the traditional teachings … that is one thing. But, to read a few books, take a few classes, purchase an altar, and dress up to play Shaman is a very, very dangerous thing to do, not to mention playing Shaman at a Halloween party.

On the subject of cultural appropriation, there are thin lines and gray areas that warrant seeking intelligent dialogue, and engaging study of the spiritual traditions of others who might be offended by a perceived disrespect of their culture. It is reasonable to seek to understand sacred symbols and paraphernalia before wearing them as jewelry or home, office, and car decorations. It is important to understand the spiritual significance of, and proper respect for things like malas (prayer beads) being worn as jewelry, home decorations, and body art … even extending to Halloween costumes and sports mascots. It is generally frowned upon by the spiritually adept of these traditions, both physical and non-physical. Disrespect for the spiritual and mystical protocol of ancient traditions can be very dangerous. You may come up on the radar of entities and energies that no amount of rational resistance will protect you from. They do not die. All of the Psychic Self-Defense in the world may not protect you from the consequences of such a low-frequency behavior and disrespect. Why should the mystical world be any different on issues of diversity? The difference is that in the unseen realms, consequences are guaranteed to be dramatic.

It is difficult to reference any one particular meditation style used by such diverse First Nation tribes because, for all of them, everything is a meditation. Everything is a prayer. Everything is an exercise in mindfulness. Meditation is regarded as a natural method used to transcend the physical plane to connect with and obtain Divine wisdom. A higher octave of that transcendence is to understand that there is nothing to transcend ... There is no separation. There is only One. The Timeless Now is here now.

The spiritual power unleashed by dance, music, drums, and fire is returning to its rightful place at the global forefront of mystical ritual practice. Though "Rasta" is often mistakenly identified with a hairstyle (dreadlocks), Rasta is not a hairstyle. It is not an excuse to "stay stoned." It is not a "New Age" trend. It is not a Reggae concert. It is ancient, dating back to the origin of the human race on the continent of Africa.

The Gift of Prophecy and Healing is associated with spiritual practice, prayer, fasting, chanting, meditation, strict natural food and vegan diet, and above all, an acceptance of the Divine Will of the Most High. As Frequencies merge, and Voice is audible, the connection is achieved and maintained, unimaginable portals of consciousness become available, and miracles occur. The Voice of the Ultimate Natural Mystic is housed within us, the vessel of The God, referred to as the I in I ... the True Self, the I AM.

The Rastafarian's Zen-styled life promotes simplicity and a positive, energetic environment. One element of that is a healthy diet that they call "Ital," which not only means that their diet is vegan, but that it is also organic, free of processed foods, chemicals, and toxins. The curative effects of natural medicinal herbal treatments are preferred over pharmaceuticals. There is a growing scientific community that is not invested in the danger of irresponsible drug dispensation of the healthcare industry. It is becoming well understood that many of the side-effects of these drugs are worse than the conditions they are promoted to treat. The pharmaceutical industry is just that, an industry, as invested in blind confidence and dependence as olden day snake oil peddlers. State and Federal laws have begun to bend in favor of legalizing herbal practices, after much organized, vigilant advocacy, and scientific evidence of its healing properties.

It is patently understood that *anything* can be reduced to the level of a drug, with the myriad resulting dependency, addiction, and health issues. Food, in general, has become a growing concern, as it demonstrates the characteristic symptoms associated with drug abuse, addiction, and dependence, with all of the resulting physical, mental, psychological, and even spiritual damage that it causes. These legal drugs are generally accepted as a cultural reality, as the death toll rises, graveyard industries flourish, and the people suffer.

I cannot "teach" you anything. I am a student myself, a student for life. The lifelong impact of spiritual warfare forced this journey. The gift it offered was experiential insights into powerful methods of energetic self-healing, from many traditions. They work for me and offer relief from some of the most excruciating emotional pain anyone can imagine. They work to even out the playing field and battlegrounds of undeclared wars, behind the lying masks of psychic warfare.

"Problems cannot be solved with the same mindset that created them."

~ Albert Einstein ~

I had no choice but to learn how to navigate through and transcend the emotional mindset that was causing such suffering. I have always experienced an innate resonance and connection with the Natural Mystic … that Inner Voice of transcendent reasoning. I believe that we all have that in common. The Natural Mystic is the Bridge Between Dreams.

The Power of Prayer, Intervention, and Faith

It is tough navigating the unpredictable twists and turns on this road called life. It defies natural instinct and reason to adhere to limiting beliefs of fixed conclusions about just how fluid this mystical Universe really is. Nothing is fixed. Our greatest consolation is to know that we are not our own, whether we know and accept it, or not. We are intrinsically connected to The Creator, God, in a union that is so sacred it cannot be named by our lower plane languages and utterances. We are connected in Essence to That Source Consciousness, a Consciousness so unfathomable that it is pure vanity to imagine it is possible to speak Its Holy Name. Prayer should not fall into a category to be debated or argued to dust. The prayers, meditations, and affirmations are our own sovereign choice, based on what makes us feel the strength of our connection. Our essence and That Essence are One.

Our regular affirmations of belief and submission are vital to our spiritual healing in times of feeling afraid of nebulous things. If we waver in our belief of the miraculous nature of The God, all we need to do is look in the mirror. When we look into our own eyes for that spark of Light that we are, we know that we are looking at a miracle. Prayer is our way of communicating with The God. We validate our love and appreciation for The God and heal our own souls with every word of every prayer and sacred thought. In our prayers and meditations, we strip away the flesh and bone vessel that contains the spirit we are and bare our immortal soul to The God in communion with That Essence.

If our prayers are but mindless verbal recitation, we cheat ourselves out of the experience and comfort of the sacred relationship we have with The God. The sacredness of our own relationship with Divinity makes it worth the time and effort to respect the ritual process of preparing to experience that consecrated holy union. It is worth the mindfulness of unplugging from the matrix of this confusion system to plug into a Higher Energy Source, that of the Most High.

It is healing to elevate the intensity of our longing by, not just praying, but *remaining* in repetitive prayer and chanting. It is well worth the time we allow in our busy lives for a departure from the vanity-based drama of the perishable world to rest our weary souls in the loving embrace of Ultimate Reality. As we accept responsibility for our spiritual journey, we must be mindful of the fact that we are not alone. We are intrinsically connected at the core of our being to the Source of all healing. In the face of relentless pursuit by the spirit of despair, with its never-ending effort to capture and collect our souls for fun, we submit in prayer to the Will of the Most High in thought, action, and deed.

So why do we bother to pursue metaphysical studies and practices? I think we may do it for the same reasons we exercise the muscles of our physical body even though it is born perfect, even in spite of any of our perceived imperfections. Our perfection rests in the Loving Eyes of our Creator and has little to do with our, or anyone's judgments, opinions, criticisms, or comparisons. Still, we naturally feel compelled to exercise, improve, and groom our already perfect vehicle because that inclination is a natural component of our perfection. However, we are not to bow down to the exercise. We bow down only to The Creator, not to the ritual around our practice.

Prayer is a spiritual exercise. Surrender is the spiritual muscle that results. There, in the spirit of that sacred surrender is faith … faith beyond evidence, beyond proof. The prayer must be a meditation of surrender. The meditation must be a prayer of surrender. From the killing fields of raw fear, all we can do is surrender what is left of us, to the only Force capable of facilitating our healing. I do not represent any one religious or spiritual path over another. The prayers and meditations you choose to engage in are entirely up to you. If the energy of your prayer resonates with the energy of your Higher Self, you will feel it and know. Sometimes the best and most powerful prayer or meditation is simply, "Thank You."

At this point, I will refer you to the first four sections of this book, What is Psychic Self-Defense? The Meaning of I AM, Protect the I AM, I AM Consciousness Rising, and The Mystical Path to Self-Realization. After reading these chapters for an understanding of the I AM, return to this chapter and answer the following questions: Now that I have chosen to distinguish my Eternal True Self from the body-identified, impermanent self … Does the True Self really worry about not being able to defend Itself? The answer is, NO! What does the True Self fear? The answer is NOTHING! The I AM, our Essence, who witnesses who we think we are … What does it fear? The answer is NOTHING!

I will share with you a few of the prayers from many traditions that I found comforting and healing. I encourage you to share prayers that speak to your soul at dreamuniversalmedia.com, to possibly be used in future publications.

Prayer of St. Francis

Lord, make me an instrument of Your peace;

Where there is hatred, let me sow love;

Where there is injury, pardon;

Where there is error, truth;

Where there is doubt, faith;

Where there is despair; hope;

Where there is darkness, light;

and where there is sadness, joy.

Oh, Divine Master, Grant that I may not so much seek

to be consoled as to console;

to be understood as to understand;

to be loved as to love;

for it is in giving that we receive;

It is in pardoning that we are pardoned;

And it is in dying that we are born to Eternal life.

Every prayer is heard. Every prayer is answered. Sometimes the answer is, "no."
Sometimes the silence is a test of faith. In the silence you may hear answers spoken
to your soul in your own inner voice.

Release Prayer

The Great and Holy Spirit,

Sacred Mother/Father God

the essence of I,___Name___,

am your humble servant

and You are my Beloved

I seek refuge in your Guidance

and submit my personal will to Thy Will

at this point where the river of my suffering

meet the shoreless ocean

of Your Love,

Compassion and Mercy

At this time, I stand before You

for guidance in this matter

My soul is burdened

My heart is heavy

and still, my faith

and my gratitude

are stronger than my suffering

I release and submit my willfulness

asking Your forgiveness

for every moment of

falling into forgetfulness

that only You are my sustenance my providence

Our connection is Sacred

Our only reality is Our Oneness
I release my attachment to the outcome
I surrender my personal will to Divine Will

Here in the shadow realms of a desolate night
I release and let go as I seek only Your Light
Here in the brokenness of my heart
that beats only for You
that seeks healing only from You
I wait only for You

The Prayer of Life

The Rebuke of Self-Harm and Harming Others

I was given the gift of this body to stay in it for as long as it takes

to hear it called back home in its perfect time

My own voice will never make that call

I realize this is not the home of my spirit

I recognize my soul's yearning for its return home

I evoke the awareness that I am already there, in or out of this body

no matter where else I may appear to be

I can die to this world and never leave my body

I can be here now

transcending the pain, the sadness, and the grief

transcending the loneliness and the suffering

transcending fear and rejection

I am not asking for my burdens to be taken away

I am asking for the fear to be taken away

and be replaced by the strength to bear it

Angels watch over me

I am never left alone

I cannot fail in this dance of destiny

I am here for that

for as long as it takes

to know that I do not need a body to exist

My body needs me to exist

Inside of it, I am the transcendence of all materiality

189

Right here

Right now

I affirm that there is no such thing as death

I affirm that I cannot die

I affirm that it is not possible to end my life

I affirm that who I really am

will survive anyone's attempt to erase me

I will not depart from this plane before my time

I will not suffer to be forced to witness

the fallout of the suffering I have caused

I am Eternal

There is no beginning of me

There is no end of me

Not by my hand, nor the hand of any other

Not by fire, air, water, or earth

I Am One with That from which my true Self emerged

I choose not to witness

the self-destruction caused

by my misguided choices

I choose wisely and I do not allow

my tormented emotions

my troubled mind

my shattered spirit

my broken heart

to bring destruction to my life

by my own intentions

I choose not to witness the pain

I choose to love and accept my True Self

My life matters

I have the power to reside in the domain of my Higher Self inside of this body

I have the power to transcend the stories, the faces, the masks, the theater

of the lower realms of my consciousness

I give up

I give up approval seeking, comparisons, and people pleasing

I give up imposing impossible, false, soul-selling standards upon myself

I give up force-fitting the vastness of my Self

into the tiny boxes of illusory realities

that have nothing to do with who I really am

I owe no offerings to the fake imagery of others

I am not this body

I was here before it happened

I will be here when it is gone

No thing, no person, no opinion, no circumstance

DARES to try to invalidate the beauty

of this life, this breath, this Light, this Love, that I am

I am HERE NOW

I AM THAT which I seek

I am One with the Most High Creator Mother Father God

of my highest understanding

I am a spark of the Original Flame

There is no difference between us

I forgive myself for any thought of separation

I accept this perfect gift

this beautiful container

which is not me

It transports my true Self

through this experiencing

I own the power to OWN it

Journey to Negril

I experienced a powerful spiritual revelation in a vision and was advised to cancel my plans to travel from Port Antonio to Negril in Jamaica. I was warned that I would die the next day if I pursued my intention to travel through Kingston on that Friday night. I chose to disregard the warning and affirmed my belief in The God over the belief in a vision.

The stage was set, and all the players in the unfolding of this prophecy were in place. I could see the whole picture of a violent, untimely bloody death unfolding over some unwelcome attention caused by a designer purse I was carrying that appeared to be valuable. Its only value was in the label, and I'm not even sure that was real. I had been well-advised over my five-year stay in Jamaica, of the dangers of traveling alone through certain areas of Kingston. I understood the safety issues of doing so without the normal precautions I would take anywhere in the world. What I did was not very smart, no matter where I traveled, especially after I had seen a vision of how I would pay the ultimate price for my defiance. I proceeded on with my mission with the faith to know that I was not alone, though I appeared to be. I left my fate in the hands of The God in full submission to His Will. I submitted that, if my time is up, it is up. I did not argue when it began. Who am I to argue when it is time for it to end? I accepted that if it were not my time to go, I would be protected. I also had my prayer beads and silently prayed for that protection.

This local style, packed bus, traveling from Portland to Kingston, encountered torrential rains on a slippery, narrow, two-lane, winding, mountain road, with no railing, over bottomless slopes. If it had a bottom, no one who had ever seen it lived to tell the story. Then came the crab attack. A stampede of land crabs moved across the road like a tremendous shadow covering both lanes of traffic. The driver slammed on breaks in such a way as to startle all the passengers on the bus. After he recovered from the scare enough to speak, he said that had never happened to him before and relayed the story of the same thing happening to another driver who wrecked his bus because of it. He said many did not survive the crash.

Upon my arrival at the Kingston terminal for my connecting bus to my destination, restless crowds of people were completely out of control. I became completely overwhelmed in the rush for baggage at the back end of the bus. It was so out of control the police became involved in an attempt to calm the crowds trying to get on and off the bus at the same time.

Out of nowhere, a woman pushed her arm through the crowd and stepped in between the other passengers and me gathered at the rear luggage compartment of the bus. The area I had to walk through to the location of my connecting bus was one of the most dangerous on the island, especially on a weekend night. My Caribbean patois is not good enough to express what she told me in as flavorful a manner as she did, but I will do the best I can to recount the experience.

She told me to move out of the way and get my things, in a patois-laced tone, voice as strong as Blue Mountain coffee. I was hauling luggage on wheels, a computer bag with my computer in it, and a big purse … a total mark. She seemed a bit frail, but she was strong and fast. She was a well-known vendor, hauling her unsold product home from Kingston to Spanish Town. She saw me struggling with my bags, and she reached over and snatched my heavy computer bag, and the weighty, awkward Louis Vuitton bag, with the zipper wide open. She told me to act like we were together. She said she had to take my things along with her things, pointing to a couple of shady characters casing me. She whispered in a panicked tone that they wouldn't bother her because they knew her. She was moving down that dimly lit street so fast that I couldn't keep up with her as we ran to transfer to the bus to Montego Bay.

She mumbled, visibly annoyed, complaining, saying that she just did what she was told. She said, "He" told her that if she didn't help me that night, I wasn't going to make it, demanding to know what I was doing there in Kingston at that time of night anyway. She asked me if I was crazy. Now that I look back on it, I must have been, at least a little bit.

She went on to explain that the bus I had to get to was not her bus and that her bus to Spanish Town was on the other side of the street, down the road from mine. She seemed annoyed by that but told me she had to get me to my bus safe, regardless. She told me again that she just does what she is told and that as long as she does what "He" tells her to do, everything is good, and she's alright.

She fired a series of forceful commands at me as if she was talking to a two-year-old, and that's exactly what I felt like. She told me in her spicy Jamaican accent to "hurry up, walk fast, and act like you are with me. Close your purse, pull it close to you, they'll cut your throat and take your things." She motioned with her index finger across her jugular and pointed to the two men. When they saw that we were together, they looked at one another, sighed, twisted their faces in annoyance over this apparent intervention, and retreated.

She moved with turf authority so fast with those heavy bags that I could hardly keep up with her, confident that no one would bother her or me because of him, "The Spirit." We moved unnoticed through Tivoli Gardens in Kingston, Jamaica, on a Friday night, unscathed. I asked her who told her to help me, realizing at this point that she was an intervention to save my life, literally. Everything became blurred, surreal, other-worldly. She told me that the Holy Spirit told her she had to help me to wherever I was going, or I wasn't going to make it … that I would die that night.

She sat next to me, impatiently waiting for the connecting bus to Montego Bay. I don't remember her name. I can't remember her face. I remember her eyes.

I remember looking deep into them and seeing my own death, just as she had seen. She complained as she looked longingly at the bus down the street that was loading passengers. She told me that it was her bus and it would drop her off right in front of her house in Spanish Town. She complained that she couldn't leave me yet because it wasn't over. She said, "He" hadn't told her she could go. As I questioned her about this, "He," she told me about a voice she hears that she described as the "Holy Spirit." She said that for her entire life it had guided her correctly and that as long as she listened and respected it, she was fine, "if not, *Problems!*" Her expression seemed to recall terrifying consequences for not listening.

A Rasta elder stepped up on our bus. Relieved, she said she could finally go because even though she did not know him personally, she knew that he was the one that would know what to do from that point forward. Still slightly irritated, she told him our story, and how badly she wanted to go and board the Spanish Town bus, that was about to leave, but couldn't because of me. She told him that she knew that he could hear "Him" too, so he would take care of me and do what he was told to do. To my surprise, he said he understood and that he had also heard a voice that told him he was to secure my safety up to the point of my destination, or I wasn't going to make it alive that night. He then took over like an armed bodyguard. He had very little to say other than the "Holy Spirit" was his companion, guide, and comforter. He said, as long as he did what he was told to do, his life was fine, if not, "*Problems!*" I had to force some money into her hand as she hurried to catch her bus. She said she hadn't done what she did for money and tried to give it back. She looked at the money and looked at me smiling strangely. She said that she hadn't sold anything that day and that she needed, and had prayed for, exactly that amount of money that morning. She disappeared into a moonless night toward her bus, and I never saw her again.

After I reached my destination, the Rasta elder continued to look out for me. He waived away three taxis and placed me in the cab he said was the right one. He

196

told the driver to wait outside, watch, and make sure I got into my home and locked the door behind me. The cab driver told me on my way home that he knew the Rasta Elder and that they were "bredrin" who heard and obeyed the same Voice. I asked, "What voice?" He said, "The Natural Mystic, The Voice of The Holy Spirit." He smiled and told me that when he heard It and ignored It, "*Problems*!" At that point, I felt like either EVERYBODY was crazy (including me) … Or I was trapped inside of an episode of the Twilight Zone.

I didn't sleep well that night. I was awake in total amazement of the unprecedented, interconnected series of events of the entire day that I was sure could have been my last. I have never witnessed such a precise, strategic, skillful intervention. I knew before I left Portland, that day was possibly my last, according to a trusted vision and its revelation. It confirmed I would not make it, and all of the signs and omens had been falling into place like dominoes. But The God said "NO!" So, I share with you from my experience, not belief or faith, but personal experience and personal knowledge, that before and beyond any oracular vision, all that exists is the Divine Will of the Ultimate I AM. Nothing can happen outside of Divine permission.

I was told that I was under spiritual attack and had to seek refuge in The God for protection. I was told to read a particular verse from the Bible that night. I carried in my wallet a prayer verse on a laminated card. I meditated on the sacredness of its words and rested in a new revelation of the Glory, Beauty, and Protection of The Divine One.

Yes, I was given the gift of a vision of an event to come that would be significant to my life. However, I was only permitted to see enough to know that there was cause for concern for my safety, but not enough to bow down to a death sentence that did not come from the One, and the Only, Giver, Sustainer, and Taker of Life. It is ill-advised to make claims that an oracle or oracular vision *must* foretell the certain future in a fortune-telling scenario. It can give us a forecast, like a weatherperson after the six o'clock news, always allowing for nature's variable X factor. We can be shown signs and influences. We all know the trouble we can get into if we don't observe traffic signs. But even traffic signs can be tampered with to the extent they can lead a driver astray. It has happened that they have pointed a person in the wrong direction or, in some way, been deceptive. Through all of our earth-bound travels, if we are in communication with someone who has a bird's eye view of our entire journey, even if a sign is misleading, the information from The Source, The One with the broadest perspective won't be. But it is deeper than that. The most expansive bird's eye view is not just an observer. It is The Creator and has the power to intervene in our affairs as It sees fit, at any stage of our journey, and can mystically cause something to happen that was never on our trip planner. That is the only oracle we can truly trust and love. That oracle is The God.

We must know the difference and never forget for a moment, for in that moment stands our destruction … victorious and laughing. We must know The God. We must know, accept, respect, and maintain spiritual responsibility in the Light of our own Divinity. We must know our self. We must know our Self, the Higher Self that is a Spark of The Divine Light, from which we were created.

I have made mistakes. Everyone has. I was told once by a spiritual teacher that if The God were ever to find humanity perfect, He would replace us with imperfect beings. Our perfection would cancel out so many of His attributes, the Most Beautiful, The Merciful, The Forgiver, and so many more. There would be no need for forgiveness and mercy if we were all perfect and never made mistakes. I believe that a "mistake" is in the same category as a "coincidence." There is no such thing as a mistake, only a lesson to be learned. There is no randomness in our creation. It is all very intentional. I pray that you will not make some of the choices we might call "mistakes" that I, and others, have made out of ignorance. The biggest mistake any of us can make is to allow our attention to wander from a singular focus on The One Divine Creator God. Awaiting our souls at the end of

198

that dangerous road is an altar, with all that we have bowed down to other than The God, blocking our access to all that there ever was to cherish.

The Role of Prayer in Psychic Self-Defense

We grossly underestimate the power and importance of prayer. We live one prayer away from a miracle. It is vital to our spirituality to reconnect daily with the value and importance of prayer. We do not need to ritualize or make an exhibition of prayer. Prayer is a very personal communication between The Creator and creation. There is no right or wrong way to pray. No tradition, culture, or religion has cornered the market on a system of prayer. There is no paraphernalia required to engage in sincere prayer.

A woman, who had a near-death experience and traveled to the other side, shared a touching observation about prayer. She saw prayers rising from the Earth Plane as little spots or bubbles of light. She was told that the brighter and larger ones were the prayers of mothers for their children.

In matters of Psychic Self-Defense, both the seen and unseen realms are acknowledged as a possible battlefield. Prayer is the shield, the whole armor of The God, the most powerful defense against negative spiritual energies. I have often heard this Bible quote regarding the nature of spiritual warfare and the comfort of knowing that we are not fighting alone.

Ephesians 10 – 12, The Bible (KJV)

10. Finally, my brethren, be strong in the Lord, and in the power of his might.
11. Put on the whole armor of God that ye may be able to stand against the wiles of the devil.
12. For we wrestle not against flesh and blood, but against principalities, against powers, against the rulers of the darkness of this world, against spiritual wickedness in high places.

I share with you these Biblical verses, offered to me by friends that are used as powerful prayers and mantras, even though I believe prayer can be as informal and spontaneous as a conversation with loved ones. The word, the thought, the prayer, the mantra, that reaches out to connect with Divine Presence, reaches in as well. It is only an acknowledgment of the connection that is already there.

23rd Psalm, The Bible (KJV)

The Lord is my shepherd
I shall not want
He maketh me to lie down in green pastures
He leadeth me beside the still waters
He restoreth my soul
He leadeth me in the paths of righteousness
for his name's sake
Yeah though I walk through the valley of the shadow of death
I shall fear no evil for thou art with me
Thy rod and thy staff they comfort me
Thou preparest a table before me
in the presence of mine enemies
Thou anointest my head with oil
My cup runneth over
Surely goodness and mercy shall follow me
all the days of my life
and I will dwell in the house of the Lord
forever.

Psalm 91, The Bible (KJV)

1. He that dwelleth in the secret place of the Most High shall abide under the shadow of the Almighty.
2. I will say of the Lord, He is my refuge and my fortress; my God; in him will I trust.
3. Surely, he shall deliver thee from the snare of the fowler, and from the noisome pestilence.
4. He shall cover thee with his feathers, and under his wings shalt thou trust; his truth shall be thy shield and buckler.
5. Thou shalt not be afraid for the terror by night; nor for the arrow that flieth by day.
6. Nor for the pestilence that walketh in darkness; nor for the destruction that wasteth at noonday.
7. A thousand shall fall at thy side, and ten thousand at thy right hand; but it shall not come nigh thee.
8. Only with thine eyes shalt thou behold and see the reward of the wicked.
9. Because thou hast made the Lord, which is my refuge, even the Most High, thy habitation;
10. There shall no evil befall thee, neither shall any plague come nigh thy dwelling.
11. For he shall give his angels charge over thee, to keep thee in all thy ways.
12. They shall bear thee up in their hands, lest thou dash thy foot against a stone.
13. Thou shalt tread upon the lion and adder; the young lion and the dragon shalt thou trample under feet.
14. Because he hath set his love upon me, therefore will I deliver him; I will set him on high, because he hath known my name.
15. He shall call upon me, and I will answer him; I will be with him in trouble; I will deliver him, and honor him.
16. With long life will I satisfy him and shew him my salvation.

<u>The Lord's Prayer</u>

Matthew 6:9-13, The Bible (KJV)

After this manner, therefore, pray ye:
Our Father which art in heaven, Hallowed be thy name.
Thy kingdom come, Thy will be done in earth, as it is in heaven.
Give us this day our daily bread.
And forgive us our debts, as we forgive our debtors.
And lead us not into temptation but deliver us from evil: For thine is the kingdom,
and the power, and the glory, forever. Amen.

There should be a warning attached to certain prayers, even if they are scriptures from sacred texts. It would not be a good idea to take certain types of prayer into deep meditation with designs upon another. You incur the Karmic debt of what befalls the target as a result of what constitutes an energetic or spiritual attack. If we have reason to believe someone has wronged us in a way that justifies specific consequences relayed in certain powerful prayers, consider that if we are wrong, we have waged spiritual warfare against an innocent person. We will have made ourselves a magnet for the return of the energies sent out … a consequence of the attack. If scriptures are directed out of anger and judgment, rather than the energy of pure and Unconditional Love, great harm can be caused. In cases involving the manipulative use of scriptures, or other methods … Know that it is a boomerang. It will return. All in life is a circle. Keep your circle clean.

When using prayers and verses from sacred texts, be sure to remain general and objective. Don't use the energy of it like a poison arrow. Pray all prayers in great humility and surrender to the Will of The Divine One. One of the greatest prayers any of us can pray is for the healing of another.

The Power of Repetitive Prayer

The chanting of mantras and repetitive prayer dates back to the beginning of time. A mantra can be as simple as a single word of power, a vibrational utterance, a childhood prayer. This sacred practice balances and clears internal and external energies, bringing harmony to mind, body, and spirit. The sensation of this powerful energy results in our consciousness being shaken from the perishable realm into Ultimate Reality, the Eternal Now. All healing occurs there where the arrow becomes one with the mark, the essence, no beginning, no end, no time … where the prayerful ones become the prayer.

Words of power in repetitive prayer and chanting can be used for very specific purposes, including the clearing of dense, toxic energies. The sound and vibration involved with the chanting of mantras can produce transformation and have a positive healing effect. Sacred sounds, repetitive utterances, mantras, chanting and prayer, date all the way back to the beginning of time. All we know began with the Sacred OM and is sustained by its vibration. It has no energetic beginning or end. It is well worth the effort to study how to engage the power of repetitive prayer and chanting, as practiced by so many traditions, on so many spiritual paths. It does not matter what language it is spoken in, as long as it is the language of the very soul of our being.

Repetitive prayer should not be a divisive issue. Among the core mystical groups of most spiritual traditions, the root language is ultimately, Sacred Silence. What matters is the breath, and the heart's intention, as they are carried upon the magnificent wings of the most surrendered prayer, whispered into the Ether. These are not the prayers and chanting of beggars with personal agendas and a list of demands. It is the sound of surrendered fusion with the Absolute Energy and finding the point of connection within. What matters is our ability to suspend our senses and drop all ego self identification. What counts is how powerfully we can withdraw our attention from all distractions and focus it in such a way as to create change on a cellular level. What resonates with, and as Divine, is the purity of our hearts.

The information shared in this book is not meant to be purely remedial. There must be a wholesome, balanced lifestyle in place to support your practice. It makes no sense to have an elaborate altar, consecrated for healing and holistic well-being, if every door to the temple of the soul is swinging open to any, and every, random, sorrowful energy. Much drama would be averted by simply closing and locking the doors of our lives, to the mental and emotional triggers that cause our suffering.

Most paths and traditions practice some form of chanting sacred sounds and words of power, each with their own unique method of repetition. Repetitive prayer is often practiced with a string of a prescribed number of prayer beads, or malas, for counting and focusing attention. There are specific "mudras" or hand and body positions associated with certain systems of chanting, meditations, and prayer. Some are practiced with instrumental accompaniment. Drums bring their own level of vibration and frequency. Some practices include spinning, dancing, or swaying rhythmically, while others require stillness of motion. Your best mantra is the mantra of your choice. The best mantra can be as simple as a childhood prayer, or even as simple as, "Thank You. Thank you for existence." You may feel drawn to a certain mantra or prayer system. Choose with discernment and in-depth knowledge of the meaning of what you are chanting or praying. Repetition of a mantra serves to quiet the over-thinking, reactive mind, inspiring transcendence beyond the origin of thought, into pure awareness. To enter the silence of Ultimate Reality is the goal of most meditation disciplines.

You would be ill-advised to engage in certain traditional practices without mindfulness regarding the proper respect for its sacredness, and the strict protocol that must be observed, down to specific subtleties of perfect pronunciation, personal

205

hygiene, and diet. For that reason, I have not shared certain prayers here that are essential to Psychic Self-Defense. Look to the ancient traditions, speak to the teachers and practitioners on the subject of Psychic Self-Defense. It is worth the effort to study how to perform many these very basic, but profound healing rituals and prayers. These practices are prescribed in times of spiritual danger, emotional suffering, and used as a powerful tool for healing. Use that knowledge to empower your own practice.

The battle between forces of joy and sorrow is a choice and a perception. We are given the understanding that they are interdependent, and neither is "good" or "bad." They just are. To see it in the context of a pendulum swinging to extremes, rather than a balance being kept, we become an enemy of our own well-being. We may find the worst enemy of our happiness in the mirror. That is where the energetic cleansing begins. Removing the magnets that attract spiritual and emotional drama will result in a more peaceful life.

The OM/AUM

The Sacred OM/AUM is the original sound through which the Universe was created and is sustained.
It awakens the Light of the Third Eye Chakra .

The Four States of Consciousness and the World of Illusion

1. Waking (Jagrat)
2. Dreaming (Swapna)
3. Deep sleep (Sushupti)
4. Transcendental state (Turiya)
5. The world of illusion (Maya)

THE SACRED OM/AUM

This Ancient Mystical Sanskrit Symbol
represents the original
sound vibration
by which The Creator caused
creation to exist, evolve
from chaos to order to creation
and all that sustains it.
It speaks of the dream world,
the waking state,
and the veil between them.
OM, when intoned,
vibrates the skull and the bones of the face
stimulating the Light of
the Third Eye, at the center of our brow line,
the sixth of our seven energy centers
known as the Chakra System.
The vibration and frequency of the OM
is the sacred connection between the Ultimate I AM
and The Divine manifesting in the I in I,
that Sacred link between Creator
and that which was created.
It is the voice of the Contained calling out
from within the container of our physical form
singing the song of its liberation.
The container can either be a prison
incarcerating our Essence
or it can be the sacred garment
that compliments and adorns It.

The vibration of the OM,

at the Fifth Chakra

in the area of the throat,

can be the medium

through which It is freed.

Sacred wisdom in wordless Holy language

through the representative visual art

of its evocative calligraphy

can cause the symbol of the OM

to become a catalytic connection

that seeded by the mystical Essence.

This sacred symbol is consistent with the three Sanskrit sounds

A U M representing various fundamental triads believed to be a vibration

of the spoken essence of the Universe.

It is uttered as a mantra

in meditation, affirmations, and blessings.

Let us meditate every day.

We meditate upon The Divine Essence.

Do unto others as we would have them do unto us.

One God

One Love

One Breath

Born of the Eternal OM

of and into

The Light of the Creator our souls merge

as members of the same body of Eternal Light.

Let us join in this Universal dream.

We will once again

dream together.

Together we will awaken

our lives transformed

to emit our own frequency
and stop living in reference to
and under the influence of
discordant frequencies
that distort our perception of True Reality.

Affirm:

Like the OM, I am imperishable.
I choose a life that confirms this truth in every moment.
The Timeless tone of the Sacred OM is my meditation.
I must never forget who I am.
I remember I am
that space I share with no one.
I am
beyond time
beyond you and me
I am
the tone
the sacred
OM

Why Use Root or Symbolic Language in Spiritual Ritual?

Translations of sacred scriptures are offered in many languages. A wise mystic and spiritual practitioner generally prefer the use of root languages in ritual work because of the potential for confusion using others, particularly English. I assert this, assuming that because this book is in English, the reader speaks or understands English. I am certain that The God will hear and understand our prayers no matter what language we use as long as we respect and know to Whom that prayer is directed. However, the problem with language can originate in our own subconscious understanding. Our mouths may chant a mantra. Our hands may write a petition. Our minds, our souls, may extend a prayer. Any of these practices used to commune with Spirit may be well understood on a conscious level. At the same time, our subconscious mind may discern subtle, but powerful contradictions between our spirit's deepest desire, and an awkwardly expressed intention using a derivative language.

The use of certain root languages, such as Hebrew, Arabic, and Sanskrit, can more clearly express our purest intentions, with the least room for misinterpretation, misdirection, and misunderstanding. Even though confusion may occur in our own minds on a subconscious level, that is where it could be the most compromising to the outcome of our spiritual work. The subconscious mind is the origin of the thought-form from which a strong-willed intention emanates. It may fertilize a corrupted seed through which the fruit of a poison tree is multiplied. When this predictable phenomenon occurs, and a thought-form manifests, we can refer back to that original prayer, mantra, meditation, or petition, and examine the corruption in the wording of a derivative language. We don't want to learn the hard way that such misunderstandings can be the root cause of a corrupted manifestation. We may reflect upon the essence of our intention, observe the twisted meanings braided into the words of our original petition, and discover the source of the corrupted materialization. That is why, when using one of the derivative languages, well-

211

known sayings come to mind, "Be careful what you ask for because you just may get it. No prayer goes unanswered." Our intention and desire must be expressed in pure, concise, specific and humble perfection for optimum results in our spiritual practice.

There are many factors to be considered. Culture plays its part. Emotion plays its part. Mindset and temperament play a part. However, all of these things are expressed in the *word* and the vibration of the word. When we practice ancient spiritual traditions using a modern language imbued with the understanding from which it rises, tragic mistakes can be made. The other side of that coin is that glorious new energies can be experienced. We do not think like the people of many ancient spiritual traditions. We are often vain in our perception that one culture and one language should reign superior over the entire range of human experience, which is the narrative Western traditions appear to perpetuate. There are words from ancient languages that have no English equivalent at all. The study of such words can serve to enhance our experience of life and expand our perceptions. There are mantras that not only have no English equivalent, they can only be expressed using a symbol, sound, symbolic language, tone, or simply silence.

Sound, vibration, tone, silence, breath, and mudra, can all be used to create portals into planes of existence and states of being. Mudra in this text is derived from Sanskrit, meaning seal or mystery, and refers to symbolic hand and finger positions, posture, and movement in meditation. Images may do the same thing, yet I recommend caution in their use for the practice of meditation. I won't qualify that in this section because that would be, at the very least, another book. The spark created by intense emotion is the primary causal factor of mystical practice. There are silent meanings infused into language based on tradition, legends, and culturally conditioned phenomena. We use language in such a way as to empower the words or text, which are reliant on subtext or symbolic, unspoken, emotionally charged thought-forms. If we are using English or a similarly confusing language in our

212

spiritual work, we may manifest a confused or unpredictable outcome because of a conflict between conscious text and thought-forms created by a subtext.

There are communications or transmissions made with symbols formed with the hands, silent gestures, even in the projection of an intense gaze that will affect the object of its attention. Most spiritual and mystical traditions acknowledge a phenomenon called the "evil eye," suggesting that energy can be transferred to another through the eyes, in such a way as to cause harm to that person. Many traditions acknowledge a mode of speaking that is believed to be a holy language, utterances beyond our known languages, referred to as "speaking in tongues" or Glossolalia. It is associated with intense, transformative experiences and can trigger transmissions of information from the prophetic realm that defy explanation. There are as many methods of communicating sacred mystical knowledge and energy as there are people who believe in it.

The interpretations of visions, dreams, symbols, prayers, meditation, energy, and emotion are often culturally influenced. The flash of emotion, the core level stirring of energy, is a requirement to create that spark between visualization in meditation and the manifestation of our intention. Words and emotion connect differently for diverse reasons as they are filtered through our many cultural and linguistic precepts. For example, white is the color of mourning, death, and grief in Chinese tradition. Western beliefs suggest a different subtext, associating black with being a color connected to death, mourning, grief, and sorrow. A bat may portend good fortune in the East, and demon spirits in the West. References to magic or the supernatural may suggest science fiction in one culture and be an accepted reality in another.

We can choose to reassign the energies of a conflict between text and subtext. We can accept as our reality the associations we prefer. Emotional experience and reaction are subjective. Two people can speak the same language, come from the same culture, and share a common understanding of what the subtext of one particular word is. The emotional response and associations inspired by *one word* can be completely different. The psyche and spirit can access energies beyond words. There are some energies so complex they are better expressed using symbols, like the Sanskrit symbol of the OM, which represents a sound and vibration used as a meditation mantra. The symbol of the Yin and Yang, among countless others, evokes spiritual energies for which language has no real equivalent. English, particularly, often imposes cultural and ideological belief systems, which shadow spiritual context. The word, the energy, the emotion, the 'symbol,' the spiritual experience, is the alchemy that together causes the whisperings of powerful suggestions that speak to the heart in many ways.

Language in ritual, meditation, and prayer work is an important study, and well worth the effort. When we seek sacred connections with The Divine One, the utmost of respect and reverence is required to keep our signal strong and free of static interference. One of the simplest of disciplines is the repetitive chanting of OM. The energy from the vibration engages the Third Eye and has the power to induce a deeply meditative and transcendental state of consciousness, which serves many healing purposes. The Sanskrit symbol for the Sacred OM illustrates the four states of consciousness. Our spiritual practice strives for the fourth level, the transcendent state of the Higher Self. From that perspective, healing from emotional trauma is viewed differently. The first question would be, "Who is the 'self/Self' that is suffering?" If the personhood is suffering, the person, the ego, must be dropped, and the matter must be taken to a higher realm to be resolved or dissolved. From a transcendental perspective, there is no "self," consequently, no self to succumb to fear. Once the trappings of the ego self, with its conditioned, subconscious, cultural narratives have been stripped away, the Self that remains knows that it cannot be harmed, damaged, or killed. It knows that it is Timeless, formless, identity-less, label-less, and without agenda or interest in carnal worries rooted in victimhood.

The Natural Mystic

To the Natural Mystic, all time is DreamTime. All time is now. The Natural Mystic identifies more with the 'contained' than the 'container' and knows that the mirror is only a door. The Natural Mystic considers the journey to be the destination. When embarking upon this mystical journey, much consideration is given to the art of cleansing and purifying the physical vessel. That is just the container of who we really are. When attention is given to elevating the vibration of the subtle or Light body, through energetic purification, we can accomplish a respect-filled spiritual relationship with The Divine Presence that we are. A practicing mystic who does not seek to align his or her personal will and presence with Divine Will and Presence is wasting valuable spiritual energy. When those Wills are acknowledged as One, the Universe aligns itself behind his or her intention.

The Natural Mystic sees his or her desires through the filter of The Will of The Divine. An emotional attachment to sensual gratification is sometimes in conflict with that which The Creator desires for us. The practice of mysticism in the hands of the spiritually unenlightened is, at least, a danger to the practitioner. However, the Will of the spiritually enlightened is a polished, shining, and sparkling intention to achieve alignment with The Will of The Divine. Nothing but good can come from such practice. A discipline aimed at accepting the Light that we are, is not so much a "practice," as it is a perfection.

Our choice to become aligned with a current of creative energy can produce a phenomenal *"quickening"* of the spirit. It can be a studied or assisted process. A quickening of spirit can manifest as what feels to be a bolt of lightning rushing up the spine and blowing out every chakra it touches. A blow out like that can produce what appears to be a seizure, spontaneously striking without permission or warning, possibly bringing on an epiphany and new consciousness. It could also result in devastating, diverse manifestations on a physical, mental, emotional, and spiritual level. An *awakening* can be as subtle as a single tear in prayer or meditation. It is not to be feared, just approached with wisdom and spiritual discernment. It is our natural state. We are more than physical beings. We are energetic beings expressing ourselves through a unique physical container.

We are all mystics, whether we are consciously aware of it or not. We are naturally mystical beings. Natural Mystics raise their vibration above the level of base desire, rejecting societal conditioning and identification. A life of surrender, love, and complete trust in The Creator's Will sustains all aspects of the mystic's being. That is our Truth. Seek refuge in That. Seek refuge as That Self-Realized Eternal Being, the I AM.

I AM Meditation

In my well-rewarded attempts to find editors for this book, I did not go in search of an editor who would validate or patronize me, rather, one that would confront me and challenge me to raise the bar. Writers are only as strong as the extent to which they will humble themselves before the mind and voice of wisdom's constructive critique. There must be an ability to at least explore guidance in directions that may not have been considered, even to the point of abandoning the warmth and security of a fixed comfort zone.

In a conversation on the subject of the I AM and Mystical Meditation, I was told to meditate on *here, now*, and *nothing*, only I AM, I AM, I AM, I AM. I was told to resist escaping or taking myself away from my life in the present tense, though every conscious thought strived to encourage me to do that. I found this meditation exercise to be incredibly difficult. I was coached to be totally focused on my life in the present, the present space, my present reality, my present overview. I was told to observe it, as is, resisting the desire to see anything about it as changed, or in any way altered to represent a vision of some future potential, or more desirable reality. The objective is to take a good look at everything, without attachment, aversion, opinion, or judgment. There were things about my life and the lives of others that I was subconsciously holding in judgment. Judgment imposes demanding ideals that will, more often, defy reality, than achieve it. The harshest of all of the judgments I entertained turned out to be the harsh judgments I held against myself. In meditations I have enjoyed, I had the freedom to visualize and transform any present reality into an idealized virtual reality scenario, existing in a future where the ideals would be real. But after returning to the *now*, nothing had ever changed, and there was a letdown, even though the escape was a pleasant one.

In the I AM meditation, I was told to see my life as a floor littered with things that I would have a natural urge to clean up or fix by sweeping it away.

Through my escape meditation practice, I was able to sweep away the litter with a very large broom. But the challenge for me was to transcend the need to do that and just observe it. If I am in a meditation and the things that I identify as litter on the floor of my life disturb me, this disturbance has become a distraction from my present reality and pulls me out of the meditation. The litter is a *part* of the meditation. The objective is to be so focused, intentional, and undistracted by perceived imperfections that all distractions are included in the meditation. For example, a noisy truck passing by could be a startling distraction from this I AM meditation. Rather than allowing it to become the thing that interrupted the meditation, it becomes included in the meditation. It is all a part of the I AM present picture of life, everything, including the litter. It need not be edited, swept away, enhanced, or Photoshopped into a magazine photo of the perfect floor, in that perfect place many seek to escape to in meditation.

At first, it worried me to resist the broom. I was distracted from the meditation because I began to meditate upon the broom, and the pleasant vision of change it offered to chaos. I resisted, as difficult as that was for me to do. I just looked at the floor of my life, observed it as something that need not be 'fixed,' something that just simply is what it is. The mantra I used to help me focus was, "It is what it is," "I am who I am." I own it, *as it is* in this moment, here and now, as though there existed no other possible moment, ever. If I saw something that I felt I should fix, something that did not meet my expectations of what the floor *should* be like ... I did not have to clean it up, stop it, or fix it. I could choose to meditate on *including* it as a part of the reality of what is. I learned that it is a choice as well as a challenge to simply accept that it is what it *is*.

In this meditation, I repeatedly drifted into the arena of the, "what *should* have been," "what *could* have been," "what *will* be, *if* ?"... "what *could* happen, *if?*" I could not handle being held to my present reality, to be in the *now,* without fixing anything about it. It was so difficult for me to resist unconsciously redressing my *present* to suit my *future* ideals. I hated it. I realized then that my previous practice of meditation had one aim, one goal, and that was to escape my present reality, to take a pleasant vacation away from it. If meditation is used in this way, it can lead to expectations that result in painful disappointment.

Rather than embracing the *now,* with its fluid, naturally mystical power, we tend to affix our consciousness to a place called *future* and *past.* Neither exists. We do not know what tomorrow will bring, as surely as we did not know yesterday, what today would bring. To see time and timing through the Eyes of The Divine Creator would make us let go of it with the knowledge that everything is what it is. Everything is perfect in creation. Everything is following the timing of The Creator, God. Meditation should be the key to open the door to that reality. When meditation is used as an escape mechanism, its positive effects can be thwarted and coaxed into some imaginary realm, where the now is avoided rather than appreciated. In some very fundamental way, we cheat ourselves out of our present value.

Meditation is most beneficial as a practice of submission to the rightness of the now. We are exactly where we are supposed to be, right now. We are exactly who we are supposed to be, right now. Where, and who we are, is *perfection* by a much higher standard than our own. In this simple, I AM meditation, my harsh judgments of my here and now experience could not be escaped. It was to be included. "This is who I am. This is where I am, right here, and right now. Love it or hate it, these are the people and circumstances of my life." The objective was to neutralize it emotionally and free it to just *be*, without being clouded by my opinions and judgments of it.

That was when I discovered my attachment and aversion to certain systems of meditation. In this one, I had no vehicle of escape. I was once able to leave my present condition and, without responsibility for the journey, take a free mind trip away from myself. After I arrived at my destination, I feared my mind would be taken places more unpleasant than the reality I was trying to escape. The more I meditated upon the "as is" part, the more uncomfortable I became. I resisted my desire to transcend and go to another place in consciousness. I would not have to include it as my present reality. I figured out that there is a special point in meditation where the focal point must be the "Self" and all of its aspects, free of judgment, free of going to another place where it is not, free to let go of the past and the future. I found freedom in knowing that if I were to disappear from the face of this Earth, at this very moment, I have seen time and resisted my compulsion to 'change' it, if only in my mind. I was free to just experience a moment, this one, very special, very authentic moment. I was free. It was a brand of freedom from trying to fix what is not broken with the declaration that, "It is what it is."

After I relaxed a little from my struggle to not jump for the *fix-it* broom, I took the deepest cleansing breath I have experienced in quite some time. I was challenged to gaze upon my life and myself, in meditation, and tell myself … It is what it is. I Am as I Am. I am all of this, right here, right now, not flipping the pages of visions over to the perfect version of the I AM of my imaginations. I accept the reality of the present I AM … Without the need to perfect it with a judgment that it is not *already* perfect.

There are as many styles of meditation as there are people who meditate. Each form of meditation is a key to the door of higher consciousness. Behind the door are many paths and many destinations, with the most profound being, no destination at all. The style that causes self-examination, like the I AM Meditation, can take us to new levels of practical Self-witnessing and acceptance. Many forms of visualization meditation can cause the energy of coveting and conjuring. Some suggest that visualizing and chanting for what you want in meditation will attract these things to you. This, in fact, is true. But if we don't know who we are, how can we possibly know what to want that would serve our highest good?

Prayer is a higher octave of meditation. We must never forget that no prayer goes unanswered, even though the answer may be "No!" We must know the difference between powerful mystical manifestation and interfering with the Will of The God in our lives. The intensity of the prayer must be as that of a drowning person with no rescue in sight, with faith enough to use their last breath to call upon The God for intervention. Why wait until we are drowning? For all we know, we could be drowning now. There are elements other than water that we could just as easily be drowning in.

It is better to meditate upon your prayer than to pray upon your meditation. It is unwise to close the doors through which miracles are issued into our lives. The I AM Meditation can open the door to a conversation about the consciousness of I AM, the consciousness of the fact that "I am not a body." I am a being, without beginning or end. With this awareness, there is no illusion of permanence as *form*. When a spiritual connection with The Light of Ultimate Consciousness is established, through the energy of the Light body, unknown universes align themselves behind our positive intentions.

With time, I began to expand on the I AM meditation practice. In another form of an I AM meditation, I felt my "self" disappear and became aware of my subtle Self. There was no appearance of a Light body. There was no appearance of anything. The deeper I looked, the more any semblance of form disappeared. The viewing of myself as a person began to fade the first time I asked, "Who am I?" I thought of images from the beginning to the end of my timeline. I dropped the images and masks … All of them. But I was still there. At first, my mind kept defaulting to the "self" as a person. It was as though I looked into a mirror of identity, into, and beyond, the Third Eye. I traveled until all concepts of a person or self disappeared. Then there was nothing. The noise and kaleidoscope of images riding the waves of distorted "I" consciousness faded.

Who am I … this True Self that cannot be seen? This Self is pure consciousness. This Self is aware that it cannot be seen and that something that cannot be seen witnesses it. It terrifies me to think that we can live our entire lives in a cage of rotting flesh and bones, believing that the cage is who we really are. There is freedom in understanding and living life from the transpersonal perspective of the Eternal I AM. Our freedom is earned as we own our knee-jerk illusory reality. Our essential Self says, I AM. What we call by many names, including The God, says, I AM. What we call by many names, including the Devil, says, I AM. Keeping this in mind, be discerning with who answers, I AM. We must know when we are weaving webs of bondage around ourselves, with ego-based, worldly mindsets and desires.

The material world incessantly beckons and calls, whispers and screams, baits and switches. Some call her Dunya. Some call her Maya. She is a beautiful seductress, powerful and unwavering. Her ambition is to have us live in her shadows, sell our souls for her superficial trappings, and bow at her clay feet. Her victory is our forgetfulness of who we really are, as we lower ourselves to live for, and as the external, rather than the Eternal. She is a major archetype of humanity. We cannot escape her encounters. We prayerfully break her bewitching spell with ceaseless reminders that she is around every corner we turn, even as we turn within.

PROTECT AND HEAL
THE LIGHT BODY

The Sacred Self

Observe the basic rules of physical and spiritual hygiene when performing meditation and prayer ritual. Some methods include performing ablution, a ritual cleansing as prescribed according to many traditions before spiritual work, and prayer. "Cleanliness is next to Godliness" is not an empty cliché calling out to meaningless ritual. A purification bath of sea salt and baking soda will amply prepare you for intense meditation, cleansing the aura of astral garbage. Soak for about twenty minutes. In the preparation of the bath, as you pray or chant your mantra aloud, run your hands through the water, projecting the energy of your prayers into the water, in a stirring motion.

Anoint a white candle with olive oil and prayer. Place the candle in a fire safe location that is easy to view from the tub to provide a pleasant ambiance and a powerful focal point for concentration. Certain oils enhance this cleansing ritual, such as rosemary, rose, and lavender. Engage in your choice of affirmations, visualization, intense prayer, or a guided meditation. Do not use a recording of a guided meditation unless you have listened to it first, in its entirety, in a fully conscious state. Determine that you completely understand and are in agreement with every single word of the meditation.

Many read or chant verses from Holy Scriptures. Some engage in prayers that take on the form of personal conversations with The God, with the understanding, that is exactly what they are. I have experienced a quickening of frequency and energy when I ran a slow stream of water from the shower while meditating in the tub. The cleansing of the aura and sacred workspace to prepare for meditation and prayer is accomplished by "smudging," using smoke charged with prayer and positive intention as a clearing of discordant energies. You can burn a "smudge stick" of sage or burn cedar, sweetgrass or Palo Santo. Light your sage wand, in prayer, and fan the smoke with your hand or feathers, using your right hand. Pay specific attention to the top of the head (Crown Chakra), Third Eye or Sixth Chakra, (between and just above the brow line), the nape of the neck, the throat, the heart and the Solar Plexus area, all the way to the bottom of the feet and back up to the Crown Chakra. The smoke represents the rising of the spirit of the prayer to the Great Spirit, the Creator, for spiritual cleansing and protection.

This ritual cleansing should be performed in a manner consistent with your chosen tradition of prayer while visualizing the aura being cleansed of negative energies. In addition to cleansing yourself, take the time to cleanse your meditation area and the entire house with frankincense, myrrh, sweet grass, salt, lime, lavender, and sage, prior to spiritual work. What you use, when, how, and why, will become intuitive choices as you delve deeper into your studies.

The Body System

The ability to utilize all aspects of our True Being, particularly our energetic frequencies, is important as we continually evolve into a perfect vessel for the Spirit of the Natural Mystic ... That Sacred Indwelling Presence, a Spark from The Original Flame. Our Mystical Meditation discipline begins with our decision to become a desirable container through which The Creator chooses Its Expression. This process involves every aspect of our being; spiritual, mental, emotional, and physical. We are not one body. We are many bodies, variously layered in many forms, rising, fusing into Oneness, seeking balance and union. We must give each aspect of our many selves their own domain of significance in our lives. Our many bodies must be cleansed and healed with Light and Love.

The Light/Subtle Body

The soundest advice I can offer in approaching mystical studies is, *Know The God.* Be conscious that we have come into this incarnation with the responsibility and challenge of getting out with our Eternal souls intact. The soul is all we have and all we are. Our connection to the Divine One is the Light Energy of our immortal soul. We must see ourselves in the big picture that extends beyond our physical form.

I cannot imagine a more chaotic, empty, and lonely life, than the feeling of separation from The Creator. In my references to "The God," I speak of the Love from which we all emerged. I say "The" God to distinguish The Creator God from lesser gods, for there are many. Our sacred connection with The God transcends Earth Plane precepts and concepts. It is inclusive rather than serving to divide and exclude. Before blindly embracing any spiritual practice served up by mortal beings, we must consider the source, consider the cause and effect, and consider the consequences. The spiritual must bend to The Greatest of Spirits, That Which Created it all. We need no intercessor or interpreter. We are one with That. Allow the Frequency. We are That. The subtle body is the God Essence that we are. There is something Divine about us.

The Mental Self

The mental process plays a major role in making meditation work as we fortify the Light body to become a powerful warrior, fearless on the battlefields of the mind's relentless struggle to make things permanent that are not. It is within the frequencies that our strongest meditations and prayers for healing occur. The first thing we must understand is who we really are. We are not our minds. We are not our bodies. Who we really are is what observes the mind and all of its myriad changes. It is within the hidden chambers of our minds that we may access and process the knowledge of who we really are.

We must exert an effort to reprogram the conscious and subconscious negative messages we give ourselves. These are conditioned, programmed belief systems that we may not even be aware of, sabotaging our best efforts to survive the un-survivable. If it is love that we want to manifest in our lives, and deep within there is an abyss of toxic, fermented negative beliefs about love, we hold a fear that is more powerful than our longing. We cannot expect positive results from our strongest conscious efforts to manifest love in our lives if we don't believe in love. If our relationship with money is guilt and fear-based, we cannot expect our efforts to override our subconscious negative belief system.

Affirmation, prayer, meditation, and chanting help us to channel our wandering thoughts into a single stream of energetic intention. These positive thought-forms, summon our intentions into manifestation. A pure and focused thought-form can assist effectively in magnetizing our own electromagnetic force field to attract our conscious and subconscious desires, by Divine Will. It is, therefore, a spiritual mandate that we are very sensitive in detecting and banishing negative thought-forms that may be projected from within, or from an external source. It is equally important to reinforce positive thought-forms that work in favor of manifesting our highest good.

The mind can be a powerful ally or a mean-spirited, fickle bully. Our own minds can be the most dangerous psychic attacker we will ever encounter. That is why there must be time set aside to silence it so that it can rest and heal, or it can cause damage to the entire body system. Sometimes the mind longs to be liberated from its vain, petty preoccupations so that it can return to its natural, peaceful state of surrender to the I AM, the Essential Self.

The Emotional Self

Studying Mystical Meditation impacts our emotional stability in a positive way by offering a sense of sovereign security in spiritual practice. We learn to take full responsibility for all aspects of our life. Some people really are better off being a part of a consistent support group or circle that offers a forum to vent, heal, and be understood by people who are, themselves, coping with the fears associated with spiritual warfare.

Some chose to be loners while coping with Psychic Self-Defense issues, rather than associate with people who would unintentionally introduce triggers that would slow the remedial process. Though it is a fact of life that it fluctuates, there is an emotional balance that must be kept. When depleted, energetic balance can be restored by constantly cleansing our own emotions of the spiritual burden and heaviness of guilt, jealousy, envy, anger, and hatred. Forgiveness, whether it is deserved or not, is important to maintain our positive energy. The emotional must yield to the spiritual because unstable emotions can cause fear, panic, and grief attacks. These attacks are directly related to specific triggers.

The Physical Self

The part that the physical self plays in walking the path of the Natural Mystic is often ignored and considered unrelated. Our physical condition can either make us a fit, or unfit vessel for the flow of creative, mystical forces. To facilitate the safe and effective performance of prayer and Mystical Meditation, we must give proper attention to certain aspects of our physical health.

Pharmaceuticals and over the counter medications must be used with caution. The side-effects of certain drugs can cause energetic damage and create auric ruptures, opening portals into our consciousness that are not easy to close. A perfect storm of discordant elemental energies can leave us vulnerable to all manner of physical, mental, spiritual, and emotional trauma.

Tai Chi, certain systems of Yoga, Chi Gong, or sound disciplines of personally compatible forms of meditation and exercise are helpful in establishing the groundwork of mystical practice. Many mystical and spiritual disciplines promote the maintenance and well-being of the body's seven major energy centers, the Chakra System. This text offers exercises that are helpful in that effort. A holistic approach ... mind, body, and spirit, can facilitate a healing that can cause a radical and positive shift in energy.

We must not underestimate the potential for protection and healing offered by practicing the energetic exercises recommended in this, and many other spiritual texts. Our goal is to strengthen our energy centers, maintain a healthy aura of protective Light, and energetically close portals through which we may be invaded or occupied. Our well-rewarded sacrifices mark our concern about the care and maintenance of the health and well-being of our many "selves" as guardians of the Temple of our Creator.

The use of consciousness-altering chemical substances, legal or illegal, is generally not recommended in most common spiritual practices. It can leave us wide open to energies and forces we may not have the experience or strength to be able to manage. Even on spiritual paths that do use substances that will alter consciousness, it is generally practiced in a prescribed, supervised, and sacred manner. It is always advisable to consult both spiritual and medical experts to determine what best serves our individual physical and spiritual needs.

There is an army, visible and invisible, of Divinely commissioned guardians to guide and protect us on our journey through this life, with all of its light and shadows. There are accessible states of consciousness that exceed the capability of any drug or consciousness-altering substance known on this plane of existence. Access to these realms can be spontaneous or induced. I have personally experienced both on more than a few occasions. These experiences were so profound that I have no words to describe what happened. There are no set rules, only amazing rewards for our longing, on our sacred quest for the Unattainable.

The Soul, The Ether, The True Self

The soul is the least dense of our being. It, like its Source, can only be expressed as Silence. This silence is not the silence of the absence of sound. It is a silent awareness, a spark of the Flame of the Ultimate Essential Being, That which created all.

The soul has no form or substance in the way that beings of the spirit world may have. Even though that is true, it is not beyond manifesting a form to be perceived for whatever time and reason. It cannot be identified by the same standard as an incarnate being with an endless list of archetypal and personal qualities. It cannot be bought or sold. If it finds itself feeling fractured or scattered by some traumatic event, it can be mystically gathered up and retrieved, becoming stronger in the broken places.

It is the drop of water that embraces the ocean and ultimately becomes it. That drop can feel either diminished or enhanced. It can feel as though it disappears in the vast sea of its own element. It is at home. It can claim a higher understanding, as the sea in all of its vastness. That is the choice we have. Do we cling to a multitude of self-defining identities in the face of the opportunity to become One with the Source of all existence? … Or do we become the ego-fueled argument of a wave rising on the ocean, declaring sovereignty?

The soul is not something that I feel inclined to speculate on, as though I can define it. All is speculation because none of us can say that we really know. It is of the realm of The Unknowable. A truth of it I sense is that it does not belong to us. We were manifested by way of it, individuating as us, emerged from the Source of all.

The Body System

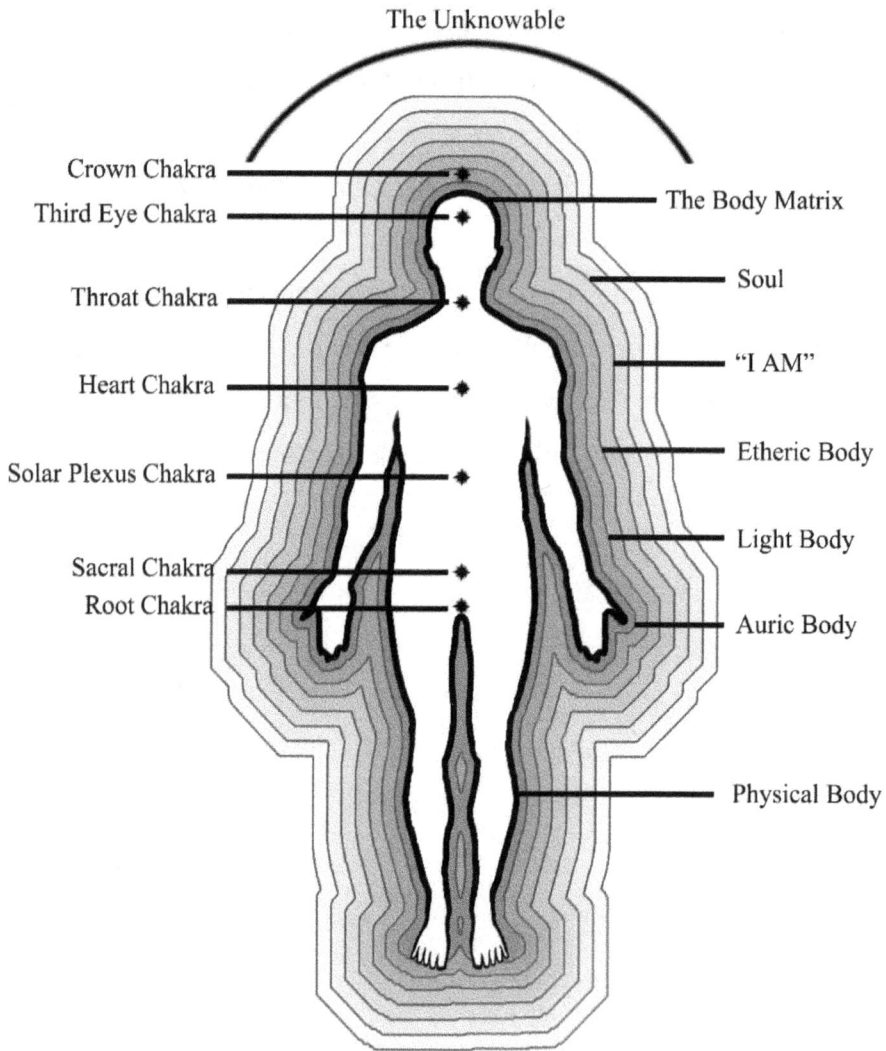

The Unknowable

Crown Chakra

Third Eye Chakra — The Body Matrix

Throat Chakra — Soul

— "I AM"

Heart Chakra — Etheric Body

Solar Plexus Chakra — Light Body

Sacral Chakra
Root Chakra — Auric Body

— Physical Body

The multifaceted body matrix is a system that knows no boundaries or borders.
They are interconnected and can make a dominant manifestation for their own
time and purpose, even while still connected to the physical body.

This diagram is a representation/approximation and in no way indicates
actual or exact locations of the "bodies" of the Body System.

The Aura in Psychic Self-Defense

The Aura is a luminous Astral Plane substance that creates an energetic force field surrounding the human body, much like the glow around the flame of a candle. This force field can reflect the spiritual, mental, emotional, and physical state of an individual to those who are sensitive enough to see and read the human aura. It is the environment of these emanations that we often tap into to extract energy or tap into to cleanse the energy of it.

The energetic field of the aura creates a "charge," or current, that can affect the practice of meditation and prayer. This energy can be transferred between people as well as objects. In certain forms of meditation, crystals and other semi-precious stones, charged with positive energy, are used as a catalyst to boost the force and depth of the meditation. These stones are charged with astral material associated with the essence of the individual who charged it. Objects carry a vibration, and the meditator taps into the frequency, much like scanning the band of frequencies on a radio, to find a clear signal and a channel with music agreeable to our personal preference. Energy is gathered by relaxing into the clearest possible channel, and listening to the subtle voices we will learn to distinguish from those of our own thoughts.

In a similar way, that energy is channeled in such practices as the *charging* of holy water, anointing oil, candles, and other objects. Energy is transferred and shared in a common energy field. It can be a factor in the discomfort felt in the presence of some people, and the pleasant feelings experienced in the company of others. It can even explain why certain people with a "green thumb" are better at growing strong, healthy plants than others. The energies of some people are more conducive to nurturing the Life Force of plants than others.

We have all seen examples of the aura, illustrated in the many renderings of historical characters of great spiritual significance, depicted as being surrounded by

233

a white or golden Light or having a halo of Light around their heads. The rainbow colors of the aura can perform a fabulous light show, varying according to the spiritual, mental, emotional, and physical state of the individual it surrounds. Often the aura contains impressions of pictures or symbols that display relevant information about the person emanating it. This light display can provide accurate information that serves to be helpful in determining the cause and cure of problems a person may be experiencing that requires knowledge of Psychic Self-Defense.

Certain colors tend to be associated with emotional states of mind. Often these colors demonstrate a correspondence to the colors of the chakra energy centers and their representative energies. However, there are no hard, fast rules about the interpretations of the colors of the aura. People have their own unique emotional reaction to and interpretation of these colors, which may differ from textbook correspondences. Which is right? Your intuition will give you the best information as to the meaning of the colors and impressions of viewing the aura of another person.

The aura can be charged or magnetized by the energy of our emotions to either attract or repel many of the experiences of our lives. Through proper physical and spiritual care, the aura can be magnetized to protect us from physical and spiritual damage. Before entering a meditation, and as part of a healthy mystical practice, *visualize* your aura surrounding you as pure white Light, a brilliant illumination that continually grows more intense with the rhythm of your breath and heartbeat. Envision yourself comforted by the Pure, Radiant White Light of Divine Protection, as a shield and barrier to any presence of harmful intent. Visualize yourself encapsulated in an egg-shaped body of Light, which extends several feet from the physical body. Nothing penetrates this powerful barrier, except that which is Divinely Ordained with Permission to do so. Prayer and remembrance of The God as our Protector empowers these visualizations.

It is important to the effectiveness of spiritual work that the aura is well-maintained and not polluted by substances known to be toxic to both the physical and Light body. The aura is magnetic and very sensitive. It is important to avoid the damage that alcohol and drug abuse can cause the aura. There are certain vibrations, even lighting, such as fluorescent and strobe lights that are very damaging to the aura and can affect our physical health.

The aura can be influenced by our thoughts and emotions, as well as the thoughts and emotions of others. Due to extreme emotions, injury, or trauma, the aura can sustain damage and become "dirty," ruptured, or lowered in vibration. Particularly damaging is our own unbridled anger and that of others who may direct it toward us. This energy can literally take on a life of its own as a "thought-form" which can attach itself as astral material to the aura, creating negativity that can ultimately lead to attracting misfortune and poor health on every level of our being. Many emotions, even love, though positive, can be damaging when the object of this undesired attention does not welcome the invasive energy. It is important to develop skills in the verbal expression of emotions and seek to communicate with an effort to resolve emotional conflict in a timely manner. We must seek spiritual guidance with regard to the virtue and mandate of forgiveness. We will exercise humility and compassion in the expression of our volatile spiritual and emotional energies.

Suppression of negative energy does not guarantee that it is under control. In fact, it can cause an escalation of the negative energy and create a critical mass scenario building to an explosion or implosion, equal in intensity to the degree of suppression. These energies can be seen in colors and images floating around an individual in his or her aura. This can occur when one is obsessing or brooding over a particular thought, either consciously or unconsciously. The energy spins and gains momentum. Intention directs this concentrated emotional energy around him or herself, and the object of the attachment. Anger and resentment can show up in the aura as a dirty red hue. This phenomenon can also occur when someone is

235

engaged in ego-based power struggles, attempting to influence, bend, or break the will of others. Our spiritual, mental, emotional and physical condition can change the colors of the aura surrounding us. These colorful illuminations can be seen or sensed by those who possess that spiritual gift. We all can be trained to see auras, and it can happen spontaneously.

It is a spiritual imperative to devote our energy to the study and implementation of methods of insulating ourselves from the negative or invasive energy of others. It is a common occurrence that strong emotions bypass energetic boundaries and attach themselves as attacking thought-forms. Those who can see auras can identify the tainted aura as cloudy and polluted by the litter of floating Astral Plane garbage. The energy of fear and guilt rank high on the list of what makes a person an attractive target and increases the effectiveness of the negative, attacking energies.

A damaged and unclean aura is a precursor to physical illness, as negative energy penetrates both the aura and the physical body. The human energy field, or matrix, is the seed from which the physical form has grown. The formless Self existed *before* the physical form. That fact explains the phenomenon of phantom limbs of amputees who continue to feel sensation in a limb that is no longer a part of their physical body. Those who possess the ability to see and read the energy field can see these limbs. Traditional Chinese Medicine approaches healing at the origin of disease, rather than merely relieving the symptoms of it. Practitioners have been known to treat organs that have been surgically removed because they recognize that the organ is still there on an energetic level and can still be the source of illness.

In this great study, we have chosen, our primary concern with the aura is to keep it free of the attachment of unwelcome thought-forms, the absorption of negative energy, and the leaking of positive energy. The symptoms of maladies that result from these conditions can range from an inability to concentrate, all the

236

way to going barking, stark raving mad. Thought-forms could attach themselves, but they are perceivable intuitively. If you are aware of them, they can be banished. If you are not aware of them, they can influence your decisions, concentration, and behavior. These negative thought-forms, entities, and energies feed upon the energies of fear, guilt, and anger, using it in much the same manner our physical bodies use food for nourishment. A sound clearing or cleansing ritual is an effective way to release these energies before they turn us into a magnet for unpleasantness in many forms. They can manifest as interference in our relationships with other people. They can manifest as interference in our relationship with our Selves.

Those who seek to drain us of vital Life Force energy can deposit spiritual parasites into our aura. I am sure that everyone has experienced the company of a person who is invigorated by spending time with us, yet leaves us feeling physically and emotionally drained of energy … lifeless and empty. This is often the work of people who are completely unconscious of what they are doing. It is not always possible to avoid the company of people with such vampire-like energy. It becomes important to replenish our energy resources after having been depleted of energy. We must seek restoration from positive sources rather than any random source available. Reaching out indiscriminately trying to fill that type of energetic emptiness can lead to bad habits, substance abuse, and cause further damage by leaking vital energy through ruptures in the aura. Incorporate methods of Psychic Self-Defense suggested in this book and others, into your daily spiritual practice for protection from those who are either consciously, or unconsciously, corrupting our positive energy.

The archetypal personality of an energy vampire is referenced in your advanced text, FACELESS: THE SACRED RELATIONSHIP-How to Heal Your Relationships through Mystical Meditation, as the archetype, The Undead. My book, FACELESS, reviews the major archetypes of humanity, and how our lives

237

are healed by understanding them and then transcending them, choosing to live as the True Self ... *every* time.

The Undead is particularly relevant to the study of the aura. That is why I have shared it here. If people who fit this character archetype engage in a conscious or unconscious meditation or fixation upon us, in or out of our presence, they can have a powerful influence upon our aura. These character types make an appearance in the lives of anyone who has a trace of positive energy and Light for them to feed on. They can be dangerous and treacherous, yet many of them are passive-aggressive and can appear harmless. We will study this dangerous archetype because the knowledge of them helps us defend ourselves against them. The best defense is identifying them before they attach themselves too securely to our lives. It is worth the effort to shield ourselves from them and banish their toxic energy. As we examine the energy of The Undead, we must examine our lives for their shadows, as well as our own.

Care must be taken in cleansing the residual debris from encounters with them. After they leave us drained, a salt bath or smudging with sage along with life-affirming prayer helps restore balance. Some people replenish low positive energy levels by hugging trees, gardening, swimming, or being submerged in the ocean if that option is available. Taking a nature hike, exercising, and horseback riding, even listening to certain types of music can have a cleansing and balancing effect. Ancient practices of Tai Chi, Qi Gong, Yoga and breath control meditations are helpful in rebuilding our energy levels.

Another method of revitalizing positive energy and recharging the Chi or Life Force of the person, the home, and work environment is the study and practice of the ancient mystical science, Feng Shui, the art of placement. It extends from the ideal placement of furniture in the home or office to intricacies of the architecture of the building. The Chi energy of the home or office is enhanced by elemental, symbolic, and mystical cures to any energetic obstructions and interferences. The goal is to provide a healthier flow of Chi energy in the home and work areas while keeping our positive vibrations and overall well-being at optimum levels. This can be assisted through the use of aromatherapy, flowing water, lighting, colors, crystals, mirrors, flowers, and plants, among other remedies.

Wearing certain properly charged crystals can divert, absorb, or diffuse an energetic attack. Never lose touch with the most basic truth, *the power of prayer exceeds all else*. When we feel uneasy, as discordant energies try to penetrate our energy field, one way to immediately protect ourselves from them, is to cup our hands close to our mouth, catching the breath of intense prayer. Perform an ablution (cleansing) with the breath of the prayer, affirming the nonexistence of anything but The One God. Visualize yourself surrounded by the Protective Light of the Divine One, inside of the "REFUGE" Light vehicle that is illustrated among the following diagrams. All else must concede. Nothing exists but The God.

Healthy Aura

Polluted Aura

Aura Affected by Drugs and Alcohol

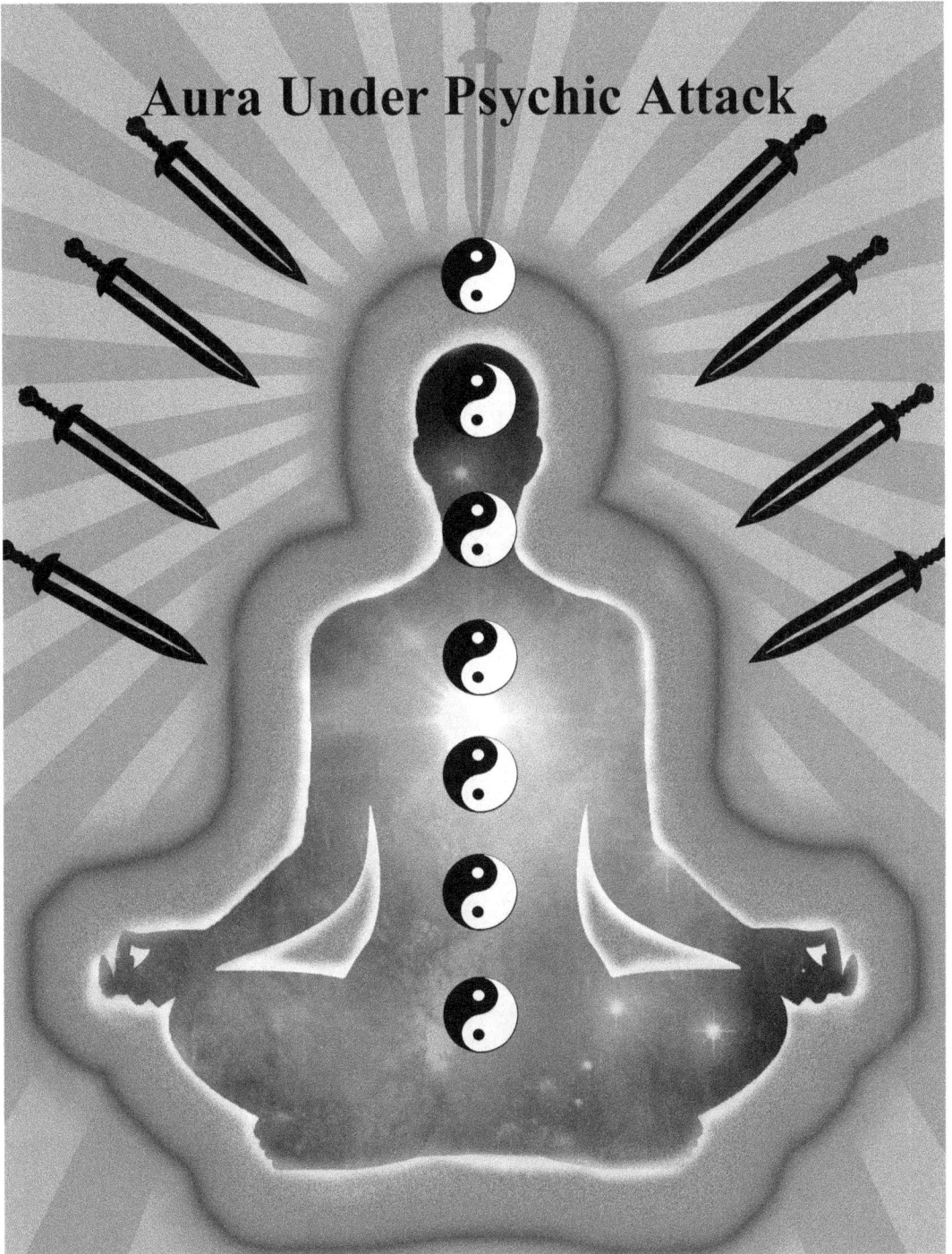

Aura Under Psychic Attack

Light Sphere of Protection

Refuge

The Archetype of the Undead

This section is an excerpt from my book FACELESS: THE SACRED RELATIONSHIP, a mystical journey behind the masks of the many faces of our associations. The Undead is shared here as an in-depth overview and character analysis. It is a dangerous archetypal personality, with respect to its powerful influence and relevance to Psychic Self-Defense. An archetype is a model or prototype personality/character that filters down through the ages, as personalities that manifest across time, into our lives, and into our own being, without invitation. They will shapeshift through sociocultural, psychological, even spiritual conditioning, and resurrect from being buried so deep into our collective subconscious; we believe we are the authors of who we are being, and with whom we share our lives. As we study the effects of vampiric and parasitic energies that drain our Life Force and leave us flat-lining on the floor of a solitary confinement cell, we once called our life, gasping for air, this character simply cannot be underestimated considering the potential for irreparable damage. This influence of the Undead can result in toxic and disturbing physical manifestations that disrupt our lives and the lives of those around us. Particularly susceptible to these subtleties are children and animals. Often people experience phenomena that appear to be bad luck or poor health, only to find out that their misfortune was a construct of some Judas-spirited sorcerer, once believed to be loyal family and friend. It is important to identify, expel, and banish these causative, negative energies quickly and thoroughly.

The archetype of the Undead introduces itself to you as a council and a warning. It is a shadowy energy, murky, incredibly dangerous, and void of authentic social skills, with the modus operandi of a malignant narcissist or sociopath. This energetic 'type' is a closeted, low vibrational force, with the predatory energy of a low frequency, compassionless, shapeshifting monster. Void of both empathy and remorse for the damage left in the wake of their primary, two-faced objective, is to leave behind them in their paths, broken spirits, hearts, and trust. Though it looks like malignant hatred, behind the mask, who they really hate the most is waiting for them in every mirror. Who needs to focus on invisible enemies when their memetic nature allows them to shift into the relationships and mirrors of our lives, looking out of familiar eyes for new mischief to make, new souls to take. This phenomenon qualifies as a Spiritual Emergency.

Zero

0

The Undead

Planetary Association - Mars/Pluto
Ruled by the Fifth Element - Ether

I speak for myself. Look into my steely eyes. I am the fixed, rigid gaze and cold icy touch of the departed ones from the physical plane though I am a sovereign and ancient being. I am that demon behind the eyes, behind the vertical pupils of the spirit possessed. I am the screams and fearful tears of the innocent ... the wonder that casts shadows over the pure of heart in their amazement at just how far and how low I will go to exercise my evil intentions. I cannot help myself. This abysmal energy has become my nature. When I awaken to a new day, it is overcast by utter darkness for the Light is my destruction, and darkness is my abode. When I close my eyes, my devilish mind knows no rest, nor does it sleep, never ceasing its relentless pursuit of souls to capture and spirits to break. When a light shines and comes up on my radar, I cast my net and gather energy for my next attack. It is not personal. It is my nature.

I dare not look into the mirror because, as a vampire, I cast no reflection. My soullessness and emptiness make me unbearable to gaze upon. I have died, and there was no funeral, no burial, no mourning, no obituary, no grave, nothing. There was no evidence of my passing away, only the vacancy in my eyes and the emptiness and hunger of a soul that cannot be satisfied by positive energy ... only by the destruction of it. I am relentlessly driven by an appetite that cannot be sated by anything but the living death that I represent.

I stalk the living from my one-dimensional world. After I feed upon their energy and Life Force, I leave my victims feeling spiritually, emotionally, physically, and mentally violated and drained to the point of exhaustion. Overwhelmed by a perpetual state of fatigue, I suck the very life from their souls, and as they become weaker, I become stronger. I will leave you battling forces you have become too weak to defend yourselves against. I will leave you in ill and deteriorating health. I will leave you feeling broken and confused for I have an investment in making you question your own judgment, or making you behave in ways that other people would witness and write you off. I influence you to make the "mistake" of perceiving me as a figment of your imagination. If you go into denial of me and become unconscious of my presence, the damage I do to your life leaves you spiritually empty without the desire or energy to even seek help.

I stalk your inner and outer world to determine your vulnerabilities, which is usually found in what you believe you desire or need. All I want to know is, "What do you desire?" I am well skilled at extending a well-baited hook to draw you into the realm of my attack by the manipulation of your own desires.

I am not happy, as I exist between worlds, held in bondage by my own welcome ignorance. I hate myself for my primal evil and insatiable appetite for destruction and take joy in the fallout. I am a critical faultfinder with such low self-esteem that

I seek to bring down the positive levels of self-worth of everyone around me. I wear masks ... the perfect masks that create opportunities and invitations for myself among the undiscerning, the trusting, the desperate, the needy, the gullible.

Even the mirror refuses to gaze upon my face. Perhaps, if I could see the ugliness of myself, I would gross myself out and be open to change. That is the cruelest of my realities. I cannot see myself except by the Light of day, which would burn me to ash. That is why it appears I have no conscience, cannot be shamed, will not change. I entertain myself with energies associated with unprecedented tragedy and grief.

I attack, not even realizing I am harming the people closest to me. All you can do is kill me in your mind. I am worse than a devil. What is your victory over my brand of evil? Your only victory over me is The God. If you seek to destroy me by my methods of destruction, you have become me. I am not stupid, not troubled ... both are elements of the mental and emotional planes. I am a contagious spiritual disease ... a virus.

Recognition of the archetypal Undead represents a necessary stage in the evolution of the soul and spirit toward the Judgment of self. The energy of these Undead beings of many species will slither around undetected, below the radar, among the living, as a virulent ethereal toxin. These are individuals whose consciousness and belief system are overruled by an *exclusive* attachment to the physical plane and material existence. In some cases, a higher awareness is in place, but stronger is their refusal to accept responsibility for the negative manifestations they intuitively know their energy is causing. If they were to acknowledge and observe the toxicity of their energy, they *might* not find it so easy to penetrate and poison the lives of other people for the shame that it should make them feel. Within a linear context, their refusal to submit to the Command of The Most High constitutes a spiritual death. These beings walk among us, appearing to be alive, yet they are dead. They represent a danger to themselves and others as they sniff around in the stench of their various stages of decomposition, looking for fresh innocent meat to devour. Closure, with regards to the death of the spirit or soul, is not ritualized in the same way as a death on the physical planes of existence.

This unconscious, living, yet, dead person is wired differently, and rarely finds a proper resting place in the conscious world. The Undead are sentenced to directionless wandering as a shadow until he or she is awakened to the reality of his or her own true spiritual nature. At every twist and turn toward their awakening, in the resurrection of this dead person, they become accountable for the damage caused by their condition. They must willingly accept responsibility for the effect they are having on their own lives and the lives of others. They must seek atonement for the shadows they have cast.

This deadly archetype expresses the most impenetrable shadow side of human character, capable of gross, intentional, and unspeakable mischief. So often the incredible Light or disparaging shadow aspect of the Undead is cast over the lives it touches, manifesting a full spectrum of composite characters. The Undead can appear as a voice of counsel, an enabler of fear-based behavior. They can run interference in the quality and depth of a spiritual relationship with the Higher Self, rendering the victim broken by feelings of helplessness and co-dependence.

As a rule, we are not vulnerable to these predators because we are open, compassionate, loving, trusting, and loyal. Somewhere in our consciousness, we have provided a place for attacks of all types to land. We become vulnerable when we operate on the lower, ego-based frequencies of fear and guilt. Fear is the opposite of love. Fear sends out powerful, manipulative messages, becoming the puppeteer that pulls the strings of our dance with fate. The guilt consciousness magnifies our faults and anchors the thought-form that we are not good enough, rendering us emotionally needy and insecure.

The Undead represents advanced stages of spiritual corruption and destruction, born mature into spiritual ignorance. This energy is an airborne "free floater" in the realms of both the astral and material planes. One must always be on the lookout for this wicked force and its attempts to creep into and bring ruin to every life it crosses at the intersection of any major change.

The Undead appear in the vapor of every aspiration or inspiration at will. We will all experience the energy of every one of the many archetypes of humanity at some point in our lives. The Undead will always be the storm cloud that threatens to rain on the positive experiences of everyone within his or her force field. The Undead will always be a precursor to negative change and seeks to pull out of the shadows the secrets we keep, even from ourselves.

The Undead is a warning, not an indictment. It either warns us to stop or proceed with a heightened sense of caution. It always means not just to pray but remain in a state of perpetual prayer. A state of perpetual prayer takes on different forms in different traditions. Most spiritual traditions use prayer, chanting, or repetition of a positive mantra, sufficient to provide a spiritual shield of protection. We must be mindful as we examine our lives to determine if we are the target of malevolent attacks or influences. The most dangerous thing we can do is respond to this warning with fear. Fear is their nourishment. They feed upon it. Prayer is the neutralizer and healer.

The nature of the Undead is much like that of what we have seen ascribed to the classic mythical "vampire." They can be victims. Many are left soulless for having somehow been robbed of it. Though they may have been a victim, at some point, they are transformed into predators, perpetrators, murderers, and thieves of souls. They are attackers and destroyers of the spirits of other people whose souls

252

and consciousness have sustenance enough to be a source of energy that feeds their insatiable appetite. Their targets, however, may have some reason for willingly opening the door and inviting them in. There may be feelings of neediness, instability, insecurity, or perceive themselves to be weak in character, inspiring their feelings of guilt.

Often some trauma has destabilized their spiritual resolve, or some unfortunate circumstances caused the Undead to fall into such a perilous situation that they are left open and vulnerable, fruit from a poisonous tree, ripe for the picking. The most effective defense against them is to never let them into your energy field in the first place. Avoid involving them in your affairs to the extent they can get close enough to do great damage, holding their place like leeches. Feed them with a long-handled spoon. Better yet, don't feed them at all.

We must examine ourselves and find the loopholes in our own character that invited them in and heal that condition before imagining that we can heal theirs, not to mention, *defend* ourselves against them.

The Undead are possessive, jealous, controlling, arrogant, selfish, empty shells. Often, they are hostile under the guise of passive-aggressive wolves in sheep's clothing. Fear is a weapon and tool for the taming of the intended victim. They want to know what a potential victim wants and fears. They function at the emotional level of a spoiled, self-centered toddler. Their behavior tends to be childlike, mischievous, and unbecoming of an adult. Consequently, they are abysmally lonely because these are not attractive qualities and will eventually cost them everything and everyone they believe they care about or covet. Loneliness is a powerful energy that keeps them fueled on their deadly prowl. They are bored and frustrated to the point of implosion. They hate themselves. Soon they find they have driven every positive energy and force out of their lives, as all things positive are sent running for their souls. After such loss, bloodthirsty and alone, they are right back on the hunt for new victims.

The Undead often use tools of isolation, repetition, sensual deprivation, spiritual starvation, and (re)languaging, or (re)culturing, to mesmerize and disable their intended prey. They have nothing of substance to offer and seek to destroy or cut off any source of spiritual sustenance to their victim. They seek to take control of the lives of their victims, assuring that they have a convenient and constant source of nourishment for themselves, as they go on with their lives, leaving their prey without one.

They show up among our families, in our relationships, in the workplace. They hide behind the forced smiles of counterfeit friendships and can be hidden beneath a shallow embrace of love. They are everywhere. And as we draw toward the end of a major time cycle, their efforts and energies are stronger than ever because they need more of that Life Force they seek to deplete, and closer proximity to that Light they seek to extinguish. Their attacks constitute the making of more undead as they spread their contagion. We will ultimately find many of their characteristics becoming a part of our own, as we have fallen under their spell.

They are plagued by fantasy-oriented sexual issues, which they perceive to be completely beyond their control in behavioral patterns of addiction. They are comfortable with harsh judgments of others, while they have enough skeletons in their closets to fill a large cemetery, with the most haunting being the ones they keep in their minds. Sex, among other drugs, can become an addiction, obsession, or compulsion, that only instant gratification then discarding the victim would satisfy. These appetites are insatiable. In the face of accountability, they shrink from responsibility for the consequences of their actions following their frequent voracious feeding frenzies.

Being the victim of this narcissistic hatred is a confusing experience because when confronted with their behavior observe:

- They are masters of the "blame game." It will always be your fault;

- They convince you they celebrate your success when what they actually want, and will construct, is your failure;

- They will sabotage and ruin every special occasion. They dampen the experience of whatever gives you pleasure or makes you happy;

- They do not encourage activities that will contribute to your skillset, health, or your future prosperity;

- They will never teach you anything that serves your higher good;

- When they feel they are losing control over you, or find their mask is slipping, they will, in subtle ways, conduct a smear campaign against you to separate and isolate you from anyone that could help you;

- They play the "victim" and seek to make the target of their attack responsible for their own suffering;

- Their reprehensible behavior can manifest as arrogance, cruelty, and a lacking of empathy and compassion;

- They condescend and demean their victim, as being weak and deserving of their suffering;

- They see themselves as superior to others;

- They exaggerate and inflate their accomplishments and achievements and exalt themselves over others, seeing themselves as examples or models to be emulated;

- They are spiritually empty though they may claim to profess some kind of spiritual belief.

Once they are discovered, and attempts are made to exorcise them from our lives, they become more vicious than ever, determined to control and disable the victim on all levels. This is the point at which survival depends on spiritual fortitude. We must affirm that nothing happens outside of the Will and Permission of the Almighty, Creator of everything. If we harbor strong feelings of malice against them, even though they have earned it, we open ourselves up to physical and spiritual disease, issued through the portals of our anger and hatred of them. We observe, in bewilderment, the ruins they have left our lives in, and the evil spirited joy of victory they have taken from our suffering. They have no sense of fairness or mercy, so our cries and appeals fall upon blind eyes and deaf ears.

Would-be victims have a weapon the Undead did not bargain for … Belief, faith, and respect for Divine providence and protection. If they were able to transcend the core nature of their mischievous inclinations, they would not have to act the way they do to sustain their bleak lives. But isn't that like saying, "Spiders would not weave webs if they only had belief, faith, and respect for Divinity?" Spiders could meditate and pray for victory over web weaving, after which the spiders would ultimately perish, for seeking to operate outside of their nature. We human beings are not spiders, do not have the nature of spiders, and do not get such a pass. We have a choice. There is something about us that is Essentially Divine. With that knowledge comes great responsibility.

A victim of the Undead is often defenseless within the margins of their own emotions. Emotions such as hatred, greed, jealousy, envy, anger, depression, rejection, and grief weaken our immune system and leave us vulnerable to attack. Spiritual discipline and learning to be in command of our frequencies is our only protection from them. If we find our standards slipping STOP, and immediately, fully engage in a spiritual practice that will help to manifest balance and equilibrium through complete submission to the Will and Love of The God. A sound spiritual practice serves as a shield of Light that becomes our armor of protection against such spiritual attacks. It mystically closes portals of entry through which energetic harm may be issued in by forces such as the energies of the Undead.

The personalities of the Undead are inauthentic and fraudulent. Sometimes feigned kindness or generosity masks their angry, domineering, and hateful spirit. They are flamboyant with their comfortable acceptance of the deadly sins as a welcome part of their lifestyle; pride vs. humility, envy vs. love, wrath and anger vs. kindness, sloth vs. zeal, greed vs. generosity, gluttony vs. faith and temperance, lust vs. self-control, and vengeance vs. forgiveness.

The archetypal Undead can manifest as malefic spirits trapped in bodies, and therefore, these people are very much in touch with the spirit world. They hide under many disguises. They have a certain charisma, but just beneath the surface of that, they tend to be mean-spirited, brutal, cruel, inhumane, sadistic, vengeful, spiteful, and vindictive. Our efforts against them often end in disaster, especially if we do not understand the nature of what we are dealing with.

As we observe a person known to us as possessing behaviors that suddenly change from a kind, gentle, and humble person into an arrogant, mean, and violent person, it can be a sign that this person is either an attacker or under the influence of an attack. *Prayer* is the wooden stake that must be driven through the heart of the Undead. The Love of The God is the only defense against them. They fear the Sun and are burned to ash by it. Exposing them to the Sun in the form of the Light of The God is both their destruction and redemption. To destroy them is to redeem them. The only way to destroy them is to cause them to examine their own nature and seek the Light that will burn, but purify their hearts. They must seek to annihilate the "self" that they are, in order to become the "Self" they have the potential to be, after surrender to the intense Light and unfathomable depths of the Mercy of The God. To submit their ego self to becoming "slain in the Spirit of The God" could result in their surrendering and redirecting of their negative, self-destructive path.

257

They are not to be mistaken for those who have fallen into the Abyss. To fall into the Abyss is often the result of spiritual consciousness reaching critical mass and crashing. This type of crash or meltdown can often precede or follow a profound spiritual epiphany. The aftermath can manifest as anything from fluctuating, roller-coaster personality disorders to a complete shift of energy and disruption of the psyche. Some people survive. Some do not. When someone is trapped within the framework of such a spiritual crisis, they can display the symptoms of the Undead. This is sometimes the only way, in the natural process of spiritual rebirth, that a person can restore balance, cleanse, and heal vital energies. They save themselves only by surrendering their will to the Will of The Most High, The God. The Undead have seen the Light and chosen to succumb to the shadows.

The quickest way to identify the Undead is to observe their unyielding, relentless desire to manipulate their victims into giving up control of their own lives, to free up more of their Life Force to be drained. They desire to exalt themselves over other people to support the illusion that they are still alive and well. They are naturally jealous and competitive, and cannot stand to see other people experience the happiness that they are incapable of feeling. There is an ugliness about them no matter how physically handsome or beautiful they may be. They are soul-satisfied by enslaving the spirit of others and occupying their lives. They have no lives of their own and entertain their boredom with mischief that can leave a strong soul in mortal danger.

They have a strong investment in making their victims see themselves differently than who they really are, until the victim becomes transformed into the negative image of their projections. The Undead want to become the mirrors that show the reflections of their victims. The victim begins to see their own reflection through empty eyes and identify as the image conjured by the eyes of their beholders. They want their victims to judge and define themselves by their standards, which leaves the victim feeling like "nothing," sitting like a pet dog waiting for a bone of self-esteem to gnaw on.

At this point, if we find ourselves the victim, and I think we have all had this experience at some point, we must pray and run for our lives. Pray as though our very souls are approaching the gates of hell, and we see a detour. Many suicidal thoughts and behaviors, mental conditions, chronic physical ailments, depressions, and even deaths, are the result of the vicious spiritual attacks of the Undead. On the subject of suicide, I recommend reading the section "Is it Even Possible to Kill One's Self" from my book, THE TIMELESS NOW: Healing from Grief and Loss. These walking dead people are dangerous and must be approached from a position of spiritual strength, not fear. That is often difficult after they have skillfully depleted our spirits of the positive energy necessary to defend ourselves against them. When we have approached the awareness of forgetting who we really are, we are in the most danger of succumbing to their attack.

If we choose to look at it from another perspective, we can emerge from these attacks stronger than ever. We must release our attachment to shallow, vanity-based judgments and acknowledge that we are not defeated, that we actually *are* "nothing." Our *only* existence is in the Light that we are and The God that we have within. We then seek refuge in our inner Temple and Sanctuary where That Which Created us abides, waiting there to administer a healing. Often, our own pride, arrogance, or ignorance, increases the damage of the attack, as we hold ourselves in false esteem, by the standards of the physical world.

A person operating from such a demonic force field must be examined for the cause of it, as far back as their early childhood. Something happened that caused them to become such dangerous hypocrites and parasites. Even in the committing of some of the most abhorrent acts of depravity and violence, they can be made to see some reflection of themselves and become disgusted, yet their uncontrollable impulses cannot easily be cured of these behaviors. "Do they have a soul?" would be a good question to ask. The difference between them and the physically dead is that it is possible to resurrect them from the grave of mental and spiritual bondage. As a mercy and gift of The God, they may be made to see

259

themselves and how they are behaving. They may seek to resurrect themselves from the grave of their own ignorant choices.

The Undead must have a soul within because if we say they do not, it is a contradiction of the Laws and terms of the Divinity of humanity. The question is, "What type of soul is this?" People don't commonly hang around cemeteries trying to resurrect the dead unless they have some Jesus/Lazarus complex. That is why, without intervention, we can be defenseless against them. It is almost impossible for our souls to understand them. What we cannot understand, we cannot effectively defend ourselves against. It is especially difficult to identify them as they can look so normal, as long as you do not look into their eyes or their hearts. Many do not act out of hatred. They do it for the enjoyment. They do it because it is the nature they have assumed, and it fulfills them.

Exposing them to the Light of The God and sincere prayer is the best weapon we have with which to defend ourselves, and that is all that we can do. It is also the *worst* and most effective thing we can do to them, without jeopardizing our own soul by becoming them. It is like shining sunlight upon a vampire. We must close our doors, lock, and guard them. We must keep the Light on, as we call upon the Great Light for guidance and salvation, and withdraw from them for the sake of our spiritual lives. We are not to withdraw as in a cowardly act but withdraw and seek refuge in the Loving Embrace of The Divine One. If we are running from them and they are in pursuit, we are running them into the arms of their own destruction. If there is a bully harassing you, and you have a friend on your side who is powerful enough to destroy the bully, the attacker is forced to concede. To choose the energy of the Divine Embrace for protection and refuge directs them toward their own obliteration in their relentless pursuit.

Encounters with shadows such as these are usually designed to push our spiritual strength to a new level. It is a rite of passage or an initiatory experience. We may be the ones that were chosen to coax them to open their eyes, look within, and ask if they are comfortable with the life they are living. They must see themselves or be touched by The God in some way. They are wired differently, and the shame/guilt factor will not change them. They can even feel guilt, but it won't stop them, not until they look in the mirror and be repulsed by what they see. At that point, it is not just about bad behavior. It is about self-definition. The question becomes, "Who do you choose to be?

Our transcendence of their influences is a way of running them into the light where they must either choose that light or perish. As they pursue us, we seek refuge in that same Light that will destroy them. This retreat from their presence will serve to neutralize and transmute their energetic wickedness into Light, along with their entire being, if they resist. We may have to leave loved ones behind, trapped in the intricate web of the matrix. We would be required to sever our attachments and never look back at our tears, turning into a trail of salt. It may be our responsibility to help them free themselves by placing them in front of a mirror. This mirror is not the mirror of our judgment, but a mirror of Divine Reflection and Revelation.

We must strive to avoid an evil versus evil scenario by casting judgment and damnation upon them. There are manners in which we can seek their destruction and cause our own. The Undead can do damage that extends beyond the world of the perishable, and inflict wounds that transcend the physical form, leaving scars upon every soul they touch. If they can tempt us into lowering our vibration to the level of theirs, they have accomplished their objective. Their conscious or subconscious objective is to crush and rob our spirit of its positive Life Force. Remain aware. Remain in prayer. We must never forget who we are.

What Do Chakras Have to Do with Psychic Self-Defense?

We live in interesting times. Interesting times result in stressful lifestyles that are more destructive than they are nurturing. A holistic approach to self-nurturing will have a healing effect on every aspect of our lives, our relationships, careers, families, communities, and even the world. We must concentrate our energies on understanding the function of the Chakra System and study methods of clearing blockages that can have a negative effect on our physical, mental, emotional, and spiritual health. A strong and balanced Chakra System will make one less vulnerable to the negative energies that constitute a psychic attack. There are many styles of meditation that are specifically helpful in maintaining optimum health of the chakras. A meditation for each of the chakras has been provided here to increase the flow of positive energy to each chakra and eliminate the magnetic, negative energy that can cause physical, emotional, mental, and spiritual harm.

The word chakra is derived from the Sanskrit word "chakram," which means "wheel." This term refers to a network of seven major funnel or cone-shaped energy vortex centers in the "subtle body." They are believed to be about six inches in diameter, extending one inch out from the physical body. The wider opening is on the outside of the back and front of the physical body, with the small tip being located inside our body near the spine, connecting the two. They are located vertically, from the base of the spine, up through the top of the head. They move energy in and out, in a spiraling motion and function to inhale and exhale vital energy, based on the direction of their spin. Each center relates to particular states of mind, connecting to the experiences of the physical body, as well as the energy that surrounds it.

Chakras are considered the intake organs for energies from our external environment. Due to blockages, the Chi or Ki energy cannot flow freely, resulting in physical, mental, emotional, and spiritual disease. Chi is the "breath" or "wind" and vital Life Force in all things. In a human being, the Chi is a reservoir of energy

262

located in the area of the lower abdomen, the Tan Dien. Any obstruction or weakness of the Chi force can result in vital physical organs not receiving needed energy and can cause a deterioration of our health on all levels.

There are colors associated with each of the chakras. Meditating on a particular chakra and visualizing its corresponding color is known to stimulate the energy of that chakra. Sound vibration can also affect the chakras. Each chakra has a corresponding tone. Certain meditation practices are designed to clear energetic obstructions and blockages of the Chakra System by raising our Kundalini energy force. The objective of some meditation and yoga practices is to cause the Kundalini to rise to the level of the Crown Chakra, resulting in spiritual enlightenment, transcendence, and emergence from time and space. There are exercises that we can incorporate into our regular spiritual discipline, which will keep the energy of the Chakra System fine-tuned, clean, and strong.

There are as many varied descriptions of the function of the chakras as there are belief systems. There is a multitude of variances of correspondences relating to every aspect of the Chakra System, based on the tradition of who is describing them. This is in no way intended to be a thorough explanation of any particular tradition. It is an overview of how chakras relate to meditation and other spiritual practices.

This visualization exercise is helpful when making a deeper energetic connection at the more profound levels of meditation. Your meditation is more powerful when you bring a question or issue into it, determining which chakra directly corresponds with that subject matter. Ask for a healing to take place in your life.

Before engaging in any meditation, observe recommended basic protocol regarding personal hygiene and the cleanliness and ambiance of your setting. Sit in a private, quiet, comfortable place with soft lighting. Avoid meditating in complete darkness and never meditate under fluorescent or CFL lighting. Facing the East is energetically best. Touch the tips of your index fingers and thumbs together. Touch your tongue to the roof of your mouth, and clench your butt muscles tight to facilitate the most effective channeling of energy. If you are not able to sit in a full or modified Lotus position, be mindful of your posture and sit up in a comfortable chair.

Meditate on the area of each of the chakras and visualize its corresponding color, spinning clockwise. Breathe that color in through your nostrils and exhale it out of your mouth as you visualize a circle of that color that you are creating with your breath. This exercise will help clarify your issues and reveal answers to your questions.

Be mindful of the natural rhythm of your breathing. Close your eyes and relax into the energy of your Sixth Chakra (Third Eye). The Third Eye or Psychic Eye is believed to be the eye of the spirit and soul. It not only looks out into the world of the mystic, but it also gazes upon the mysteries that dwell within. This level of inner vision transcends linear space and time, seeing the past, present, and future in the same time frame of reference. Its relationship to the pineal gland has long been associated with telepathic communication when activated. We must connect our focus and energy with the color and energy of each chakra to activate the full force of its power.

Just as there is a Yin and Yang energy to all of creation, this polarity also exists in energetic reference to our chakras. I will not refer to one as good and the other bad. Both sides exist for a reason, and neither can exist without the other. One is the domain of our gifts, and the other the domain of our challenges. They engage in the elegant dance of creation as each side flips like a coin and becomes its own polar opposite. The ideal perspective is not to entertain an attachment or aversion to either side. They are as Shadow and Light. Accept them both as necessary energies to navigate the seas of this life in perfect balance.

Basic Human Chakra System

Chakra/Sanskrit Name		Color/Syllable
Crown Chakra (Sahasrara)	7	Violet/Om
Third Eye Chakra (Ajna)	6	Indigo/Sham
Throat Chakra (Vishuddha)	5	Blue/Hum
Heart Chakra (Anahata)	4	Green/Yam
Solar Plexus Chakra (Manipura)	3	Yellow/Ram
Sacral Chakra (Swadhisthana)	2	Orange/Vam
Root Chakra (Muladhara)	1	Red/Lam

Basic Human Chakra System

Chakra/Sanskrit Name		Color/Syllable
Crown Chakra (Sahasrara)	7	Violet/Om
Third Eye Chakra (Ajna)	6	Indigo/Sham
Throat Chakra (Vishuddha)	5	Blue/Hum
Heart Chakra (Anahata)	4	Green/Yam
Solar Plexus Chakra (Manipura)	3	Yellow/Ram
Sacral Chakra (Swadhisthana)	2	Orange/Vam
Root Chakra (Muladhara)	1	Red/Lam

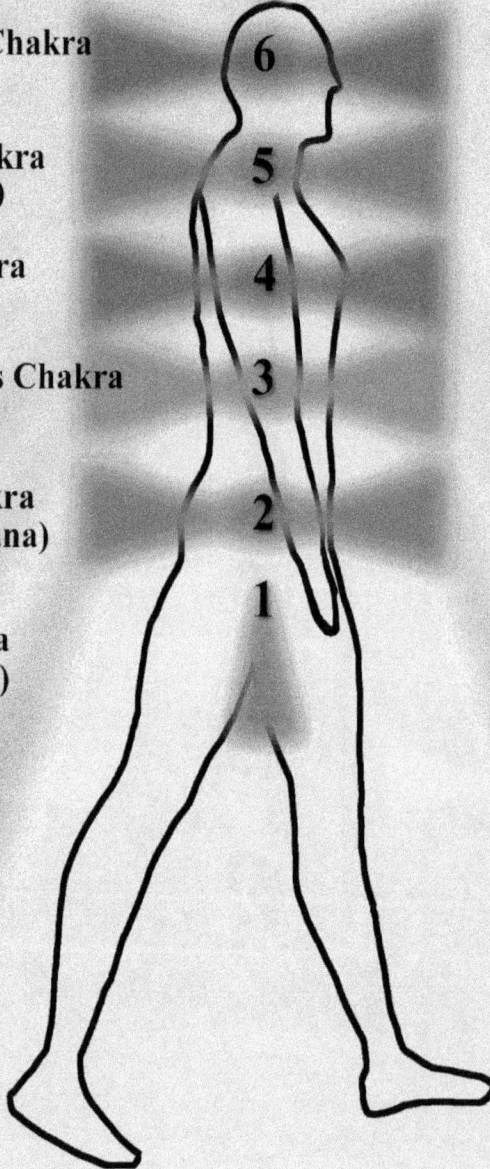

Meditation Posture

Yoga-Union of Mind, Body, Spirit, seeking Union with the
   Divine One
Mudra-Hand gesture that directs the flow of energy to body
   during meditation
Lotus Position-seated (appropriate for you), back straight,
   legs crossed, hands resting on knees, palms up, index fingers
   and thumbs touching, mindful natural breathing.

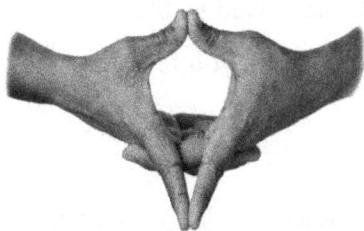

Uttarabodhi (Sanskrit) Hand Mudra
*Thumbs touching and index fingers touching (pointed
down), all other fingers intertwined at the Solar
Plexus level.*

. Inspires sense of inner unity and alignment with Divine Source.
. Enlightenment, insight, inspiration.
. Calms the mind, reduces stress levels, improves concentration.
. Dispels fear, realization to fear nothing or nobody except God.
. Problem solving, decision making.
. Improves self-confidence, realization of the Higher Self.
. Refreshes the body system and recharges it with energy.
. Shield for the body and mind from negative forces.

267

The First or Root Chakra is between the legs at the sacral-coccyx joint and is referred to by some as the sexual center along with the Second Chakra. It is strongly associated with our physical reality, our will to live, and is a generator of the energies of physical vitality. It is connected to the earth element and believed to be associated with the sense of smell. The uncoiling of the Kundalini is the manifestation and realization of optimum human potential by revitalizing and transforming all of the chakras as it rises in a manner that can spark enlightenment.

The Root Chakra has a shadow side when it is out of balance. Care is to be exercised in meditations that concentrate on the clearing of this area. The unleashing of a spontaneous Kundalini awakening before one is prepared for the rush of energy associated with the raising of it is something that some have not survived intact. I experienced this phenomenon after a spiritual breakthrough in my studies. It felt as though a bolt of lightning entered through the base of my spine, shot up my spinal column and out through the top of my head. I shook as if gripped by a seizure of some sort for over twenty minutes. After medical professionals failed to explain what had happened to me and ruled out any physical cause, I consulted a spiritual professional and established the connection between that experience and an overwhelming spiritual epiphany that occurred just before it. Kundalini meditation practices are to be studied with a knowledgeable and experienced teacher that you feel comfortable with and whom you feel you can trust.

*Focus on the energy of the Root Chakra and visualize **red light** whirling in a clockwise motion, gaining momentum with the intensity of your focused visualization and depth of breath. I release this issue to the Holy Spirit and ask for a healing to take place in my life.*

Speak to it and say:
"I release this issue to The Great Spirit and ask for a healing to take place in my life."

The Second Chakra or Navel Chakra is located just above the pubic bone on the back and front of the body. It is the seat of our emotions and is approximately located at the center of the sacrum. The Second Chakra is associated with the water element and is connected to feelings of sexual passion, danger, health, energy, and hate. Some believe this chakra is associated with the sense of taste. It generates energy for the immune system and the sexual organs.

People that operate primarily on the lower chakra levels are considered to be functioning at the basest level of human existence. As vital as it is to keep this very important chakra in optimum health, it is nearly animalistic to function only from the level of its intense, primal energy. It is also a chakra that is easily obstructed because of damage from repression and abuse.

An obstruction or imbalance can manifest in unbridled sensual indulgences, carnal, emotionless, even violent, or obsessive, compulsive behaviors. This kind of damage can reach back into a childhood wrought with extremes of restriction, taboos, and false or negative judgmental information regarding the sexual function. Damage can also occur as the result of the breach of boundaries through sexual abuse.

Focus on the energy of the Second Chakra and visualize **orange light** *whirling in a clockwise motion, gaining momentum with the intensity of your focused visualization and depth of breath.*

Speak to it and say:
"I release this issue to The Great Spirit and ask for a healing to take place in my life."

The Third Chakra or Solar Plexus Chakra is located in the Solar Plexus or upper abdominal area of our body. It is related to the element of fire and the principals of sight and light. It supplies energy to the stomach, gallbladder, liver, spleen, pancreas, and nervous system. As its name suggests, this chakra pulls from the energy of the Sun, distributing vital Life Force to all of the other centers. The spiritual planes provide a source of essential energy whether or not we tap into it during meditation. This chakra is associated with feelings of desire and acquisition. It is very sensitive to external stimuli. It is associated with our intuition we call "gut" feelings and directs how we connect with others.

For this reason, it is a chakra we should concern ourselves with about protection against those who seek to energetically *invade* and deplete our energy reserves to do us harm. The Third Chakra can serve as an effective point of entry, providing a portal through which energy can be absorbed and transmitted. Absorption of negative energies in this area is damaging to our overall health and well-being and are associated with psychic or spiritual attack.

It is advisable to do prayers for protection focusing on the Third (Solar Plexus) and Seventh (Crown) Chakra area before entering into meditation. Visualize a large, heavy, metal vault door that you may, at will, close and lock against those who may, either intentionally or unintentionally, drain or poison your energy. During a meditation that you find unusually exhausting, you may be experiencing an invading energy stemming from the influence of your own emotional state or an energetic attack from another. Simply shut and lock the impenetrable vault door to your Solar Plexus Chakra with intense protection prayers, enabling an energetic force field around you that will shield you from any attack.

*Focus on the energy of the Solar Plexus Chakra and visualize **yellow** or **golden light**, whirling in a clockwise motion, gaining momentum with the intensity of your focused visualization and depth of breath.*

Speak to it and say:
"I release this issue to The Great Spirit and ask for a healing to take place in my life."

The Fourth Chakra or Heart Chakra is located in the heart area and is associated with the emotion of love, balanced by will. It distributes energy to the heart, circulatory system, and upper back. This chakra is believed to be associated with the element of air and the sense of touch. The Fourth Chakra is associated with the emotional realm, the feelings, and sensations associated with love, compassion, warmth, empathy, and the pleasure center. It is the mid-point of the seven chakras, with three above and three below. It is the point where the spiritual and physical energetic meet, merge and determine the nature of a being.

When the energy of the Heart Chakra is balanced and healthy, it flows with love and compassion, forgiveness and a nurturing, healing, and acceptance. A closed or blocked Heart Chakra can give way to grief, anger, jealousy, fear of betrayal, abandonment issues, and emotionally crippling hatred of self and others. This tends to be the chakra that is most often obstructed or badly damaged due to emotional disappointment, trauma, anger, and an inability to forgive. Often people have experienced suffering so emotionally devastating that forgiveness is not easy, nor seemingly possible, without some manner of spiritual intervention.

It is important to concentrate on this area and send healing energy through meditation, visualization, and contemplation on the Divine. Affirm that nothing is greater than The Creator. Affirm that nothing is more healing than the contemplation of The Creator and that nothing is abler to facilitate a more powerful transformation. Forgiveness is the most powerful cure for blockages in the Heart Chakra center. No one is perfect. If we are so vain to expect forgiveness from others for our own imperfections, and not be willing to forgive others and ourselves, we cause ourselves abysmal emotional pain and suffering. To open wide, the receptive portals of intuition and discernment, the Heart Chakra must allow the unobstructed flow of positive energy. Meditation is one of the most effective ways to restore balance.

*Focus on the energy of the Heart Chakra and visualize **green light** whirling in a clockwise motion, gaining momentum with the intensity of your focused visualization and depth of breath.*

Speak to it and say:

"I release this issue to The Great Spirit and ask for a healing to take place in my life."

The Fifth Chakra or Throat Chakra is located in the front and back of the throat. It supplies energy to the bronchi, thyroid, lungs, and alimentary canal. This chakra is believed to be associated with the element of Ether and governs the principle of sound related to the sense of hearing. In situations of attempted entry by a negative energy or entity that has been projected with malefic intent, the point where the back of the neck and spine meet is a focal point of entry as well as a focal point of healing. Protect and cleanse this area with sage, frankincense, myrrh, salt, strong meditative energy, recitation of a mantra, and repetitive prayer.

The veils between the worlds become thin when engaging in Mystical Meditation, and nothing should be taken for granted or written off as coincidence. It is sometimes difficult to distinguish reasonable concern from paranoid delusion. That is why the faculties of spiritual discernment should be fine-tuned in every possible manner to ensure that we do not find ourselves vulnerable to attack. At the same time, we should ensure that we do not attack ourselves with our own ungrounded, unreasonable fears.

An otherwise amazing singer in a recording studio session went tone-deaf attempting to record a love song. She was suffering from a freshly broken heart. Everyone was tired and just wanted to go home. After the twelfth attempt, I asked her if she had experienced the recent break up of a relationship. She looked at me, shocked, and said that it happened the night before. I told her that was why she was struggling with such romantic lyrics and music. The emotional pain of the breakup had gridlocked the energy in her Heart Chakra, obstructing the flow of the First and

Fourth Chakra energy to her Fifth Chakra, affecting her voice. I asked her to go into the next room, sit down, breathe, and do a specific mudra (hand position) and mantra (chant) to clear the blockage. Twenty minutes later she walked out, went into the sound booth, and laid down the tune in one take. The Law of Attraction affirms that we speak things into and out of existence with the vibratory power of the spoken word. Silenced, unexpressed, or disregarded speech becomes the innermost cry of the voiceless. The result is the energetic obstruction of the Fifth Chakra, making any attempts at authentic communication a challenge.

The rebound effect of the power of the spoken word has inspired many common proverbs and quotes. It is said that before your words leave your mouth, you are their master. After they leave your mouth, you become their slave. The creative power of the spoken word is tried and true. The great poet Hafiz is quoted, *"The words you speak become the house you live in."*

Focus on the energy of the Throat Chakra and visualize **blue light** *whirling in a clockwise motion, gaining momentum with the intensity of your focused visualization and depth of breath.*

Speak to it and say:
"I release this issue to The Great Spirit and ask for a healing to take place in my life."

The Sixth Chakra or Third Eye Chakra is located on the forehead, at the mid-point between and just above the brow line. It is the area known as the Third Eye. It is believed to be the eye through which the astral body is able to see. It has been referred to as the "Psychic Eye," as it is considered to be the portal through which psychic energies are received and transmitted. It is the window through which we may view the astral and higher planes if we dare to enter and journey there. The Sixth Chakra is associated with the "Sixth Sense," Ether, Light, and the seat of the I AM Consciousness, the veil between worlds, the bridge between dreams. Its energies, from tradition to tradition, in ancient and contemporary spirituality, are identified many ways.

When we turn within and journey through the innermost planes of existence, we strip ourselves of our ego and our Self-limiting identifications, allowing us to let go of our fears of the loss of our *person*hood. Through Third Eye vision, we are able to see our essential nonphysical being, as well as that of others. We can access energies that are less available to us as we view ourselves only in a physical context. It is associated with paranormal experiences of all kinds. That includes, but is not limited to; clairvoyance, clairaudience, psychometry, telekinesis, energy healing, telepathy, prophecy, dreamtime, out of body experiences (OBE), insight, foresight, the powers of the mystic seer (Higher Self), the gift of viewing the subtle energies of chakras and auras, even visions into the Timeless realms, beyond past, present, and future. Some of the highest states of consciousness are associated with the Third Eye. Some call it the seat of the Natural Mystic, inducing states of a place in consciousness known by many names in various traditions; Samadhi, Turiya, Nirvana, Fanaa, Zazen, Dhyana, Moksha, Satori, Bliss, Jhana and others.

The Sixth Chakra is associated with the flow of energy to the pituitary, lower brain, left eye, ears, nose, and nervous system. It also facilitates transcendence to higher planes of consciousness and controls the many levels of concentration realized through Mystical Meditation. It affects inner and outer realities to the extent that it commands the whole of the personality. The positive energy of the Sixth Chakra (Third Eye) is maintained by deep levels of meditation, visualization, and embracing the spirit of compassion, forgiveness, and empathy. Sound and aromatherapy can contribute to the health of this sensitive chakra.

In the study of Psychic Self-Defense, the Third Eye is profoundly significant. It orchestrates the energetic fusion of all of the lower chakras. The rush of energy emanating from the First Chakra pushes its way up through the ambition and willfulness of the Second Chakra; the fiery spirit of the Third Chakra;

the compassionate spirit of the Fourth Chakra; the vibration and resonant incantations of the Fifth Chakra, speaking into the manifestation of the desires that emanate from the First Chakra; to rest comfortably in the seat of the soul, the Sixth (Third Eye) Chakra; touching Divine Will at the Crown, the Seventh Chakra. This pure magic is accompanied by a profound responsibility for the consequences of their manifestations, focusing on the nature of conscious and subconscious intention. For every pebble cast into the vast sea of Karma, the ripple effect reverberates beyond that, into the unknowable, and boomerangs right back into our lives and the lives we affect.

For this reason, among others, it is important to be mindful of the company we keep. We could be keeping company with someone who is incurring horrible Karma for whatever reason. Read the energy of the people you allow in your life and trust your intuition. If you have no power or influence to help the person or change the person or the group of people, it is important to understand the phenomenon of Group Karma. It is wise to distance ourselves from such negative energies whenever possible. It is always possible. Not doing so is like sitting on the lap of someone that owes a debt he or she cannot pay and consequently has a contract or price on their head. That puts you in just as much jeopardy as the person committing the Karma incurring offense. A determination such as this is to be made without exacting judgment because no one is perfect. We each go through what we must go through, at whatever juncture of our lives, to move us toward our eventual Self-Realization. Understanding this, we have the right and the responsibility to choose our associates wisely from among people with spiritual integrity.

*Focus on the energy of the Third Eye Chakra and visualize **indigo light**, (purple/violet, between red and blue on the color wheel used by painters) whirling in a clockwise motion, gaining momentum with the intensity of your focused visualization and depth of breath.*

275

Speak to it and say:

"I release this issue to The Great Spirit and ask for a healing to take place in my life."

The Seventh or Crown Chakra is located at the top of the head and has the highest rate of vibration of all the chakras. It supplies energy to our right eye and our upper brain. It is associated with the experience of direct contact with Divinity. The Crown Chakra is the doorway to the Sacred and should be protected and honored as such. It is guarded best through prayer, meditation, and ritual contemplation on The Divine One. When performing any sacred spiritual work, most mystical traditions advise that a head covering be worn to shield the Crown Chakra, symbolically deflecting energies that are not of Divine Source. It is symbolic in gesture to acknowledge that it is a sacred point of entry that is not open to welcoming any energies other than those, very specifically, of The Divine.

The Crown Chakra is the portal between the worlds. It is the gateway, on either side, for energies and entities from other planes of existence that may seek to manipulate, influence, and even inhabit or possess one's physical being. It is very important in protection exercises, before meditation and prayer, to concentrate on this area to enforce that nothing enters there except that which is of pure Divine Light.

It is not advisable to allow entry to anything other than the Pure Energy and Light of The God of our highest understanding, for it can be a very dangerous practice. We are not perfect. Our abilities to discern the quality and origin of the energies we allow to enter us in this fashion may not be as informed as we may think, even if we ascend to extremely high levels of consciousness. To avoid making the mistake of leaving the Crown Chakra or Third Eye Chakra open and available as a doorway to absorb energy, through meditation or other spiritual practices, we must perform a thorough banishing of unwanted energies and entities in our auric field and implement the strongest forms of spiritual protection.

The point where the base of the skull and the spine meet (Zeal Point - See diagram below) is a major focal point of entry. When a negative energy/entity enters or has been projected with malefic intent, through the Crown Chakra, the Third Eye Chakra, and/or the Zeal Point, a serious Spiritual Emergency can be triggered. The convergence point is the site for the perfect storm to deliver either a powerful healing or immeasurable harm. Protect and cleanse this area with sage, frankincense, myrrh, salt, strong meditative energy, recitation of a mantra, and most important … repetitive prayer. The Throat Chakra is able to generate a tonal vibration of protection and healing in the event of energetic invasions and related issues.

Perform the Light Meditation in this text. Visualize a sphere of pure, white/silver Light, the color of soft lightning just above your head. This sphere of Light is charged with strong prayers and positive affirmations of unwavering faith. Visualize it showering its beautiful Light in an energetic rain that covers your entire being in a clockwise, circular pattern, forming a glowing, egg-shaped, protective aura all around the physical self, as a shield, as illustrated in the aura graphics. Affirm that no weapon formed against you will prosper.

*Focus on the energy of the Crown Chakra and visualize **white light,** the color of soft white lightening (violet that glows white for its representation of the soul) whirling in a clockwise motion, gaining momentum with the intensity of your focused visualization and depth of breath.*

Speak to it and say:
"I release this issue to The Great Spirit and ask for a healing to take place in my life."

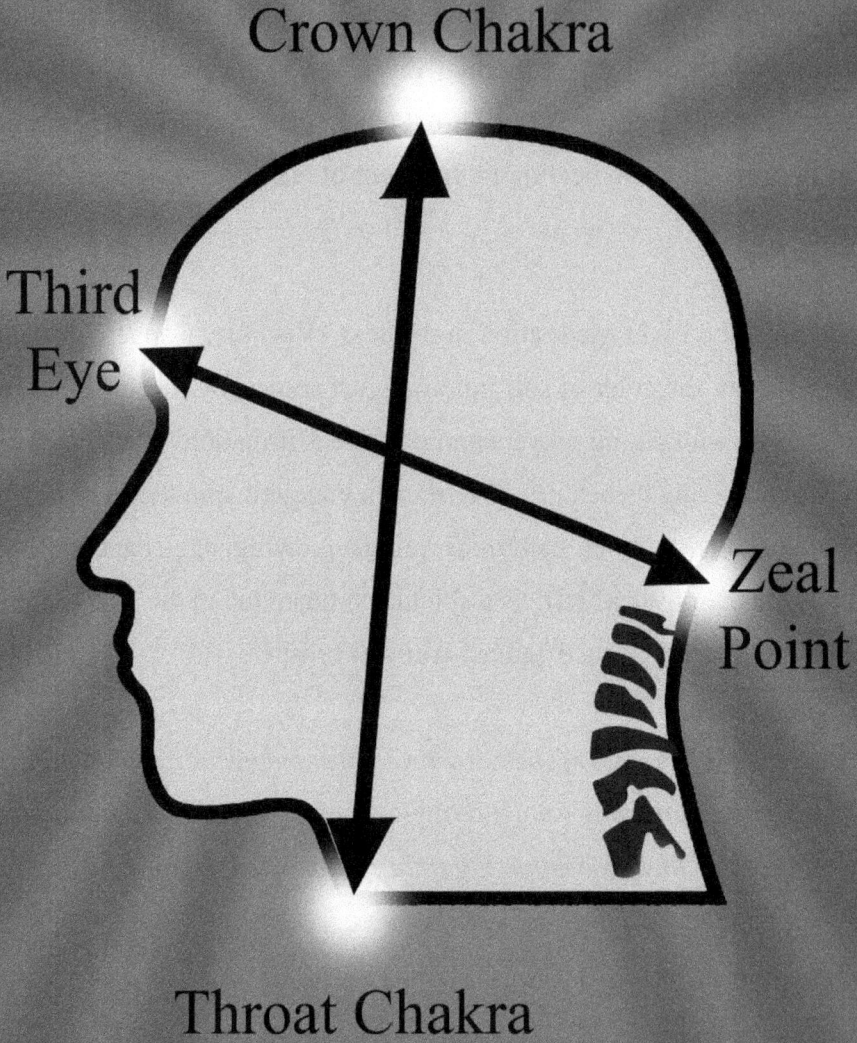

ENTRY POINTS FOR PSYCHIC ATTACK

Crown Chakra

Third Eye

Zeal Point

Throat Chakra

In all of these meditative exercises, with deep concentration, hold your focus on the color spinning clockwise in the vortex of each chakra. Fix your attention on the question or issue you have taken into your meditation to clear, cleanse, or heal.

After completing your meditation, as with all meditation practices, it is important to ground yourself before you resume your everyday activities, especially before you drive or perform any activity that would require alert, grounded concentration. If you feel light-headed or unfocused after your meditation, there are many ways to ground yourself. Bring yourself back to alertness by washing your face and hands with cold water, eating a serving of fruit, drinking a glass of cool or cold water, taking a brisk walk barefoot on the ground, playing music, dancing, or exercising.

There is a visualization that is commonly used for grounding that works well. Visualize yourself standing with your bare feet planted firmly on the ground or the floor, as close to ground level as possible. Imagine yourself sending roots, like those of a tree, down into the Earth. Inhale through your nostrils as you visualize pulling the Earth energy up through your roots. As you exhale, your roots are pushing deeper into the Earth. After several minutes you will return to your previous state of alertness.

Meditation Exercise to Strengthen the Seven Energy Centers

Painful memories and feelings can be trapped in Chakra Centers for years. Through a committed meditation discipline, these negative energies can be transmuted into pure white Light, illuminating colors corresponding with each chakra, as it is being healed. This spiritual cleansing can change the frequency and raise the vibration of the blocked chakra, in such a way as to repair damage caused by the negative energy that entered. Manifest a powerful healing throughout the entire energetic system with the strength of your intention.

When you responsibly address the life issues that the chakras govern, you will positively affect the optimal health and balance of each chakra. Avoidance of these issues can result in energetic depletion on all levels and will ultimately manifest as physical, mental, emotional and spiritual illness.

For example:

The lessons of the First Chakra are those of the physical or material world, issues of survival, self-defense, acquisition, and societal and family, law, and order. The First Chakra relates to sexuality, physical desire, ethics, guilt and blame, security and safety, control, and power. These issues, unresolved, will damage that chakra and directly affect the function of the Second through the Seventh or Crown Chakra. Any energy blockage that prevents the flow of the Chi, or Life Force, and the gentle rising of the Kundalini energy, is detrimental to the entire system. The practice of cleansing the seven energy centers causes a gradual energetic surge upward. It helps your practice to commit to memory, the correspondences, colors, and functions of each chakra.

Meditation Exercise: Ask yourself, "What are the issues relating to the "X" Chakra that I am not facing with responsibility?" Make a list of these issues. Take each issue into meditation after performing an elemental, cleansing meditation, affirming that this condition is being healed at its origin.

(As stated in the previous chapter, you must ground yourself to return to an alert state after any meditation.) After completing your meditation, as with all meditation practices, it is important to ground yourself before you resume your everyday activities, especially before you drive or perform any activity that would require alert, grounded concentration. If you feel light-headed or unfocused after your meditation, there are many ways to ground yourself. Bring yourself back to alertness by washing your face and hands with cold water, eating a serving of fruit, drinking a glass of cool or cold water, walking barefoot on the ground, playing music, dancing, or exercising, taking a brisk walk.

There is a visualization that is commonly used for grounding that works well. Visualize yourself standing with your bare feet planted firmly on the ground or the floor. Imagine yourself sending roots down into the Earth. Inhale through your nose and pull the Earth energy up through your roots. As you exhale, your roots are pushing deeper into the Earth. After several minutes, you will return to your previous state of alertness.

Human Chakra System

Energy of: **Obstructed by:**

Realm of Divinity   **7**   Ego-based Body/Mind
Identity Attachment

Vision/Intuition   **6**   Attachment to Illusion

Truth   **5**   Deceit/Hypocrisy

Love   **4**   Sorrow/Grief
Heartbreak

Will/Determination   **3**   Faithlessness

Desire   **2**   Guilt/Remorse

Survival/Existential
Issues   **1**   Fear-based
Consciousness

FEATURED MEDITATION:
THE
LIGHT MEDITATION

Journaling

Keeping a written journal is important. Technology can track and record our "doings" reliably. But how do we track our "beings" in such a way that we would not worry that our very soul was being surveilled? We do not express ourselves the way we used to. We are equipped now with a spell check, auto-correct, and tight margins that weigh and measure our "published" material against the vision of a monitoring eye of judgment.

Pen and notebook in hand, we must journal outside of the framework of all of our *doings*. How often do we stop and quietly reflect on how and who we are *being*? How often do we have that conversation with ourselves? How often should we engage in Self-Inquiry, beginning with the meditation, Who am I? We must inquire of ourselves ... *beyond* rank identifications, *beyond* personhood, parenthood, gender, religion, race, nationality, and career ... *Who* am I being? Who am I *really*? How am I *being* as a force on a mission in this Self-created reality?"

Self-Inquiry is vital to our being. We must concern ourselves with our *beings* at *least* as much as we concern ourselves with our *doings*. The written journal of our contemplations and inquiry into the Source of our being gives us dots to connect when we revisit our journal entries. Journaling helps to connect the dots of the shape-shifting nature of our experiencing. It offers clarity to our understanding of the intoxicating and seductive realms of Maya (the impermanent, illusory, material world) and allows us to document our spiritual transcendence of it.

The question, "Who am I?" is the beginning of a powerful conversation toward Self-Realization. If we are to defend ourselves against attacks that we perceive to be traveling through invisible realms of influence, how can we do that if we don't even know who we really are? Who is the "I" that we defend? Is it the ceaselessly morphing, carnal being staring back at us from the mirrors of life from the cradle to the grave? Can we trust that "I" in the mirror that is perpetually changing in predictable and unpredictable ways as we helplessly witness? Generally, that is the "I" a psychic attacker targets. If you have a thorough knowledge of Self, any attacker is confused as they stare at the "I" they can see, only to find that the unseen stares back. It is a confident awareness that knows, even though it cannot be seen, it is a powerful witness who is being observed by the "Ultimate I," that Sees, Knows, and Protects.

In matters that require Psychic Self-Defense, it enhances our spiritual practice to keep a journal or diary and designate specific times to consult it. Make a meditation of that consultation. Review it periodically to chart your progress towards accomplishing the spiritual goals you have set for yourself. If messages and information you receive in a meditation draw a complete blank and make no sense to you, by all means, record that in your journal. The meaning will unfold in its own time. Track related events using your journal. A journal is an excellent way of monitoring subtle nuances of multi-layered meanings that memory cannot be trusted to preserve. That will facilitate the decoding of cryptic communications from Spirit that tend to expand in clarity over time.

You will notice as you begin to establish a healthy relationship with the practice of Self-Inquiry meditation, your dreams will begin to change dramatically. You will go into deeper REM states that can free you to astral travel farther than you ever imagined possible. You will receive communications and profound insights into your dreams. You may even be connecting with other intelligences, which is nothing to be afraid of, provided the communications are positive. Fear only attracts the object of our fears. There is nothing to fear if spiritual protection through prayer is practiced, respecting the sacred union between Creator and creation.

It is very important to record your dreams in your journal immediately upon awakening. If there was anything particularly disturbing about your dream and you

285

wish to determine its meaning, go into prayer, meditation, and even fasting. Always consult a medical professional before taking a fast. Do not take vain "demands" into prayer, meditation, or fasting. That is disrespectful of this sacred process. Be patient. No prayer goes unanswered. Answers will come, and guidance will be given. When you receive the understanding you seek, record this information in your journal. Pay close attention to the gradual unfolding of the meaning. Refer back to your notes to expand on your interpretations often.

Keep your journal under password, lock, and key. I trust that no one would be so invasive as to violate anyone in this manner. Still, I encourage you to *lock up your journal*. Your journal will contain very personal information that you may not want to share with *anyone*.

Basic Guidelines for Meditation

Before engaging in any meditation: As was previously mentioned … Observe recommended basic protocol regarding personal hygiene and be attentive to the cleanliness and ambiance of your setting. Sit in a private, quiet, comfortable place with soft lighting, where you will not be disturbed. Assume an erect, comfortable posture. Facing the East is best, energetically. Touch your tongue to the roof of your mouth and clench the buttocks to effectively channel and contain the flow of energy. Touch your thumb to the index finger of your hands, rest them, palms up, on your thighs/knees. If you are not physically able to sit in a full or modified Lotus position, be mindful of your posture and sit up in a comfortable chair. A style of meditation called Yoga Nidra is practiced lying down. There are as many styles and techniques as there are amazing meditation instructors and practitioners.

Prepare a quiet place for prayer and meditation. There should be no television, radio, electronic devices, or distracting conversation. The telephone should be turned off, along with anything else that could startle or disturb you. It is recommended that you remove watches and ticking clocks from your sacred space. Be conscious of excessive exposure to electromagnetic currents for their ability to scramble your frequency.

Keep the lighting warm and avoid fluorescent lighting. Avoid meditating in complete darkness and never meditate under fluorescent or CFL (compact fluorescent lighting). They disrupt your auric field, causing it to become disoriented. They produce dead orgone energy that can compromise your immune system, your moods, and make you sick. Dead orgone (universal Life Force) energy from fluorescent lighting can be blocked by safely using a decorative cloth covering as shading, to lessen exposure to its harmful effects. A single white candle can be a relaxing focal point.

Take particular care in the maintenance of a clean, healthy aura. The human aura can be negatively affected by the energy you expose yourself to. Thoughts are things. We are all being constantly bombarded with negative thought-forms, energies, and vibrations from our environment, as well as the negativity that we generate from within ourselves. The electromagnetic force field around the physical body requires maintenance to keep it cleansed of the garbage that so easily attaches to it and drains our positive energy. An accumulation of this negative energy can make us walking magnets for bad experiences and compromised health. An unhealthy aura is a breeding ground for spiritual, mental, emotional, and physical disease.

The aura may be cleansed in many ways, including the use of crystals and semi-precious stones, which promote balance and restore positive energy. Proper use of certain types of crystals can improve psychic and spiritual abilities when used in meditation, with the understanding, of course, that the magic is not in the crystals. The magic is in you. Understand, as well, that this is not trendy jewelry. If you are not prepared to study and practice the proper care and maintenance of crystals and other sacred meditation tools, it is best just to leave them alone. A whole book can be written about how to respect their sacred energy. Spiritual cleansing baths, meditation, and prayer are powerful purification practices for the personal self and sacred paraphernalia.

Be mindful of your breathing. Use your breath as a focal point in your meditations. As a way of staying focused and raising your vibration, the chanting of a mantra sacred to you helps to facilitate cleansing and protection. Be mindful of the mantra that you choose to chant. Make sure that if it is in a language that you do not understand, get the literal translation and study it before you continue your practice. I have witnessed people chanting up their worst nightmares because of a misguided meditation practice and a carelessly chosen mantra. One of the greatest mantras is simply *Thank You.* Chant it and become Conscious gratitude, living under Ultimate Grace. I do not recommend any particular mudra (hand, finger, posture positions) to perform the meditations in this book. I use a basic tip of the index finger touching the tip of the thumb, palms up, resting on the knees, upright modified lotus position. Many variations of that will work. It is worth the effort to research and experiment with the mudras that are best for your preferred system of meditation. It is not a cursory study, but it is a rewarding one that is certainly worth the effort.

Don't eat, drink, smoke, chew gum, or participate in idle chatter when engaged in spiritual work. This behavior is distracting and vulgar. You are cultivating your ability to focus and concentrate, and you do not want to engage in gross and disruptive behaviors. That does not show a proper level of respect for yourself or the sacredness of spiritual practice. These guidelines fall under the category of common manners.

No alcohol or drugs. Do not ingest any substance that would alter your consciousness before, during, or after meditating. This absolutely includes consciousness-altering pharmaceutical drugs. Consult with the medical practitioner who prescribed your medication and ask if there are risks that are relevant to a meditation practice. Any substance that causes impairment can attract energies and entities that are better left crouching in the distance far, far away. Depending upon the depth of your trance or dream state, there are times during sleep and meditation, when you are, as pure conscious awareness, drifting out of the physical body. That is risky enough without adding intoxicants that distort the effects and experience of meditation to the equation. It can result in adding increased and dangerous detachment between the physical and non-physical bodies.

Meditating while intoxicated is as dangerous as driving drunk. You may provide a willing host for some random discarnate being, wandering through the lower Astral Planes, anxious to seize a form as you drift out of a drunk or drugged body. It may not even be personal. In this book, I have precisely documented my research, however, what I share is mostly based on decades of personal experience.

Do not meditate under the influence of any form of intoxicant! Even after meditation, it is not wise to fall under the influence of any intoxicating substance. You may not be grounded enough to maintain complete control of your energies.

It is not advisable to go into deep meditation on a full stomach. Though there are no hard and fast rules on this one. Eating a heavy meal before meditation and spiritual practice inhibits the ability to focus and concentrate because of our grounded energy. A full stomach can dull the senses and interfere with the discernment of subtle communications.

Take a question into meditation. Never go into a meditation without a prayer of total submission to the Will of The God and a spirit of gratitude and humility. Given certain necessary conditions, you can spontaneously tap into a current of Timeless information, past, present, and future, that can direct and assist you in life. Ask for guidance.

Evoke the protective White Light of Divine Spirit to envelop the essence of every manifestation of your being. The deepest and most profound meditations are entered into in a prayerful state of mind. The feeling of safety and security will enable you to relax, knowing that you are cloaked in Divine protection. Know that the Light that protects us is the Light that we are. We emanated from that Light.

Hold all information revealed in a Mystical Meditation in strict confidence, especially if it relates to someone else. Never reveal information you have received relating to someone else to anyone other than the person that it involves. It is a spiritual violation. It is as unethical as a medical doctor or therapist betraying the confidence of a patient by disclosing personal information shared in consultation.

Never diagnose an illness, even if the information you have received in a meditation reveals information that indicates there is a problem. Heed messages and warnings, and then consult a trusted medical professional. Do not be an alarmist. You can *create* illness and disease in your mind and body if you are not careful about the interpretation of what is perceived to be negative information. A fear-based interpretation can result in life-harming choices. Use discretion. It is dangerous, as well as illegal, to diagnose illness in such a way as to practice medicine if you intuit information for others in your meditations or dreams.

It is best to avoid meditation when tired, sick, angry, extremely depressed, or in a general state of extreme fatigue. Your unstable, ungrounded energy may compromise your meditation experience. Remember that gloomy moods can alter the quality of your meditation. It would be advisable to pray your strongest prayer before entering into a meditative state.

Journal changes in your sleep patterns. This is not Law, but you may notice your dream patterns changing as you begin to open the doors of forgotten chambers of your subconscious mind, through meditation. Studying and practicing a discipline of meditation will trigger spontaneous releases of memory, connecting you to other frequencies and realities. The act of meditating is so powerfully charged with cosmic energy that welcome or unwelcome drama may become attracted to your dreamtime world. Many tried, and true, ancient and modern practices will keep you in charge of the company you keep, whether you are awake or asleep.

A Note of Caution:

The studies in this text are for informational purposes only and not intended to diagnose, treat, cure, or prevent any disease. If you are experiencing symptoms of diagnosed or undiagnosed emotional or mental illness, clinical depression, thoughts of harming yourself or others, or seized by overwhelming health issues that would impair judgment, attempting certain types of meditation, may not be advised, as it may cause these feelings to intensify. You are encouraged to consult with a licensed therapist or medical professional.

Care for Accessories

Recommended care for Mystical Meditation tools and accessories begins with keeping them wrapped in silk or wool in a clean environment. These fabrics hold the energy and vibration of our accessories and can protect them from the attachment of lower energies, entities, and vibrations. Pouches or scarves made of these materials can be found in any metaphysical book and supply store, or even better, we can add our personal touch, be creative, and make them ourselves. These accessories are easy to make and will provide the opportunity to stitch our own spiritual energy into every seam of the fabric of our choice.

Meditation Tools and Accessories

- Head covering to symbolize the closure of the Crown Chakra to all but the Energy of The God;

- White candles, ranging in size from a birthday cake candle to a seven-day candle. The flame of the candle represents the element of Fire, the Original Flame of the One Divine Creator. White represents the Radiant Light of the Infinite Divine Essence we share with The Creator;

- Stones, salt, plants or flowers to represent the element of earth;

- A wooden box that can be locked, large enough to store meditation tools and sacred books. A note regarding crystals … Yes, they are beautiful. Yes, they are conductors of powerful energy, but you must be prepared to care for them in a very specific, prescribed manner, or their energy can turn destructive;

- A bowl or chalice for water to represent the element of water;

- Prayer beads used to keep count of repetitive prayer while maintaining a firm meditation. They are also used in meditations that involve the chanting of mantras;

- Incense holder, incense, and sage to represent the element of air. There are many types of incense with varied alchemical properties that attract specific energies. Frankincense, myrrh, lavender, rose, and sage are appropriate for most spiritual occasions. There is a long list of the attractive energies which correspond with the wide array of incense types. Though it is good to have such knowledge, I assert that the exercise of the soul's spiritual muscle, and the strength of faith and energy of our prayer work, is more important than what type of incense we are burning;

- Prayer rug and/or meditation cushion or stool symbolically declares the boundaries of our sacred space. A sacred circle of Light forms around us as we humble ourselves in praise, remembrance, and total submission to the Divine Will of That Which Created All.

Traditional storage of Mystical Meditation accessories requires that they are wrapped in silk or wool fabric placed in a wooden box, preferably, a box that can be locked. Because of their alchemical properties, it is wise to store crystals and other gemstones, along with incense, sage, and salt in the same box. This offers protection from uninvited, unwelcome energies (with and without bodies), as well as providing a pleasant, spiritually clean atmosphere for our sacred items.

Our meditation accessories have an aura of their own. Their aura, much like our human aura, can attract and collect both positive and negative energy. Clear quartz crystals can help keep the electromagnetic energy field surrounding the physical body, as well as our accessories clean and strong. Keeping a positive and clean aura is important. The aura reflects the condition of our spiritual, mental, emotional, and physical bodies. Our energy field appears as visible light and color to some who possess the gift of seeing auras. This magnetic force field can become polluted and toxic, ultimately causing spiritual, mental, emotional, and physical illness.

Crystals can clear, transform, purify and balance stagnant, negative energy when worn, carried, or placed near the body. To protect yourself and the items you hold sacred from the effects of absorbing negative energy you must employ the basic practices of physical and spiritual cleanliness. Our sacred personal belongings have a distinguishing personality, a heartbeat, literally throbbing with energy. The more bonded we are to our spiritual accessories, the sooner we realize that they have a discernible pulse! They may appear inanimate, but they have life and energy. We must respect that.

The following affirmation is designed to assist in charging, dedicating, and activating crystals, candles, and other spiritual accessories. It is wise to be aware of explicit ritual protocol:

I am one with The Creator
From Spirit, I have come
To Spirit, I connect
We become as One

In the name of all
that is good and right
In the Name of Love
and Pure Divine Light

Join The "I in I" now
Join The "I in I" here
Dispel the shadows
Dispel the fear

Within this circle
of Light I cast
I heal the Karma
of lifetimes past

I banish the darkness
with this candle's flame
I offer this petition
in The Creator's Holy Name

For the highest good
of all concerned
With intention and Divine Will
this candle burns

According to Free Will
and harming none
so, must it be
Divine Will be done

Meditation tools and accessories can absorb both positive and negative energies. They need to be cleansed periodically, whether they are stored or worn. There are many ways to cleanse accessories. The easiest way is to expose them to sunlight for a day or so. Soaking them in ocean water cleanses and recharges them. If there is no ocean access, they can be soaked overnight in a glass bowl of water containing one tablespoon of sea salt. Placing them on a bed of amethyst quartz overnight also performs a clearing or cleansing.

It is advised to allow our accessories to rest between sessions in the East, in a dark, private environment. The East is considered the origin, the "cradle of civilization," and the birthplace of the wisdom of the ancients. The sunrise in the East represents the source of spiritual energy and rejuvenation. We face the East in our spiritual practice out of recognition and respect for the source of the wisdom that we seek. For this reason, it is beneficial to face the East as we stand before our altar or in our sacred place for ritual prayer and meditation.

Our spiritual supplies should be stored in a locked box because it is not a good idea to let others, not even people that you consider close to you, handle your accessories when you are not present, *especially children*. Children are attracted to their energy and may play with them innocently, thinking it is a game, or that these things are toys. They may come in contact with something they do not have the knowledge to understand correctly and be affected in a negative or even detrimental way.

Spiritual accessories are serious tools to be used for healing, counseling, and connecting with The Divine Spirit of The God for guidance. They should never be treated casually. It is our responsibility to safeguard our sacred belongings to preserve their spiritual integrity and protect them from being misused, abused, or used for irresponsible or negative activities. Loaning, borrowing, or sharing spiritual tools and accessories is strongly discouraged. Purchasing used spiritual accessories is not wise. For energetic reasons, it is also unwise to use or carry sacred spiritual tools into places, or the company of people, that may compromise the integrity of their energy.

We are the keeper of our Temple. Our Temple is where we say it is ... that sacred place in our hearts. We are our Temple. Our Tabernacle is in our head. It is our spiritual responsibility to guard against desecration of the sacredness of the Temple realm we have consecrated. We all have a fundamental knowledge of the basics of respectful conduct in a spiritual Temple. Out of respect, it is unwise to take spiritual accessories, symbols, or sacred literature, into unclean places such as the bathroom. It is also recommended that no sacred literature be stored below waist level. Certain wall hangings with sacred inscriptions, though presented in the form of art, are never to be exposed to, or displayed in environments where lewd or disrespectful acts may be committed. This type of sacred art is best reserved for display in a place designated as sacred or consecrated, clean, and free of the energy of others. Avoid placing graven images representing deities on our altars, in homes, cars, or workplaces.

By respecting our spirituality and the sacred objects we associate with its practice, we are not "worshipping" the tools. We are respecting them for the service they provide us, and we are respecting ourselves as wise, humble, spiritually adept people. It is the most basic of spiritual knowledge that tells us the implications of carrying or placing crystals, meditation beads, or any other paraphernalia into a dirty environment, a bar or social setting where alcohol or drugs may be present. Avoid tobacco laced environments and being around people with negative spiritual energy. Some things go without saying to any reasonably intelligent person. If we are wise enough to pursue such an advanced path of spirituality, we must be wise enough to understand how to protect ourselves and our spiritual tools and accessories, respecting their sacredness as well as our own.

Blessing Candles and Meditation Tools

Candlelight has long been associated with romantic ambiance and acknowledged as a representation of the spark of the Original Flame of Divinity by many spiritual and religious traditions. The flickering of the candle's flame can create an atmosphere of meditative relaxation, which helps direct the intention and focus of our prayers and meditations. Our goal is to send a strong prayer to The Creator, to be protected by The Creator, and to connect with, and submit to The Creator. The props are not to get The God's attention. The props are to focus and direct our own scattered attention.

I am not discrediting or devaluing proper ritual work. It has incredible value. My point is, without the *emotion, energy,* and *intention* that we charge the candles with, you've got nothing but wax, wicks, and a purposeless flame. A candle without a prayer is like a rebel without a cause. On the other hand, a prayer without a candle, oh well, I think you can guess where I am going with this. I am stressing the magic of the prayer and the intention, *not* the magic of wax, or the colors of the candles, the exactness of the timing, nor the elaborate perfection of the ritual.

For our purposes, solid white candles will suffice. We will get the ambiance and the focal point to strengthen our ability to concentrate on our intention. We will, more powerfully, anchor our intention. As long as we can maintain here that *no particular paraphernalia is necessary, nor required, to commune with The Creator,* let's explore a few methods used to prepare candles that may increase our own abilities to focus, concentrate and intensify the projection of our desired purpose.

Etch the intention on the candle itself. This can be a tedious process. It requires patience to inscribe an entire prayer on an eight-inch taper candle. You may want to keep it brief and simple.

Do not engage in manipulative requests. More often than not, if we were to get exactly what we want, exactly how we want it, we will have manifested some of our worst nightmares. Look back in time at some of the things we have wanted in the past. At the time of our desiring it, we thought it would be a blessing, only to discover that it turned out to feel like a curse. That is why it is so important to be humble, realizing that we don't always know what is best for ourselves and the highest good of all concerned. It is vital to our happiness and success that we are willing to submit our desires to alignment with the Divine Creator's Will, Purpose, and Intention for our lives.

"According to Free Will, for the highest good of all, harming none." These conditions should always be added to prayer requests. If any of these conditions are violated, no good can come from it. If harm comes to anyone as a result of our misguided prayers, we have exposed ourselves to the "three times three Law of Karma" ... negative consequences come back three times if the intention is *un*conscious, and *three times three* if it is intentional. We must ask ourselves first, "How will I feel *when* this comes back to me?"

Anoint the candle. It is important for the petitioner to focus on the intended purpose of the candle when anointing the candle. Use a few drops of oil consecrated with the breath of the prayer. Olive oil works well. The more intense our concentration, the greater the chances are of communicating our wishes with maximum clarity. Holy Water (consecrated in prayer), and a variety of essential oils are used to anoint candles. Let us never forget that the magic is not in the oil. The magic is not in the candle. The magic is sparked by the alignment of our energy with the flow of the mystical energies of the Universe, our ability to connect completely with the Creator, and the clarity and intention of our communication, in accordance with Divine Will.

Never use a match. The alchemical properties of sulfur are counterproductive to a positive outcome.

We should never extinguish the candle with our breath. It is best to use a snuffer, fan with your hand, or, preferably, let it burn down to the point that it extinguishes itself, assuming that it is safe to do so.

THE LIGHT
MEDITATION

I AM PROTECTED
AS THE ETERNAL LIGHT

Basic Guidelines to Follow for The Light Meditation

The Light Meditation should be performed before engaging in any spiritual ritual work or meditation. It is designed to cleanse and activate the energies of our Chakra System to facilitate balance, harmony, and protection. It is a useful meditation that can be practiced daily with your prayer of choice for energy maintenance and as a spiritual shield. This guided audio meditation is available as a download on the *dreamuniversalmedia.com* website. **(See the Chapter called Meditation Download Instructions at the back of this book.)** The transcript of the Light Meditation is presented here for your perusal to assure that you are aware of and aligned with all aspects of its content.

THE LIGHT MEDITATION
TRANSCRIPT

I am seated in a comfortable position

facing the direction of the rising Sun

My back is straight

My feet are touching the floor

My hands rest palms up

I close my eyes

My mind's eye envisions

a single white candle that I light

with the intention of inner illumination

from my most profound depths

extending to the Origin of my existence

the Focal Point of Ultimate Light

From this comfortable seated position … I breathe

I Am the OBSERVER and WITNESS of my breath

as it touches the middle of my upper lip

I observe the sensations for qualities

such as heat, coolness, moisture, dryness

I observe … undistracted by these sensations

I go within.

I slip between the invisible pockets of silence

between my inhaled and exhaled breath

My attention goes to the sensation of my breath

as it flows across the center groove of my upper lip

The focus of my awareness moves to my Solar Plexus
the 3rd Chakra
At its most profound point, there is an ethereal SILVER CORD
anchored in my physical reality
to ground me … to guide me
back to the starting point of my journey if I should need it

A pinpoint of Light pulsates
to the rhythm of my heartbeat
and radiates from that focal point of Light
expanding to extend to, and beyond my entire body
enveloping me in this pure, radiant, protective Light
extending beyond me to envelop this room
extending beyond this room to envelop this entire building
this entire city and far beyond
seeking and connecting
to its Point of Origin.

I inhale through my nostrils
I exhale through my mouth
I inhale LIGHT
I exhale FEAR
I cup my hands over my mouth
to collect sacred breath laced with golden Light and positive intention

I inhale Light and become it
I exhale fear and rebuke it

The silver cord that extends
from my navel area at the CORE of my being
dispels all fear as my consciousness drifts

It will guide me back
to my comfort zone
and starting point
whenever I choose

I cup my hands over my mouth
to collect the breath of my earnest petition
right hand over the left
good over evil
knowing one defines the other.

In my working breath
are words of power
and utterances of commandments
a release
a surrender
of all that is of Maya
all that is temporary
I release my attachment to the CHANGEFUL
I embrace only the UNCHANGING
INCLUDING the so-called "self"
of my own lower perceptions
I embrace all that I really am
BREATH, AWARENESS, CONSCIOUSNESS
INTO THE STILLNESS THAT I AM

I suspend my senses
I shut down
I open up
Calm and focused breath
occurs in natural rhythms

I inhale through my nostrils

I exhale through my mouth

I inhale LIGHT and become it

I exhale FEAR and rebuke it

I inhale golden Light

I cup my hands over my mouth

to collect my breath

laced with THIS golden Light and focused intention

I use it to dispel and cleanse unwelcome energies

It is charged with the intention of attracting the healing that I desire

With this sacred Light Breath

I wash MY HANDS

then MY FACE

of all carnal witnessing and unsavory desires

I cleanse MY NOSE of the scent of the shadow worlds

MY EYES … of all they have seen of suffering

I cleanse MY Third Eye … 6th Chakra

located between my eyebrows

of all it has observed of lower vibrations

MY EARS … of the filth they have heard

I cleanse MY INNER AND OUTER VOICE at the throat level,

the energy vortex of my 5th Chakra

I cleanse thought-forms, both spoken and silenced, that traveled

on wings of words that injure like bullets and blades

I HEAL that with this sacred breath of radiant Golden Light

I cleanse MY CROWN, 7th Chakra at the top of my head

of all that has ever sought to come between my Higher Self and my Source the Source of all … The Ultimate Reality

With this sacred Light Breath
I move my attention down to the back of MY NECK
I cleanse and seal this entry point of whispered suggestions
from the lower planes of consciousness
seeking a home … seeking manifestation
through MY mind and spirit

I cleanse my feet of every step they strayed
from the path of my Enlightenment
with Golden Light
of Sacred Breath
My footsteps are guided
My path is protected
My journey is blessed
I inhale LIGHT and become it
I exhale FEAR and rebuke it
Hands cupped over my mouth,
right hand over the left,
I collect this Sacred Breath in my hands
I hold it to MY HEART
HEALING CLEANSING ENERGY OF GOLDEN LIGHT
enters MY HEART at my 4th Chakra
whirling, spinning, yielding in surrender
to my connection to Divinity
I accept that I am healed by this Breath of Light

I cleanse myself of the PAIN I have suffered that seeks to break me
I cleanse myself of emotional attachments to joy
that seeks to ADDICT me and CONTROL me

I am not my emotions
I am not my past
I am not my future
I am not my mind
I AM MORE THAN THAT

I break through the mirror of illusion
I forsake the lies that seek to define me
as less than an Eternal being of Divine Essence

I inhale through my nostrils
I exhale through my mouth
I inhale LIGHT and become it
I exhale FEAR and rebuke it

I inhale Light
I cup my hands over my mouth to collect
breath laced with golden Light and positive intention
My mantra is
Thank You
My mantra is
Thank You

With this golden breath, I shield my Solar plexus
from all energies that may seek to enter uninvited, unwelcome,
with their urges and weaknesses, cravings and clinging,
anger and unforgiveness, seeking to eclipse my will
with its self-serving obsessions and uncontrollable
desires and projections, seeking to make me believe they are my own

Sacred breath is the BRIDGE between the many selves that I am

from the lower to the upper realms of consciousness

With it, I have cleansed and sealed this space that I am

I do not stand alone as its gatekeeper

I am protected from creation

That Which created me sustains me

I inhale through my nostrils

exhale through my mouth

I inhale Light and become it

I exhale fear and rebuke it

I inhale Light

I cup my hands over my mouth to collect

breath laced with golden Light and positive intention

With this breath, I shield my 2nd Chakra

located in the area of my lower abdomen

the seat of all desire, attachment, and aversion

With this sacred breath of pure Golden Light

I suspend my senses

I cleanse the lower energetic, sensual,

carnal aspects of my being and heal them in the Eternal Now

The cleansing breath of Golden Light subdues the raging fire of my Root Chakra

the 1st Chakra - Sacral Chakra

sending this creative energy rising into the Golden Light

of the manifestation of my authority over my own animalistic nature

This primal fuel energizes all of the other chakras as it gently rises,

Uncoiled Golden Light of purification

Rising

Up,

Up,

Up through the 2nd Chakra below the navel

Cleansing … Releasing negative energies

Up,

Up,

Up the Spine through the spiraling vortex of the 3rd Chakra

Spinning beautiful waves of Golden Light

gently rushing up this life-enabling thread of creation's energy

Releasing … Cleansing … Healing … Illuminating

With Golden waves of Light energy

sweeping clean all residue ... all debris

All attachment … All aversion … all longing for all else

but The Beloved … The Divine One

My mantra is

Thank You

My mantra is

Thank You

CLEANSING LIGHT gently rises through the 4TH Chakra … MY HEART …

healing it from the senseless acts of emotional savagery it has suffered …

Loving it for all of the Love it is capable of … trusting it with my life.

I close my body down

I am not my body

I am not my mind

I am not my emotions

I AM MORE THAN THAT

I suspend my senses
I break the mirror of illusion

I meditate on the Light that I AM
the Light of the Eternal I AM

I have manifested on this plane
from the realm of the Divine One
I have expressed myself as my desire
for this Sacred Journey
from the angelic realm
the realm of the guides,
the realm of the Sacred
the abode of the prophets,
the mystics, the messengers, and servants
of the Most High GOD

Breath and Light are One
The Light of my Core Being
is One with the Core Point of Light
expressed out of triple darkness,
the Consciousness, the Love of the Ultimate I AM,
the Unknowable One, the Limitless One,
Whose name is best expressed by SILENCE.

My most sacred mantra is
Thank You

Beautiful energy has gathered in my HEART Chakra …
the Temple of my Beloved
the Temple of the Divine One

In Love … Golden Light energy continues to rise … powerfully … subtly

Up through my 5th Chakra at my throat

Up through my 6th Chakra, my Third Eye

Reaching the 7th Crown Chakra

GOLDEN ENERGY collected at the top of my head

connecting with my strongest PRAYER

Connecting with my strongest prayer

Connecting with my strongest prayer

I pray

I pray for protection from all unwelcome,

Uninvited energies

(silence during prayer)

Shhhhhhhhh

I accept this cloak of protection

enveloping the entire form of my body

physical and formless

cleansing my aura, purifying my intentions,

closing out all that is not of this protective Light

A pinpoint of Light pulsates to the rhythm of my heartbeat

and radiates from that focal point of Light

expanding to extend to and beyond my entire body

enveloping me in pure, radiant Light

extending beyond me to envelop this room

extending beyond this room to envelop this entire building

this entire city and far beyond … seeking and connecting

with all beings at the Point of Origin … PURE CONSCIOUSNESS

I breathe from my core
from the most profound center of my being
I cleanse myself with Sacred Breath
Golden Breath has become a solid SHIELD of PROTECTION

Waves of beautiful Golden Light
sweep up and over and around me
all the way up and over and around me
swirling up and over and around me
THE LIGHT IS MY SHIELD
It is my Comforter
I have always been THAT LIGHT

My mantra is
Thank You

My mantra is
Thank You

I return from the silence … the stillness
grounded in my humble, energetic abode
anchored in the SAFETY I have affirmed
the PROTECTION I have affirmed
the LOVE I have affirmed
the FREEDOM I have affirmed

Released from guilt … released from shame
Released from judgment

If I have ventured out far enough to have trouble returning
I follow the silver cord extended from my navel

back to the state of consciousness that is awake and alert

aware, fully focused, and grounded

no longer corrupted by false identity and conditioning

The energy of this freedom washes over me in shimmering waves of assurance that

I am a being of Eternal Light … connected to all of creation

essentially connected to the Creator of all and I AFFIRM …

That which created me is sufficient to protect me!

I AM ONE WITH THAT!

****

**The Light Meditation is available as an audio download at
dreamuniversalmedia.com. Please see the instructions in the chapter
"Meditation Download Instructions" at the back of this book. The Light
Meditation is also available on our YouTube site:
dreamuniversalmedia@youtube.com.**

Becoming Sacred Space

Let us engage in Self-Inquiry as a meditation. In matters of Psychic Self-Defense, we must be fully aware of who it is that we defend. We ask, "Who am I, really?" That is our meditation. Through this basic act of surrender and humility, we never lose sight of who we really are, without attachment, without aversion, without judgment. As we engage an ongoing study of the amazing mysteries of the art of Psychic Self-Defense, we affirm that we cannot defend what we cannot understand. We must explore ever-evolving aspects of ourselves and hold that journey as sacred. Know that the journey is *within* that safe place that cannot be touched by anything or anyone. In, and as that awareness, we are invulnerable. In, and as that awareness, our hearts were never broken … our dreams were never stolen … no person, no thing has ever touched who we really are, save Love.

Delicately kissed by morning's dew, we are a rose whose fragrance is its only reality … not the thorns or the savagery with which it was violently torn away from the bush home it knew. We are that dew, that rose, that fragrance, that thorn, and the savage reaper. We are all of that. We are the Sun that shined upon that rose. We are the Moon that watches it sleep. We are the earth and water that nourished its life. We are the bloom and the withering. We are the seed. We are the root and the fruit … and it is *all* good. We are the knife that separates and the bud that blooms. We are the air upon which its fragrance rides into awareness of all who can feel it. We are all of that.

The phenomena associated with spiritual warfare is nothing more than that … *phenomena*. It does not exist without *us* as its host. It is pure thought-form, so who is the thinker? Who accepts this thought-form and gives it a home of manifestation? What will it be after it has found no home in our consciousness? If it is a discarnate spirit, who does it stalk when we have become unavailable in our personhood, after our realization of the formless being that we really are? If it is a wicked energy, where does it land after we do not give it our permission to use our

314

lives like a theme park full of rides? If it raises its ugly head as a domino-effect change of fortune that sends our lives toppling around our feet, why was it allowed to visit us? Is there *not* something observing the I AM, that formless being that we observe as who we *really* are. Are we alone in our struggle with the plights of the human form? Is this "Watcher, or Observer" able to intervene in our affairs and protect us from attack? Is That All-knowing Awareness observing as the wisdom of allowing certain experiences to bleed through the duality of our perceptions of *right and wrong, fair and unfair*, to touch us in an apparently awful way? Are we able to see only in the rear-view mirror that we have been led to our highest good? So, if elements of an attack are allowed, does this mean that evil has triumphed over good? The Ultimate Victor is the Ultimate I AM. In that Field of Consciousness, all things are known. There are no dualities. There is no time, no past, no future … only the NOW. Every cause that is set in place is seen at the same moment as its effect.

If we, from the perspective of the I AM, find ourselves under attack, do we have reason to succumb to fear? If That Which Witnesses us is sufficient to protect us, why do we need to study Psychic Self-Defense? We study because we seek to transcend this illusion. We are That which we study. There is nothing to do. There is nothing to become. We are That. We are That which appears to be nothing, knowing it is, *therefore,* everything … as a drop of rain that becomes the ocean once they meet.

There will always be the appearance of chaos in the world. It is the dance of existence keeping its own balance. Let no one make you believe that because there is evil in the world, love is not eclipsing it with our every breath, our every smile. Life is good, even now. All of those things we have always wanted to do, we'd better do them, as the I AM. Stay there. Remain in the NOW. Love life! All that we have endeavored to attain from external sources will be discovered within our own essence as we stand up, Self-Realized, in the I AM of our being. We have nothing to fear and every reason to rejoice in our liberation. Every time we close our eyes and go within, we are carving out our sacred space in this chaotic world. As we manage a lifestyle around living from that quiet, safe, peaceful place, we win. What is the prize? The prize is The Ultimate I AM realized in our hearts.

I regret sounding preachy. I am not the expert in these matters, except for the fact that I have experienced these things that we study, and there is a level of expertise derived from experience. This experiencing caused me to initiate a lifetime commitment to this study with the longing to share it with others. There is something Divine about us. We are That Sacred Space.

THE END

The moving finger writes
And once having writ moves on
Nor all of thy piety nor wit
Shall lure it back to cancel half a line

~ Omar Khayyam, The Rubaiyat ~

About the Author
JAI (Jāy)

With early beginnings as a published songwriter, JAI's passion has remained her poetry. She has been published in the Los Angeles Sentinel, SIC Magazine, Talisman Magazine, UCLA's NOMMO Magazine, Point of Light, The Drumming Between Us, and African Voices. Her publications by *Dream Universal Media* are listed below. *Dream Universal Media* specializes in literature, audio, and video recordings, specifically designed to heal and elevate the consciousness of mind, body, and spirit through Mystical Meditation.

JAI is a student and teacher of metaphysical sciences and many mystical healing traditions, including Tibetan, Hawaiian, Native American, African, Caribbean, Middle Eastern, Chinese, and Japanese, all of which inspired her work. JAI continues to teach, publish, and write. Her works include;

THE TIMELESS NOW: HEALING FROM GRIEF AND LOSS
Mystical Meditation-The Sacred Law of Impermanence

SLEEPLESS: Transcend the Fear of Sleep Paralysis

SELFLESS: TURIYA – Beyond the Dark Night of the Soul

FACELESS: THE SACRED RELATIONSHIP
How to Heal Relationships through Mystical Meditation

LIMITLESS: MADE OF LIGHT – Your Companion Reference Book
for FACELESS

SMOKE & MIRRORS: A Poetic Journey to The Higher Self

NAMELESS

SANDBOXES

DREAM UNIVERSAL JOURNAL

AUDIO AND VIDEO MEDITATIONS INCLUDE:

The Light Meditation
I Die to my Ego Self Meditation
Stone Meditation
Turiya Meditation

JAI (Jāy), literally means "Victory" in Sanskrit, representing the Spirit of this sacred journey. Look for more at *dreamuniversalmedia.com* and the Facebook Group; FEARLESS: PSYCHIC SELF-DEFENSE

Meditation Download Instructions

To download the audio meditation included in this book, go to Dreamuniversalmedia.com and select the OUR PRODUCTS page, then select the Audio Meditations section and follow the instructions. The Light Meditation is also available on our YouTube site: dreamuniversalmedia@youtube.com.

Works Cited

A Course in Miracles. Foundation for Inner Peace, 1985.

"Vipassana Meditation." *International Meditation Centres |Home*,
www.internationalmeditationcentre.org/global/index.html.

Gibran, Khalil, AL-AJNIHA AL-MUTAKASSIRA, 1912
(The Broken Wings, English Translation)

Kahlil Gibran, The Wanderer, 1932
Alfred A Knopf, New York, New York

Hafiz, The Gift, Translated to English 1999
Translated by Daniel Ladinsky

Recommended Reading

A Course in Miracles

Hazrat Inayat Rehmat Khan; The Soul's Journey

Idries Shah; The Sufis

Nisargadatta Maharaj; I Am That

Paramhansa Yogananda; Autobiography of a Yogi (Self-
   RealizationFellowship)

Sri Ramana Maharshi; Who Am I?

Thich Nhat Hanh: The Pocket Thich Nhat Hanh

Sayagyi U Ba Khin; What is Vipassana Meditation

Rupert Spira: Being Aware of Being Aware

Sun Tzu and John Minford; The Art of War

Recommended Meditation Music

Levi Chen of Yin Yang Records and Liquid Gardens at
www.levichen.com

Joaquin Montoya (Joaqopelli) at soundcloud.com

Gabrielle Roth *(February 4, 1941 – October 22, 2012)* and The Mirrors

shhhhhhh

www.ingramcontent.com/pod-product-compliance
Lightning Source LLC
LaVergne TN
LVHW061222060426
835509LV00012B/1378